Word Magic for Writers

*Your Source for Powerful Language That
Enchants, Convinces, and Wins Readers*

BY
CINDY ROGERS

Writer's Institute
Publications
™

I am a painstaking, conscientious, involved and devious craftsman in words, however unsuccessful the result so often appears, and to whatever wrong uses I may apply my technical paraphernalia. I use everything and anything to make my poems work and move in the direction I want them to: old tricks, new tricks, puns, portmanteau-words, paradox, allusion, paronomasia, paragram, catachresis, slang, assonantal rhymes, vowel rhymes, sprung rhythm. Every device there is in language is there to be used if you will. Poets have got to enjoy themselves sometimes, and the twisting and convolutions of words, the inventions and contrivances, are all part of the joy that is part of the painful, voluntary work.

Dylan Thomas, *Notes on the Art of Poetry,* 1951

Editor: Susan M. Tierney

Cover Design and Production: Joanna L. Horvath

International Standard Book Number 1-889715-24-7
Printed and bound in Canada.
10 9 8 7 6 5 4

Table of Contents

Hooking the Audience

Introduction

Chapter 1: The Alchemy of Language

The Alchemy of Language

A schooled baker knows the importance of ingredients and how to use them. She knows, for example, the difference between baking powder and baking soda: Both interact with liquid, though one is slower; one works with certain ingredients and not others; one can be substituted for the other, but not vice versa. A good baker's cakes and scones rarely flop, and—because of her knowledge about the alchemy of ingredients—she can experiment. Her baked goods always sell.

A master magician has the ability to pull a lop-eared rabbit out of a top hat and slice his beautiful assistant in half or make a tiger appear and a castle disappear. He has collected props and techniques and practiced illusion and sleight of hand until his art is not only seamless, but spellbinding. He's an alchemist of smoke and mirrors, pizzazz and power. The enchantment of his show leaves a lasting impression on his audience.

A brilliant op-ed essay or an engrossing novel or a surprising poem is also an experience of alchemy. Each pleases a reader in many ways—not just because of the subject, but because of its voice, its rhythm, its way of pulling on the emotions in an alchemy of words, a powerful potion, word magic. Like that schooled baker or master magician, the astute author takes mere words and animates them with allusion and artistry. Drawing on numerous tricks and techniques of the trade, the word alchemist knows how to captivate, persuade, charm, enchant, empower, inspire, even mesmerize the audience.

An excellent writer knows the importance of an interesting turn of phrase, of a crisp image that leaves an impression, of a parting thought that lingers in a reader's mind. A word alchemist knows how to extend a group of words to grab or sway or enchant an audience. An author makes the effort to find a rich metaphor, a playful simile, or an apt analogy that transports readers from one world to another, increasing their understanding along the way.

Any of us can be a baker or a magician or a writer. But most of us long to be a master at what we do. By becoming more knowledgeable about our craft, we can elevate our baking or magic or writing from the mediocre to the excellent. Real art—whether in the small form of an essay or meditation or children's story or the long form of a novel or major poem—goes beyond the average, the temporal, the cliché. Art is a melt-in-your-mouth chocolate raspberry cake. Art is a chorus line of colorful scarves pulled out of your ear. Art is a scene on a lurching train in which an elegantly dressed woman pours tea with careless ease, and the reader feels not only the rumbling wheels, but the woman's confidence.

Throwing a bevy of words around an idea and hoping it comes off as genius is naive. By selecting a specific detail, like a red-winged blackbird, or a device, like personification, a knowledgeable writer create an image. He plays around with the language until the paragraph or the phrase communicates exactly what he wants it to convey. The payoff of a terrific scene or ad or speech versus a mediocre one is substantial, for it compels an audience to pay attention.

That's where this book will give you sleight of hand. *Word Magic for Writers* provides dozens of techniques, devices, recipes, along with published examples to study, practice, or mimic. The examples come in the form of excerpts from classic and contemporary fiction, from newspapers, magazines, reference books, children's books, speeches, poems. In this amazing cornucopia, you'll see how writers of every kind have made terrific use of language by employing specific devices and clever techniques.

Your Array of Ingredients

The first and largest section of the book introduces the tricks of the trade, the many language devices—from alliteration to zeugma—that compare, expand, accentuate, diminish, and enliven a scene or an idea. Dive into this half of the book where you will.

The first three chapters of Part 1 introduce simple and delightful devices that provide sound, repetition, rhythm. For example, here's a quote from Ralph Waldo Emerson: "By necessity, by proclivity, and by delight, we all quote." Emerson could have written a rather unremarkable sentence (e.g., "We quote for different reasons"), but instead augmented his words with assonance and parallelism—language devices that offer balance, emphasis, and sound.

These devices and techniques are not new. They're at least as old as the language of ancient Greece and its literature and as common as backyard chats. Comparative devices, introduced in the next three chapters, are probably the most powerful devices a writer can use. The metaphor is the cornerstone of our language—used on the street, on billboards, in the political arena, often to the point of cliché. When you revise the characteristics of a person's voice from that of being brittle as glass or shrill as a fishwife's to "brittle with sorrows, as tart as curds, and shrill enough to grate meat from a coconut" (as Jhumpra Lahiri does in *Interpreter of Maladies*), then you've elevated the description from the mediocre to the memorable. *Word Magic for Writers* identifies both the simplicity and the subtle complexities of the metaphor.

Each section of Part I introduces you to language devices that will strengthen your writing. Some of these devices you've heard of, some you haven't. Some you've purposefully used in your writing, some you've stumbled upon, not knowing their true value. Learning more about these techniques will not only fascinate you but—if practiced—will allow you to own them. Each chapter provides ways to help you create your own rhythm, your own fresh metaphor.

The first section of Part II offers not only more examples of these devices, but glimpses into the vast worlds of vivid imagery, subtle text (the kind that says more than it states), and interesting styles. Novelist Mark Salzman describes a parish priest in *Lying Awake:* "He was a large man with eyebrows that patrolled his forehead like gray battleships, ready to meet any threat to his parishioners' souls." The author expanded on a single detail to describe a character, yet the imagery of that detail is so vivid that it suggests more: This priest will go to great lengths not only to protect his parishioners, but also his church and his religion. A more mundane description would simply describe the man as large with bushy eyebrows. Vivid imagery, implication, and a device (a simile) make the difference between so-so writing and compelling writing.

The final section of *Word Magic for Writers* reminds you about the hooks that grab a reader's attention: a title, a headline, a first page, a last paragraph. The word *ax*, for example, can raise an eyebrow, but without specificity and action, it means nothing. E. B. White put that word in the form of a child's question at the beginning of *Charlotte's Web* and a whole new world is set in motion. "Where's Papa going with that ax?" captures the reader because of the choice of words, the action implied, the question it raises. What child—what parent—could not read further?

Each of the book's parts provides new material to show off classic tricks, tools, and techniques. Along the way, you'll be gathering tidbits of useful information and overviews in the form of wrap-ups. Each chapter gives you opportunities to try on these techniques, to empower your own writing. But you'll need more than a few writing exercises. Like a master baker or magician, a writer needs regular practice and experimentation. Of course, the subject or idea behind the writing is of critical importance, but the book's message is the same from start to finish: Specifically, artfully displayed words enhance the subject by evoking an image or an emotion or a hook that will draw in the audience. We're talking about the kind of language that requires a response—the goal of every screenwriter and speechmaker, novelist and poet.

This book is not about the basics of writing. It's not a cookbook or a magician's assistant. But there are similarities. *Word Magic for Writers* is a treasure trove of techniques that will show you how to invest more into language, so that you don't sell yourself and your writing short. Whether you're a businessman or an essayist, you have an amazing array of ingredients and tricks at your disposal. The success of your project—an ad, an article, an essay, a book, a play—depends in large part on how you use them. This book contains a working knowledge of all the possibilities.

Whether you use *Word Magic for Writers* as a resource, jumping there, or as a cover-to-cover read, the chapters ahead will help you to become a keener reader and a more interesting writer. A creative writer. Someone whose words delight or charm, persuade or empower, captivate or inspire. Someone who knows the alchemy of baking powder and baking soda.

Part I

Language Devices, from Alliteration to Zeugma

Devices of Sound & Repetition

Sound Devices to Tickle a Title & Snap Up a Sentence

A s readers we may think of the sounds of words as less affecting than we would as listeners, but sounds and how they are used play an important note in the music of writing. Poets, newspaper headliners, novelists, advertising copy writers, and children's writers—especially picture book writers—are among the authors who favor the devices of sound: Alliteration, assonance, consonance, and onomatopoeia may bring subtlety or solidity to language, and frankly, they're fun.

Alliteration, From the Tongue-Twister to the Sublime

The repetition of initial consonant sounds in successive words or stressed syllables is called *alliteration*. It's the stuff of children's tongue twisters (Peter Piper picked a peck of pickled peppers) and newspaper headlines ("Ventura Vetoes Plan; Budget Woes Worsen") and poetry ("My luve is like a red, red rose"). Alliteration peppers our conversation in expressions like *a dime a dozen, bigger and better, sink or swim, do or die, the more the merrier, live and learn.*

One reason alliteration bounces around our language so much is that sounds help a reader or listener remember sense. It naturally gives a certain rhythm and pacing to a line. With alliteration, a writer can make a scene move quicker (the railroad ran right through town) or slower (she stalked stars in the evening skies), or make a highway billboard a quick read (Best Buy Is Bigger and Better than Ever).

As a rule, do not alliterate simply for alliteration's sake. It will come off forced or pointless, like a tongue twister. Exceptions include periodical headlines, ads, and some children's books.

Alliteration is an aural tool, not a visual one, although good alliteration may have image as a side effect. The same repeated written letter doesn't always make the same sound, obviously: *City* and *castle* don't alliterate, nor do *knight* and *kite*. *Pheasant* and *finch* do.

If alliteration didn't support sense, if it weren't functional, it wouldn't have the broad appeal it does. It would be fun for a silly verse or an entertaining children's rhyme, but no more than that. But successful alliteration furthers meaning and pace. A reader's excitement in an action scene or a depiction of a news event, for example, is enhanced by alliteration. Here's a line from an article about Babe Ruth by Steve Hoffbeck:

> Ruth lived up to his title of Whoozit of Wham by hitting the horsehide over the fence six times.
>
> "A Visit from the Babe," *Minnesota Monthly,* June 2003

Notice that this sentence doesn't use the same initial letter to create alliteration, but rather the same initial sound, the *h* in *Whoozit, hitting, horsehide.*

Lauren Slater, in "Dr. Daedalus," elevates the energy of her profile of a plastic surgeon by alliteration. Note how easy it is to read this passage. It rolls off the tongue and is fun, to boot. Slater also makes good use of *assonance*, repeated internal vowel sounds.

> "It could be anthrax," he says as he hurries to the car, beeper beeping, sleet sleeting, for it's a freezing New England midwinter day when all the world is white. . . . [W]e're in the car now, speeding toward the hospital where he reconstructs faces, appends limbs, puffs and preens the female form.
>
> *Harper's,* July 2002

Novelists may rely on alliteration to create more energy, more noise, more action, more emphasis. Here's an example from *Peace Like a River,* by Leif Enger: "Davy smacked, swallowed, sank to yet more earnest sleep." And from Richard Peck's *Fair Weather*: "By and by I felt boy-breath on the back of my neck," and in dialogue: "Well, I'm an old sod-bustin' son of the soil . . . I got more toes than teeth" and "They's green as gourds and never seen nothing." Even in Charles Dickens's description of old Scrooge in *A Christmas Carol*, there's a decisive energy conveyed by the alliteration: "Hard and sharp as flint, from which no steel had ever struck out generous fire; secret, and self-contained and solitary as an oyster."

The same sounds can mingle and jingle in the same sentence. Peck alliterates in the following example from *Fair Weather* with a mix of *s*'s, *c*'s, and *cr*'s in a line that is not only full of energy but beautiful to the ear. Note that the *c* and *r* don't necessarily have to be side by side in the same word to bring off a *cr* sound, as in *curly*:

Exercise: Slogans That Alliterate

After 9/11, a United Way newspaper advertisement in Silicon Valley showed an Associated Press photograph of the Manhattan skyline, followed by the slogan: "Remember. Resolve. Rebuild." A successful ad campaign by Northwest Airlines pitched "Frequent Fliers." The "Jolly Green Giant" became a company's marketing slogan for vegetables.

Use alliteration to create an ad about a unique kitchen device you want to sell or a new lawn care service you want to promote, or provide a young fictional character with a slogan for his roadside stand.

It was another man entirely, in a once-cream-colored suit, badly creased, and a curly-brimmed Panama hat, a high celluloid collar, and a silk cravat.

Extra! Extra!

Newspaper editors must have a great time using wordplay to create headlines that stand out. Alliteration often pumps up otherwise dull articles with energy. Headlines can get away with the kind of alliteration that, in any other medium, sounds forced or contrived. Here are a few from a local newspaper:

- "Emphasis Won't Be on Big Bucks" (about a deer management program)
- [Senator] "Moe Mum, but Mom Spills the Beans"
- "On Thin Ice: Lessons Learned and Lives Lost"

In the same way that it pumps up headlines, alliteration can add snap to leads, or opening lines. A profile about Katharine Hepburn not long after her death began like this: "Feisty, formidable, fiercely independent describe Katharine . . ." A review of the Antoinette Perry (Tony) Award results for Broadway's *Frog and Toad* starts like this: "The bouffant bowled over the bullfrog at the 57th annual Tony Awards. . . ."

Sound repetition works in the body of articles too. In a news piece about U.S. Senate action, the alliteration mid-article gives the article energy, action, sound: It's a quote straight from the mouth of a U.S. senator who spoke of the "sneaky, slimy, and

Writers of Old

Writers of old used alliteration even more than we do in modern times, and more openly. Anglo-Saxon (also called Old English) poetry, like *Beowulf*, depended heavily on the art of repeated sounds. Poets continued to use it in Middle English, as in the fourteenth-century *Piers Plowman*, and in Modern English—Shakespeare wrote in Modern English. The modern translation of lines from *Beowulf* and *Piers Plowman* here reflect the alliteration in the original language.

Now Beowulf bode in the burg of Scyldings,
Leader beloved and long he ruled,
In fame with all folk since his father had gone.
Beowulf

In a summer season when soft was the sun,
I clothed myself in a cloak as I a shepherd were,
Habit like a hermit's, unholy in works,
And went wide in the world, wonders to hear.
Piers Plowman

In *A Midsummer Night's Dream,* Shakespeare parodies alliteration, although he is the master of it himself in other instances:

Whereat, with blade, with bloody blameful blade,
He bravely breach'd his boiling bloody breast.

sordid shenanigan" about an airline's policy decision.

Statesmen are big fans of alliteration when making a point prominent in the plethora of political words. Here's one of the better ones, the kind that gives the ear a tickle and the memory a boost, from Benjamin Franklin's memoirs:

All expressions of positiveness in opinion or of direct contradiction were prohibited under small pecuniary penalities.

On a lighter note, Franklin wrote this line, although listen to how the alliteration choice slows the pace:

When the well's dry we know the worth of water.

Abraham Lincoln, too, used rhythm and alliteration in his remarks:

> The ballot is stronger than the bullet.
> [L]et us, to the end, dare to do our duty . . .

The potency of alliteration is evidenced by how often it can be found on tombstones, especially if the entombed is someone who believed in beautiful language. These are the words, the epitaphs, that abide with the remains of famous writers:

> Steel True, Blade Straight. *Sir Arthur Conan Doyle*
> So we beat on, boats against the current, borne back ceaselessly into the past. *F. Scott Fitzgerald*
> Nothing of him that doth fade/But doth suffer a sea-change/Into something rich and strange. From William Shakespeare's *The Tempest*, on the grave of Percy Bysshe Shelley
> Cast a cold eye/On life, on death/Horseman, pass by! *William Butler Yeats*

Assonance & Consonance, Sound-Alikes in the Middle of Words

Assonance is a repetition of the same *internal* vowel sounds in successive words. *Consonance* is the repetition of the same *internal* consonant sounds, as opposed to alliteration repeating the same *initial* sounds.

Here's a line from a *Harper's* article ("The Ones Who May Kill You in the Morning," Marc Nesbitt, August 2000) that uses both assonance and consonance: "We shuck each other's clothes like husks." The *u* sound in *shuck* and *husks* is an example of assonance, and the *k* and *th* sounds are both consonance. In the same article is found this phrase that rolls off the tongue with its lovely alliteration, consonance, and assonance—*l*'s, *a*'s, and *awn/ong*: "a lawn long as allegory."

Like alliteration, assonance and consonance tickle the ear and jog the memory, which is why a phrase like "how now, brown cow?" sticks with us from first grade. Or why we remember little adages like Franklin's "Haste makes waste" and "Little strokes fell great oaks." These devices heighten the effect of the sentence's tone; they intensify it. So if a sense of calmness is needed, assonance will add to it. If excitement is needed, consonance will underline it. Can you hear the hurry in *haste and waste*? The heaviness in strokes and oaks? "A long lawn" slows the reading because the words take a while to say; they're *looonng* in sound and slow in tone.

Poets and lyric writers often use assonance and consonance to create internal rhythm. Sing that old Perry Como song lyric by Paul Vance and Lee Pockriss (inspired by seventeenth-century poet John Donne's "Song") that goes like this:

> Catch a falling star
> And put it in your pocket;
> Never let it fade away.

You should immediately hear the alliteration of *p*'s in the middle phrase, but also note the assonance in the short *a* sound of the first phrase and the short *e* and long *a* sound of the third. Another golden oldie, "Downtown," employs all three devices, including two assonance/consonance combos in the title itself:

> Just listen to the music of the traffic in the city;
> Linger on the sidewalk where the neon signs are pretty.
> How can you lose?
> The lights are much brighter there . . .

Do you hear the alliteration of the *s* and *w* sounds and the assonances of short *i*'s, long *i*'s, *oo*'s, and long *e*'s? Can you catch the consonance of *ic*'s and *ght*'s?

Verse is fun and easy to memorize when it makes use of these devices, but serious biblical and literary passages use them well too: "Thy kingdom come, Thy will be done." Of course, rhythm helps. Take a look at two sets of familiar lines:

> O, my luve is like a red, red rose
> That's newly sprung in June . . .

That Robert Burns verse is memorable for alliteration in the first line, and assonance in the second, while this Samuel Taylor Coleridge verse from "Kubla Khan" shows assonance and alliteration in both lines. Note that *decree* carries its own assonance.

> In Xanadu did Kubla Khan
> A stately pleasure-dome decree . . .

Advertising and copy writers take advantage of the rhythm and easy recall of sound devices. "Don't get mad, get Glad" is, of course, an ad for garbage bags. "The glimmer of gold, the shimmer of silver" touts a *Bon Appetit* table setting. Older ads by two different car companies used sound devices to make them memorable: one with assonance and rhythm, "See the USA in your Chevrolet," and one with alliteration "There's a Ford in Your Future."

Exercise: A Rich Blend

A descriptive line from Charles Dickens's *A Christmas Carol* has a rich blend of three sound devices—alliteration, assonance, and consonance. Notice how the word choice adds movement and the image of plumpness to the scene while the sounds of these words heighten that very energy and tone. In the first line, the alliteration is boldface, assonance is underlined, and consonance is italicized. Can you find these in the line that follows?

There were **gr**eat, round, pot-**b**ellied **b**askets of che*st*-nuts, shaped like the waist-coats of **j**o*ll*y old **g**ent*l*emen, lo*ll*ing at the doors, and tumbling out into the street in their apop*l*ectic opulence.

There were ruddy brown-faced, broad-girthed Spanish onions shining in the fatness of their growth like Spanish Friars.

The headline (another form of an ad, meant to hook your attention) of a review on two books about bungalows is "The lowdown on bungalows." Note the repetition and assonance of *low*, resulting in a play on words, a pun. Ad writers like to tickle the ear.

So do statesmen. Lincoln, in his second annual message to Congress in 1862, said, "We shall n*ob*ly save, or mean*ly* lose, the la*st* be*st* h*o*pe of Earth." This line uses parallel construction (see more about parallelism in the next chapter) with its double verb phrasing and alliteration, and it uses consonance and assonance. It is no coincidence that lines like these, full of meaning but also memorable in sound, are often quoted.

Don't think that only statesmen, poets, and songwriters use assonance and consonance. So do novelists, biographers, and memoirists. *Angela's Ashes,* by Frank McCourt, has a lyricism often achieved through alliteration, assonance, and consonance:

> ‣ [T]he shiftless loquacious alcoholic father; the pious defeated mother moaning by the fire; pompous priests . . .
> ‣ [T]he walls of Limerick glistened . . .
> ‣ [H]e'd have a drop of the Irish to celebrate his decision and departure . . .
> ‣ a cacophony of hacking coughs . . .

Exercise: Reflecting Sounds

If a character or person hisses a line of dialogue, the words that come from the character's mouth should be hissing sounds, that is, words that contain *s*'s, *z*'s, *sp*'s, *st*'s, etc. The effect of the verb is lost if a character hisses, "Don't move!" Those words simply aren't hissing words.

What would you have the character say instead?

Finally, unbelievably, so do op-ed columnists like Mark Morford from the *San Francisco Gate.* Repeat this line aloud. Listen for the assonance and consonance, beautifully paced:

A never-ending fire hose of chaos and destruction and wanton human corruption streaming in like a nasty fever dream from the global atrocity machine . . .
"Please Write More About Rape," May 14, 2004

Exercise: Novel Approach

From Richard Russo's novel *Empire Falls* comes this scene, in which a character is introduced through sound effects. Note how alliteration, assonance, consonance, and onomatopoeia are all there, but Russo doesn't allow them to take over. Instead, the devices underline the scene's rhythm and energy:

> The bell jingled above the door, and Walt Comeau danced inside, his arms extended like an old-fashioned crooner's, his silver hair slicked back on the sides, fifties-style. "Don't let the stars get in your eyes," he warbled, "don't let the moon break your heart."

Using Russo's excerpt as a guide, create your own scene: Bring a lively character (nothing drab or quiet about her) into a setting. Give something in the setting some sound, like an alarm, a blender, a baby, a lawn mower. Give your character one line of dialogue. Use one, two, or more sound devices.

The Sounds of Onomatopoeia

Onomatopoeia. (a-na-ma-*te*-pee-a) What a mouthful. But what fun to say. In Greek, *onoma* and *poiein* mean *to make a name*. Onomatopoeia means to name a thing or action by an imitation of the sound associated with it. It's a sound inside a word. When bees buzz and gongs bombilate, the reader's awareness is pricked. As with the other sound devices, the ear picks up on something new. Whether characters or objects rattle, screech, wheeze, fizz, growl, roar, crackle or pop, the reader is thrilled and the writer has reduced the need for description. It's no wonder that comic books and comic strips, where space is at a premium, revel in ono-matopoeia: CRASH! BANG! ZZZZAP! BIFF! BOOM! ZOOM! WHOMP! CRACK! AWK! AHHH! BOING!

Edgar Allan Poe's poem "The Bells" is a well-known example of the use of onomatopoeia, specifically with the word *tinkle* below, but even more so with the word *bells* itself:

> Hear the sledges with the bells—
> Silver bells!

What a world of merriment their melody foretells!
How they tinkle, tinkle, tinkle,
In the icy air of night!
While the stars that oversprinkle
All the heavens, seem to twinkle
With a crystalline delight;
Keeping time, time, time,
In a sort of Runic rhyme,
To the tintinnabulation that so musically wells
From the bells, bells, bells, bells,
Bells, bells, bells—
From the jingling and the tinkling of the bells.

The poetry of Gerard Manley Hopkins used words in new and remarkable ways, sometimes stretching those that did not begin as onomatopoeia and making them sound the thing they are. See how he does so with the italicized words below in one of his most remarkable sonnets, "God's Grandeur":

The world is *charged* with the grandeur of God.
 It will *flame* out, like shining from shook foil;
  It gathers to a greatness, like the *ooze* of oil
Crushed. Why do men then now not reck his rod?
Generations have trod, have trod, have trod;
 And all is *seared* with trade; *bleared*, *smeared* with toil;
  And wears man's *smudge* and shares man's smell: the soil
Is bare now, nor can foot feel, being shod.

Children's book writers also love the device, especially those whose genre is the early picture book: horses clip clop, clip clop; kittens mew; dogs bark; old cars pop, rattle, and bang; faucets drip drip drip; owls hoooot.

Author Phyllis Root is especially deft with sound devices in her many picture books. *What Baby Wants,* for instance, makes use of onomatopoeia in nonsense words and real words. Notice, the alliteration, assonance, and consonance:

WAAAAAAH! said Baby.
Pikola, pokala, the flowers prickled Baby's nose.

Kitchita, kootchita, the feathers tickled Baby's toes.
Slurpilla, sloppilla, the cow slobbered on Baby's chin.
Nibbitty, nubbitty, the sheep nibbled on Baby's hair.
Tawitta, taweeta, the birds twittered in Baby's ear.

Other books by Root use the same devices, especially onomatopoeia:

▸ Aunt Nancy starts to sit in a chair, when *creak,* crack the chair's lying on its side with one leg broken and *ka-thunk* Aunt Nancy's sitting on the floor. *Aunt Nancy and Old Man Trouble*
▸ Ten dragonflies *zoom*ing through the skies *whir* to the duck. *Zing, zing.* No luck. The duck stays stuck deep in the muck down by the muggy buggy marsh. *One Duck Stuck*

Here's a delightful example from *Maniac Magee,* by Jerry Spinelli, in which you can literally hear the scene unfold:

A faint tiny noise. A *rattling.* A *chittering.* A *chattering.* And getting louder—yes—chattering teeth. Arnold Jones' teeth. They're chattering like snare drums.

That's a simile in the last line, and the repetition of *chattering* is amplification, a repetition that emphasizes, and in this case, amplifies the sound and thus the tension.

Novelists and essayists use onomatopoeia to add sound and diminish the need for extended detail. Check out these lines for the tone and intention of their authors:

▸ . . . but hearing Dad wrack and hawk, and bits of his lung hitting whang in the pan. *Peace Like a River,* Leif Enger
▸ We put back our hoods expecting the chuffs and growls of plow trucks . . . *Peace Like a River,* Leif Enger
▸ . . . kissed me bang smash on the mouth . . . *Journals,* Sylvia Plath
▸ A *squeezing, wrenching, grasping, scraping, clutching, covetous* old ˙ sinner! *A Christmas Carol,* Charles Dickens
▸ The insufferable snobbery that *oozes* from every pore . . . *Baltimore Sun,* Kevin Cowherd
▸ I clipped the last two wires and ripped out the hunk of fence just as a *splash* erupted from the pool. *Dying for Chocolate,* Diane Davidson

And So . . .

Alliteration, assonance, consonance, and onomatopoeia not only diminish the need for detail in a line or scene, but they infuse the writing with tone, energy, action, and sound. Alliteration, especially, can beef up the sense of excitement and action, while assonance and consonance heighten the tone of the piece, whether it's harsh, mellow, wild, or peaceful.

Onomatopoeia, on the other hand, offers the exact sound an author may be looking for.

As with all figurative language, these devices must be used sparingly to heighten their effect in a piece of writing. But beware: Unique can become bizarre. Above all, match the specific wording of the device to the overall tone of the piece. Have some fun with devices of sound!

By Necessity, By Proclivity, By Delight, We All List

W riters adore lists. Fiction writers itemize particulars in treasure boxes, above the mantle, on the dining table. Journalists name the personalities in a courtroom, at a gala event, on a team. Biographers list historic names and events. Often, writers favor lists of three, just as myths and folktales usually work through three wishes, three tasks. Trios have a balance, and a visual, aural, and symbolic appeal. Yet, more than three—a multiplicity—is often key to a story, scene, or paragraph. Several writing devices help to create that effect without itemizing every last thing, without forcing the reader's eyes to glaze over.

Asyndeton, a Series without a Conjunction

In *Charlotte's Web,* E. B. White went out of his way to create marvelous lists of interesting items beloved by rats, pigs, and a girl, Fern. Some of his lists are common series that incorporate *and* at the end, signaling the finality of the list. Other of his lists make use of a rhetorical device called *asyndeton* (a-*sin*-di-ton). Take a look at the subtle difference between the two in this excerpt:

> Fern loved Wilbur more than anything. She loved to stroke him, to feed him, to put him to bed. Every morning, as soon as she got up, she warmed his milk, tied his bib on, and held the bottle for him.

The asyndeton is in the second sentence, a series uninterrupted by a conjunction. It implies multiplicity, that there's seemingly no end to the things Fern would do for Wilbur. White used this device to show Fern's unconditional love in an economy of words. The third sentence, on the other hand, uses the common and more familiar series of clauses in which there is a definite end to the list; Fern does these exact three things for Wilbur every morning.

White also uses asyndeton in the very middle of a sentence, set off by a pair of dashes—a *parenthesis*—in a line of dialogue in which the speaker lists the places rat booty can be found. Note that the lack of a conjunction implies that many more places than these are available to explore:

> Everywhere is loot for a rat—in tents, in booths, in haylofts—why, a fair has enough disgusting leftover food to satisfy a whole army of rats.

In an even shorter example, White lists the things that Wilbur feels are seriously lacking in his life; the reader also infers that the list is incomplete.

> . . . but he never had any fun—no walks, no rides, no swims.

The author has created the effect of multiplicity in just a few words. At the same time, he has defined the word *fun* from a pig's world-view. Notice how the lack of a conjunction and the repetition of the single word, *no* (an example of *anaphora*, discussed in the next chapter), adds emotional tension. As simple as the differences seem, the other option would be less rhythmic and emphatic: "He never had any fun—no walks, rides, or swims."

Coordinating conjunctions are "equal opportunity" connectors that link words, phrases, and clauses: *and, but, or, nor, yet, for, as . . . so.*

Trigger Words & Punctuation

Asyndeton's omission of the conjunction that usually binds words together causes a cataloguing to seem longer and open-ended. Asyndeton also gives the impression of an extemporaneous accounting rather than a labored one. Pair that with the use of words such as *everything, every time,* and *everywhere* and the multiplicity is driven home for readers. Here's an example from Wallace Stegner's *Crossing to Safety*. The author's italicized words, indicating a change in emphasis, add to the point of the girl speaking.

> "You must have brought *something*. Books? I never saw you without a green bag of books." To her mother she says, "He reads *everywhere*—in the subway, between the acts at plays, at intermissions in Symphony Hall, on picnics, on *dates*."

Lying Awake, by Mark Salzman, provides another example. The trigger word *everything* creates the sense of a longer list of items found in a certain room. Note that the list stands in its own sentence without subject and predicate, adding emphasis to the list:

> Everything in the room was designed for either measurement or analysis. Scales, thermometers, charts, probes, diagnostic manuals, tongue depressors, reflex hammers.

Exercise: An Admirable List

Create your own asyndeton by copying E. B. White's structure in the sentence below. Note that the author has added emphasis to the character's feelings of self-importance by repeating the same possessive pronoun (*his*) and adding at least one modifier (*silky, white, curly, kind, radiant*) to each item in the list, in a parallel construction. The implication is that there are more than three admirable traits.

> Dozens and dozens of strangers stopped by to stare at him and to admire his silky white coat, his curly tail, his kind and radiant expression.

Using this same structure and some of the wording, describe your own positive characteristics. Have fun with it!

An article by Julie Salaman in the *New York Times* listed items in a room because the setting was important to the context of the article. In this opening sentence, asyndeton implies more than three items:

> Her apartment contains reminders of the nomadic life they lived during their almost four years together: a framed piece of colorful

fabric from Jaipur in India, a large mask from Zaire, a coffee table made from an old door from Delhi.

"A Widow, But Spare the Pity: Resisting Pressure to Sentimentalize over Daniel Pearl," October 6, 2003

The author used parallel construction here: Each item is accompanied by a modifier and its point of origin, which makes the passage more effective, more memorable. (See more about parallelism at the end of this chapter.)

Asyndeton can have a punch that makes a mark in the advertising world. Decide whether the advertiser, www.finaldraft.com, made the right decision to draw out the idea in this example from *Book* (November/December 2003), or whether author Nick Hornby should have stopped the listing earlier in the sentence, after *teach*:

> I write because I can't do any of the following: paint, sculpt, sing, take photos, play an instrument, commute, wear a suit, remember appointments, return phone calls, work for a boss, concentrate in a meeting, serve food and drink, teach, or do anything else at all, really.

Commas don't need to be the punctuation of choice in asyndeton. Here's a dense inventory of the things the main character loves in Virginia Woolf's *Mrs. Dalloway*. It's not the small items divided by commas and conjunctions that create the asyndeton, but the overall listing divided by semicolons:

> In people's eyes, in the swing, tramp, and trudge; in the bellow and uproar; the carriages, motor cars, omnibuses, vans, sandwich men shuffling and swinging; brass bands; barrel organs in the triumph and the jungle and the strange high singing of some aeroplane overhead was what she loved; life; London; this moment in June.

Brachylogy (bra-*kil*-e-jee) comes from the Greek word meaning *short speech*. This device can be used in dialogue by a character that needs to be portrayed as hurried or harried. The speech pattern is short and hurried, as in "Jean! Get up! Dress! Eat!" Although these quick words or short phrases are listed without conjunctions, don't confuse brachylogy for asyndeton, which suggests an endless listing and doesn't give the same impression of haste.

Question marks, almost surprisingly, can serve asyndeton well:

> What of the more than 800 languages of Papua New Guinea? The 410 of Nigeria? The more than 300 in India? The unknown and as yet uncounted languages in the Amazon?
> "The Last Word," Earl Shorris, *Harper's*, August 2000

Statesmen and theologians who are known for their rhetorical ability to convey strong ideas and beliefs find asyndeton invaluable. Lines such as the following are often quoted because the specific word repetition and the idea of multiplicity create powerful, memorable statements. You may recognize this first line from John F. Kennedy's inaugural address. It places a list of promises mid-sentence, but once again, implies a longer list:

> Let every nation know, whether it wishes us well or ill, that we shall pay any price, bear any burden, meet any hardships, support any friend, oppose any foe to assure the survival and the success of liberty.

Theologian John Wesley, the eighteenth-century founder of Methodism, employed asyndeton in one of his most quoted lines:

> Do all the good you can, in all the ways you can, to all the souls you can, in every place you can, at all the times you can, with all the zeal you can, as long as ever you can.

In both examples, the repetitions of words that carry the phrases—*any* and *you can*—highlight the authors' intentions. Word repetition of this kind is called *epistrophe,* discussed more in the next chapter.

Polysyndeton: Here & There & Everywhere

The sense of multiplicity can be created in another way, seemingly the opposite of asyndeton: *Polysyndeton* makes good use of the conjunction, placing it between each and every word, phrase, or clause. A polysyndeton's repetitious effect creates a feeling of building up, of extemporaneous enumeration, of an endlessness, in fact, an emphasis—not dissimilar to asyndeton (which should be noted in this sentence). The primary difference between the two is one doesn't use conjunctions, and the other does, but polysyndeton can draw even more attention to itself.

White or his editors chose to place commas after each verb in this example from *Charlotte's Web,* but they aren't necessary. The rat intends no misunderstanding on Wilbur's part. The continuous use of the conjunction adds weight to Templeton's list of demands:

> "Struggle if you must," said Templeton, "but kindly remember that I'm hiding down here in this crate and I don't want to be stepped on, or kicked in the face, or pummeled, or crushed in any way, or squashed, or buffeted about, or bruised, or lacerated, or scarred, or biffed."

Polysyndeton can intensify, whether the feeling affected is magnanimity or pity, joy or woefulness. The effect of multiple conjunctions generates force and pacing in whatever direction the author desires. Frank McCourt, in *Angela's Ashes,* repeats one of his father's stories in a childlike voice. The series of clauses strung along with conjunctions in the first sentence points out Frank's young age. The mix of polysyndeton and asyndeton in the last sentence calls attention to the endless list of troubles brought on by Setanta's action.

> Setanta had a stick and ball and one day he hit the ball and it went into the mouth of a big dog that belonged to Culain and choked him. Oh, Culain was angry and he said, What am I to do now without my big dog to guard my house and my wife and my ten small children as well as numerous pigs, hens, sheep?

From *Harper's* comes an example of how a historian provides several exhaustive lists of places, things, and names in an economy of words. Author James A. McPherson employs polysyndeton and asyndeton. Notice how both devices emphasize the "greatness" this road deserves:

> [The Magnus Via] of ancient times ran from the Hellespont and Byzantium to Aleppo and Mesopotamia and Ur, with connecting routes to Cairo and Carthage and Spain. Many, many centuries of human history—men and camels and elephants and trade goods and

food and wine—traversed this road. Almost every personage prominent in history breathed in its dust: Hammurabi, Ramses, the Queen of Sheba, Cyrus the Great, Alexander the Great, Caesar, Pompey the Great, Marco Polo, Napoleon.

> "Reflections of Titus Basfield," April 1850," James A. McPherson, *Harper's,* June 2000

Sacred texts, too, create such effects through polysyndeton and asyndeton. The shift from the former to the latter in this King James version of *Isaiah* 24:1-2 is impressive. In these verses, the devices also keep the reader's attention on the point being made.

> Behold, the Lord maketh the earth empty, and maketh it waste, and turneth it upside down, and scattereth abroad the inhabitants thereof. And it shall be, as with the people, so with the priest; as with the servant, so with the master; as with the maid, so with her mistress; as with the buyer, so with the seller; as with the lender, so with the borrower; as with the taker of usury, so with the giver of usury to him.

Exercise: Polysyndeton for Emphasis

Try your hand at polysyndeton by using nouns rather than verbs. List the flavors of soup cans or the cereal boxes in your kitchen cupboard or the genres of literature in the library or the kinds of gadgets in your junk drawer.

Did you notice the use of polysyndeton in the previous sentence? It gives the impression that the list of items you could list for this exercise is endless.

To add to the flavor of this mini-assignment, assign a specific voice to your sentence. Here's an example of a kid's voice from Jerry Spinelli in *Maniac Magee:*

> There were fiction books and nonfiction books, who-did-it books and let's-be-friends books and what-is-it books and how-to books and how-not-to books and just-regular-kid books.

This example also points the way to the final section of this chapter, on parallelism or a balanced construction, an important tool in the writing craft that you'll find demonstrated in every chapter that follows.

Exercise: Fix It!

Faulty or bland sentence construction is often cured by parallel reconstruction. Decide on the minor shifting that these two sentences need to read more clearly and sound more balanced:

> ▸ She enjoyed keeping score more than she liked to play volleyball.
> ▸ I like to walk the mall more than I like purchasing anything.

Parallelism for Balance: Of the People, for the People, by the People

The repetition of certain words and the balanced construction of parts of a sentence—shown in both the phrasing in the subhead above and in the verse in the preceding example—speak to the idea of parallelism. Good writers strive to use parallel construction in every possible way, though often subtly. Parallelism comes from the Greek word *parallelos*, meaning *side-by-side*. It is basically a similarity of structure with a series of related words, phrases, and clauses.

Parallelism occurs all the time in simple everyday sentences—with verbs, nouns and modifiers, adverbs, prepositional phrases:

> ▸ Because of allergies, she needed *to drink* soy milk and *to avoid* cow's milk.
> ▸ My brother's favorite sports teams are the *Minnesota* <u>Vikings</u>, the *Chicago* <u>White Sox</u>, and the *New York* <u>Rangers</u>.
> ▸ I have *often entered* but *rarely won* a race.
> ▸ The fox ran *across* <u>the field</u>, *through* <u>the woods</u>, and *down* to <u>the stream</u>.

Parallelism has to do with a paragraph's syntax or a sentence's construction. Parts of a sentence or even several sentences are expressed in a similar way to show that the ideas are equal in importance. Parallelism adds balance, rhythm, clarity and, often, beauty:

> ▸ . . . an *outward and visible* sign of an *inward and spiritual* grace.
> *Book of Common Prayer*

> ▸ The White House has ordered a major reorganization of American efforts *to quell violence* in Iraq and Afghanistan and *to speed*

34

reconstruction of both countries . . .

New York Times, October 6, 2003

Devices like asyndeton and polysyndeton go hand-in-hand with parallelism in sentences, paragraphs, and even larger units, such as chapters or essays. Parallelism may be embedded in writing through a series of words, as in other examples presented here: *in the swing, tramp, trudge.* The three action nouns are parallel in size and voice. It may take form in longer single-word series: *who-did-it books and what-is-it books and how-to books.* The book types are each constructed with hyphenated modifiers.

Parallelism becomes larger with phrases and clauses. Remember the line from Kennedy's inaugural address? That series of phrases uses a parallel construction that includes a verb, a repeated modifier, and an object. The list includes five examples but the intent is many more (asyndeton):

. . . that we shall pay any price, bear any burden, meet any hardship, support any friend, oppose any foe in order to assure the survival . . .

Verbs: pay, bear, meet, support, oppose
Modifier: any
Objects: price, burden, hardship, friend, foe

Parallelism creates order and clarity via independent clauses:

▸ Readers are plentiful; thinkers are rare. *Harriet Martineau,* Florence Fenwick Miller
▸ Beareth all things, believeth all things, hopeth all things, endureth all things. *Corinthians* 13:7

Exercise: Two Horses, Side by Side

An ad by Purina Mills for Equine Senior, a feed product for older horses, captures the change in both a relationship and a horse. One of the lines uses parallelism to show the aging process in an interesting and beautiful way:

And now, while your eyes see a proud old man, your heart sees a dashing young steed.

Create a line about a young man or woman, someone who's no longer a child. Use parallelism to show the change through the eyes and heart of a parent.

35

Exercise: A Line of Speech

Parallelism makes a sentence more interesting and memorable when the words are carefully chosen, as in this line from one of Lincoln's speeches: "We shall nobly save, or meanly lose, the last best hope of Earth." Or in this one, by Ralph Waldo Emerson (the one from which this chapter's title was taken): "By necessity, by proclivity, and by delight, we all quote."

Using these parallelisms as models, make up your own line for a speech on pollution, peace, literacy, gay rights, smog, or animal rights.

Example: By irresponsibility, by ignorance, by inconsideration, we all pollute.

Note that the deletion of the conjunction opens the listing for more reasons than those listed.

Note that the last example uses asyndeton to imply a longer listing.

Full sentences benefit from parallelism too, as in these two examples from *The Way*, by Lao-tsu:

> ‣ He who knows others is wise. He who knows himself is enlightened.
> ‣ When the people of the world all know beauty as beauty, there arises the recognition of ugliness. When they all know the good as good, there arises the recognition of evil.

Parallelism is even found in paragraph construction, as illustrated by this extremely short paragraph from *Crossing to Safety:*

Expressive shrug. Enigmatic smile.

Essays, speeches, information articles often list their points in a parallel construction, which gives the work form and clarity and beauty. On an even bigger scope, this book—like many nonfiction books—is set up in a kind of parallel construction: Each chapter has a final summary, for example, headed with the words "And So." A pattern set up in chapter after chapter of a textbook presents an ease of navigation for the reader. That's a form of parallelism.

Finally, parallelism is the stuff of titles, as in these two headlines from the *New York Times* (July 1, 2003):

Exercise: Everything

1. Certain words—*everything, anything, something*—suggest the possibility of a list. In Ann Bauer's story, "The Drunkard's Gait" (*The Sun,* April 2004), the narrator says the following about a sibling's intelligence, but the implication is of much more:

> He knew a little bit about everything: European history, quantum physics, Islam.

Write a description about a certain character's abilities or behaviors or hobbies or pets in which you use a clue word followed by a listing. (Note the polysyndeton in this instruction; your choice is unlimited.)

2. In the same issue of *The Sun,* an anonymous reader writes a letter to the editor. His use of polysyndeton in the first sentence underlines his personal anguish, while the asyndeton and parallelism in the third sentence provide more fact, a listing of information.

> I sit in my cell and write unanswered letters full of pain and hate and need and love. I write my mother, but she never writes back. She has a new church, new kids, a new prescription to fill.

In a similar way, write about someone with whom you have a close relationship. Describe this person both emotionally (with polysyndeton) and more factually (with asyndeton). Use a parallel construction, if needed.

- "The Mystery of Itch, The Joy of Scratch"
- "Sleeves in His Heart, Thread in His Veins"

You can guess the general topics of the articles from the titles, but just in case you're unsure of the second, here's a bonus parallel construction taken from the text of the article: "He is the son of a suitmaker and the grandson of a pocket maker."

And So . . .

Asyndeton, a listing without conjunctions, and polysyndeton , a series divided by conjunctions, are two devices that allow a writer to create a sense of multiplicity and building up—an emphasis, whether in speech or description or action.

Punctuation and conjunction choices, as well as sentence construction, allow many options in these devices.

Parallel construction adds not only balance, but beauty and rhythm to these devices. In fact, parallelism comes part and parcel with many aspects of writing, as you'll note in the remainder of the book.

Chapter 4

Worth Saying Once,
Worth Saying Twice

Redundancy is to be avoided. *Repetition* is arguably one of the single most powerful tools in the English language. Whether it's used as a signal of danger in everyday language—"No, no!"—or as a refrain in songs and poems—"Rage, rage against the dying of the light," repeated four times in Dylan Thomas's poem of six stanzas, "Do Not Go Gentle into That Goodnight"—the careful use of repetition can make a line or passage powerful and memorable. The repetition of a single word accentuates a point in a speech, a scene in a story, or a commandment in the Bible. This repetition can be enhanced by its arrangement or its amplification.

Anaphora: Repetition of Leading Words

The repetition of the same word or words at the beginning of successive phrases, clauses, or sentences is called *anaphora* (a-*naf*-er-a). *Anapherein* is Greek for *to carry back* or *to refer.* Anaphora adds emphasis to the point being made; it makes reference to and creates relationships between segments of a sentence, verses, or paragraph. Two examples, one from a speech and the other from a story, illustrate the power of single-word repetition. The first shows anaphora in clauses, the second in phrases:

> Every gun that is made, every warship launched, every rocket fired signifies . . . a theft from those who hunger and are not fed . . .
> *Dwight D. Eisenhower,* April 16, 1953

Scrooge was his sole executor, his sole administrator, his sole assignment, his sole residuary legatee, his sole friend and sole mourner.

A Christmas Carol, Charles Dickens

In both cases, the repetition of a single leading modifier asserts the writer's point. Compare them to the more mundane usage: "Every gun, warship, and rocket signifies" and "his sole executor, administrator, assignment, legatee." These versions simply don't carry the weight intended or the emphasis the situation deserves. By repeating the modifier several times, the authors hammer home an effect. Read the examples. Don't you immediately understand the singleness—the aloneness—of the relationship between Scrooge and his friend, Marley ? Don't you feel the cost of each and every weapon on humanity? That's the goal of anaphora: to evoke emotion in the reader.

Dickens's famous line from *A Tale of Two Cities* uses the same kind of modifying anaphora with just one repetition, but it is one of the great memorable lines in English literature:

It is a far, far better thing I do, than I have ever done; it is a far, far better rest I go to, than I have ever known.

Not merely a simple modifier, anaphora can also come in the form of an entire clause, as in this memorable 1940 speech by Winston Churchill. The repetition of *we shall fight* makes the point in no uncertain terms that England will take every measure not to "flag or fail":

. . . whatever the cost may be, we shall fight on the beaches, we shall fight on the landing grounds, we shall fight in the fields and in the streets, we shall fight in the hills; we shall never surrender.

Confused about several *A* devices that have similar definitions? **Anaphora** is the repetition of the same leading words. **Alliteration** is the repetition of the same initial sound. **Asyndeton** gives the impression of an endless listing without the benefit of conjunctions.

Because of the repetition, the final clause is all the more powerful: An entire people becomes empowered; it agrees to go to war.

Anaphora is such a classic rhetorical device, many examples can be found in classical literature, including the Bible. The Beatitudes, *Matthew* (5:3-10) are a famous example of anaphora. They are among the most powerful of the words Jesus spoke because anaphora assures that readers understand the concept and the blessings.

Blessed are the poor in spirit, for theirs is the kingdom of heaven.
Blessed are they that mourn, for they shall be comforted.
Blessed are the meek, for they shall inherit the earth.
Blessed are they which do hunger and thirst after righteousness, for they shall be filled.
Blessed are the merciful, for they shall obtain mercy.
Blessed are the pure in heart, for they shall see God.
Blessed are the peacemakers, for they shall be called the children of God.
Blessed are they which are persecuted for righteousness' sake, for theirs is the kingdom of heaven.

Ecclesiastes (3:1-8) also makes use of full clauses with anaphora:

To every thing there is a season, and a time to every purpose under the heaven: A time to be born, and a time to die; a time to

Exercise: Mood

Louise Erdrich uses anaphora in a hilarious scene in *The Last Report on the Miracles at Little No Horse* in which an elder entangles himself in an old fishing boat being pulled by a moose. Because of the repetition, the author has created a mood of extreme frustration:

Nanapush cursed the moose, cursed himself, cursed the fishhooks, cursed the person who so carefully and sturdily constructed the boat that would not fall apart . . .

For practice, create the mood of boredom by placing a teen in a scene in which he or she is stuck in study hall or in traffic or in front of the TV. Use the repetition of a single verb to emphasize the teen's boredom.

plant, and a time to pluck up that which is planted; a time to kill, and a time to heal; a time to break down, and a time to build up; a time to weep, and a time to laugh; a time to mourn, and a time to dance; a time to cast away stones, and a time to gather stones together; a time to embrace, and a time to refrain from embracing; a time to get, and a time to lose; a time to keep, and a time to cast away; a time to rend, and a time to sew; a time to keep silence, and a time to speak; a time to love, and a time to hate; a time of war, and a time of peace.

As long as this list is, it contains no conjunctions between the major components of the passage (although *and* is used for balance in the internal phrases). The repeated semicolon suggests more possibilities. The concept builds with each repetition, creating a rhythm and strength that has spoken to an audience over many centuries. And of course, thou shalt remember the Ten Commandments: "Thou shalt not " The rhetoric of continual repetition through a listing commands a reader's or listener's attention. The repetition establishes the importance of the list's contents. Note, however, that asyndeton and anaphora, used together, are *high rhetoric* that have to be used sparingly or their effect is diminished.

In her novel *The Last Report on the Miracles at Little No Horse*, Louise Erdrich uses anaphora to start each new sentence, and she uses asyndeton when she describes how Father Damien's letters flowed everywhere. This time, the list evokes multiplicity as well as priority. By the time we are done with this listing, we readers are as exhausted from the writing as Father Damien must have been. The combination of anaphora and asyndeton is effective for that very reason in this representative portion of the passage:

> He wrote to the governor of North Dakota, to the Commissioner of Indian Affairs, to . . . He wrote the President of the United States and to county officials on every level. He wrote to Bernadette Morrissey and to the sick former land agent . . . . He wrote to the state senators and representatives and . . .

Emphatic Epistrophe, Memorable Antimetabole

Epistrophe (e-*pis*-tro-fee) is a partner to anaphora. It's the repetition of the same word or words at the end of successive phrases, clauses, or sentences. The epistrophe is a most emphatic device because it places a heavy stress on a particular word, idea, or concept, as in Lincoln's line that talked of a government "of the people, for the people, by the people." Or in the biblical line: Love "beareth all things, believeth all things, hopeth all things, endureth all things." (1 *Corinthians* 13:7).

Here's another example from Erdrich's *The Last Report on the Miracles at Little No Horse,* an epistrophe that evokes the feeling of steadiness, steadfastness between two characters:

Fleur sat on the shore for a long time with her daughter's weight heavy against her and the water rolling in, and rolling in, and without pause rolling into the shore.

Antimetabole (*an*-tee-me-*ta*-bo-lee) comes from the Greek word meaning to turn about in the opposite direction, a counter-change. Specifically, for the writer, it's the repetition of the identical word or phrase in reverse grammatical order. The device,

Exercise: Antimetabole

In the chapter's text, the examples of antimetabole—the repetition of the identical words or phrase in reverse order—illustrate a reversal of an entire phrase or clause. How about a single word? Make your own antimetabole by choosing a single word (perhaps with two meanings) and placing it at the beginning and the end of the sentence.

Example: May spring sprout soon, perhaps in May.

Epizeuxis (e-pi-*zook*-sis) is the repetition of one word for emphasis, as in Samuel Taylor Coleridge's "The Rime of the Ancient Mariner": "Water, water, everywhere,/And all the boards did shrink;/ Water, water, everywhere,/ Nor any drop to drink." Remember Edgar Allan Poe's poem "The Bells," cited in Chapter 2? "How they tinkle, tinkle, tinkle . . . From the bells, bells, bells, bells"? That's epizeuxis.

Exercise: Clarifying Evil

Here is how a nonfiction article in a special 2003 edition of *U.S. News and World Report,* titled *Spy Stories,* uses amplification to give the reader a definition of evil:

"Philby was truly evil, truly sinister," says Bruce Thompson, a history lecturer at the University of California—Santa Cruz. "He was a traitor without scruples."

Try your own version of amplification by mimicking this passage, but choose a different characteristic: angelic, childish, stubborn, lonely, controlling.

like any form of repetition, gives emphasis to the content, helping the listener to remember:

> ‣ When the going gets tough, the tough get going.
> ‣ You can take the boy out of the country but you can't take the country out of the boy.
> ‣ Ask not what your country can do for you; ask what you can do for your country.

Amplification & Climax Emphasize & Clarify

Two other devices sometimes used with rhetorical repetition are *amplification* and *climax.* Amplification means exactly what you might think—to amplify or augment the idea or situation already expressed. It adds more detail by repeating a word or expression in order to accentuate what could be missed or passed over. In its simplest form, amplification is the expansion of a single detail.

‣ She stared at him, at the flap-soled sneakers. *Maniac Magee,* Jerry Spinelli

‣ A tiny spider crawled from the sac. It was no bigger than a grain of sand, no bigger than the head of a pin. *Charlotte's Web,* E. B. White

‣ . . . because Harry Potter wasn't a normal boy. As a matter of fact, he was as not normal as it is possible to be. *Harry Potter and the Chamber of Secrets,* J. K. Rowling

The importance of amplification in adding power to an argument or statement of principle has no better representation than in one world-altering political document. The Declaration of

Independence is a model of clarity and precision, an ideal of logic and reason. Its second paragraph uses amplification to define the truths that are self-evident. Note how the use of that word, *self-evident*, sets the logic, clarifies, and draws the connections between sentences:

> We hold these truths to be self-evident, that all men are created equal, that they are endowed by their Creator with certain unalienable rights, that among these are life, liberty and the pursuit of happiness. That to secure these rights, governments are instituted among men. . . That whenever any form of government . . .

Although both clarify, a *modifier* and *amplification* differ in the repetition of a pivotal word. "She loved him dearly" is a rather simple sentence using a single modifying adverb to explain how much she loved him. "She loved him, loved him more than any other man, loved him more than herself" uses amplification to clarify—to emphasize the intensity of her love.

Frank McCourt's delightful opening to *Angela's Ashes* makes great use of both epistrophe and amplification by clarifying the differences in miserable childhoods, his own being the worst, of course:

> When I look back on my childhood I wonder how I survived at all. It was, of course, a miserable childhood: the happy childhood is hardly worth your while. Worse than the ordinary miserable childhood is the miserable Irish childhood, and worse yet is the miserable Irish Catholic childhood.

A writer can repeat the simplest adjective or article to create the effect of amplification, as in this example from *The Last Report on the Miracles at Little No Horse*. The reader is forced to understand the child's abandonment; each additional *a* phrase—a ditch, a washout, a pothole—adds clarity about the depths of the child's despair:

> That's when I came to know that to be left, sent off, abandoned, was not of the moment, but a black ditch to the side of the road of your life, a sudden washout, a pothole that went down to China.

In the last two examples, McCourt and Erdrich use another rhetorical device, a *climax*. A climax is the arrangement of words, clauses or sentences in ascending order of importance or emphasis. There's no getting around the idea that a miserable Irish Catholic childhood and a pothole to China are the extreme. The magic of three is present in both excerpts; three strong examples are all that's needed to make a point, and that's why these two quotations are not lists but clarifiers that make the character's or author's point.

Whether in drama or comedy, a sentence climax can elevate a scene, making the situation much more memorable for the reader. Out of a fire scene in *A Child's Christmas in Wales,* Dylan Thomas created three sentences that build on each other and climax, exactly as a child would think. The effect of this scene would have been completely different if Thomas had reversed the sentences. This time anaphora is implied through the use of *as well* and *and*:

> We ran out of the house to the telephone box.
> "Let's call the police as well," Jim said.
> "And the ambulance."
> "And Ernie Jenkins; he likes fires."

In *Maniac Magee,* Jerry Spinelli does an equally fine job of using climax, and anaphora, when he introduces the humorous book's serious theme:

Exercise: Wiley Climax

Sheila O'Connor in her novel, *Where No Gods Came,* uses both anaphora and climax to emphasize her narrator's disdain of a character named Wiley. Can't you hear her disgust, punctuated by the final Wiley clause?

> I despise Wiley for showing up in our lives and ruining everything. . . .Wiley hooting and hollering until the morning. Wiley, with his long sideburns winding down his face, his brown teeth. Wiley telling my dad it was a waste of a life to work for a living.

Think of something you love to hate. List four disgusting things about it. Number them in ascending order of importance. Finally, follow O'Connor's lead and create a paragraph.

And some kids don't like a kid who is different.
Or a kid who does dishes without being told.
Or a kid who never watches Saturday morning cartoons.
Or a kid who's another color.

The second of the two sentences below from Kate DiCamillo's *Because of Winn-Dixie*, uses three rhetorical devices. The technique of the multiple conjunctions, polysyndeton, mimics a child's voice and raises the emotional tension. The repetition of words, anaphora, creates an added stress that builds the sentence's power and the teenager's heartache. If the author hadn't used the same verb three times already, the effect of the final usage would have been diminished. The biggest heartache for this boy is the final item of the list, to the climax:

He cried just like a baby. He missed his mama and he missed his daddy and he missed his sisters and he missed the boy he used to be.

Adding Parallelism to the Mix

As you may have noticed in the last two examples, a parallel construction heightens the effect of a climax, offering a sense of order, balance, and continuity.

A declaration ascribed to Julius Caesar is a simple and famous example: "Veni, vidi, vici" or "I came, I saw, I conquered." The list ascends in order of importance with the most weight given to the final word. The parallelism is in the same verb structure all three times, simple past tense, and the phrase in Latin has the added strengths of alliteration and assonance.

A longer excerpt from Michael Chabon's award-winning novel *The Amazing Adventures of Kavalier and Clay* shows off epistrophe and asyndeton in a parallel construction:

Anadiplosis comes from the Greek term meaning *to double again* or *to redouble*. It's the rhetorical repetition of one or several words that ends one clause, line, or sentence and begins the next. It creates a connection or a binding together: "The love of wicked men converts to fear, that fear to hate, and hate turns one or both to worthy danger and deserved death." *Richard II,* William Shakespeare

She told him that he snored too loudly, laughed too loudly, simply lived too loudly, beyond the limit of tolerance of civilized beings.

Parallel construction comes easily to most of us when we speak, because of its simple effectiveness. A *New York Times* article (October 6, 2003) on a book about Daniel Pearl, the *Wall Street Journal* reporter who was kidnapped and murdered in Pakistan, quotes his widow. Do you see how the first sentence uses a parallel construction, how the second sentence uses amplification, and the third, a metaphor (to be discussed in chapter 5):

One day I was living in Bombay with Danny, and now I'm living in New York with Adam [her baby]. We've lost that sense of normalcy, of things having coherence. That highway I thought was my life doesn't exist anymore.

And So . . .

Repetition of leading words, anaphora, or ending words, epistrophe; the extension of a detail, amplification; and the ascension in emphasis, climax, are all rhetorical devices that empower words. Place these four in a parallel construction along with a few sound devices, and you may be a Henry Wadsworth Longfellow writing "The Song of Hiawatha":

By the shores of Gitche Gumee
By the shining Big-Sea-Water,
Stood the wigwam of Nokomis,
Daughter of the moon, Nokomis.
Dark behind it rose the forest,
Rose the black and gloomy pine-trees,
Rose the firs with cones upon them;
Bright before it beat the water,
Beat the clear and sunny water,
Beat the shining Big-Sea-Water.

Comparative Devices

Chapter 5

Metaphor:
The Core of Language

Metaphor is the most important figure of speech. Ralph Waldo Emerson suggested that it is at the core of our language and, beyond that, our understanding. In *Nature*, he wrote,

> Parts of speech are metaphors, because the whole of nature is a metaphor of the human mind.

When we feel strongly, we speak in metaphor: "That issue is a bear cat. This place is a dump. My car is a lemon." We use metaphors so much that they have become clichés: "What a little devil! She's lost her mind. I died laughing."

Even the military and the government speak in metaphor:

- The Defense Department weathered the storm.
- A cloud hangs over their credibility.
- The Secretary of State is feeling the heat.

Metaphors are the cornerstone of the advertising industry:

- Renee Fleming: A voice so beautiful it can break your heart.
- Hawaii: The pearl of the Pacific.
- Diamonds: A girl's best friend.

Our lives are shaped by an amazing mix of metaphors.

What Is Metaphor?

Taken at its core, a metaphor is a comparison of two dissimilar objects or actions that have some quality in common, a quality that can relate one to the other. A mechanical bunny is a literal metaphor for Energizer batteries because it "keeps going and going."

Take a look at two clichéd metaphoric expressions in the English language: "He's the apple of his mother's eye" and "she's got two left feet." He isn't really an apple, and she doesn't really have two left feet. Yet there's an indirect comparison of two things going on here: Her clumsiness is being compared to two left feet and his dearness is being compared to a favored fruit.

A metaphor eliminates the need for much explanation by enhancing meaning through this indirect comparison. Abstract ideas or difficult topics often need an image to clarify. That's where a metaphor makes all the difference. Think: "Men are from Mars; women are from Venus."

Despite its everyday usage, the metaphor is also one of the writer's most powerful tools. It transfers meaning or bears meaning beyond the obvious. Well-placed, fresh metaphors create striking images or surprising and engaging ideas. In the hands of a good writer, they clarify, enhance, create layers of meaning.

A Good Metaphor Supplies an Instant Image

Periodicals, books, and speeches are full of simple, apt metaphors—instant images. In an article about plastic surgery, for instance, author James Poniewozik makes this claim:

> Plastic surgery is the new Vegas; once laced with glamour and vice, now for boring, normal people.
>
> "Trading Places," *Time*, July 2003

Two dissimilar things are compared (a surgical procedure paired to

---

Defined, a **metaphor** is an implied or indirect comparison that refers to or describes one thing as if it were the other. Literally, it comes from the Greek *meta*, meaning *beyond* and *pherin*, meaning *to bear.*

a city) as if one were the other. The metaphor works because of the connection between them—glamour and risk.

An essay in the *Minneapolis Star Tribune* (July 27, 2003) discusses the life of a basketball superstar, Kobe Bryant. Note how the author inserts a metaphor and then extends it to the end of the sentence:

> The larger truth is that, like other rich and famous entertainers, Kobe has lived in a golden cocoon for years—one we fans helped spin.

A cocoon—a silk protective covering—links us to the idea of spinning. Kobe has lived in a sheltered environment of his and his fans' making. The golden color of the cocoon, of course, refers to his wealth and fame, and at least subtly, the notion of spinning evokes the sense of both a basketball in motion under the superstar's control, and the fact that his life now seems out of control. This simple metaphor layers meaning both explicitly and indirectly.

Politicians speak in metaphors, especially in the midst of crises, giving listeners instant images meant to inspire or explain. Winston Churchill characterized the Soviet Union on a 1939 radio broadcast and the complexity of forecasting its actions:

> It is a riddle wrapped in a mystery inside an enigma.

During a 1940 fireside chat, Franklin Roosevelt said, "We must be the great arsenal of democracy." George W. Bush, in his 2002 State of the Union speech, named Iraq, Iran, and North Korea "the axis of evil." Each of these examples is a powerful metaphor—figurative speech that provides a concrete picture through indirect comparison.

War coins new metaphors. The Korean War brought *brainwash* to

Exercise: A Dream of an Image

Actress Bette Davis made the following observation, comparing her vocation to a meal:

> To fulfill a dream, to be allowed to sweat over lonely labor, to be given a chance to create, is the meat and potatoes of life. The money is the gravy.

Try creating a metaphor for your life's dream.

Exercise: Hidden Metaphors

Some metaphors are so hidden by common use that they're practically invisible: the mouth of the river; in this neck of the woods; by the skin of his teeth; toe the line; stabbed me in the back; she shot down his argument.

Can you think of others?

the collective vocabulary; from the immediate post-World War II era, Churchill gave us *iron curtain*; from Desert Storm came *smart bombs*; from the latest war in Iraq, *shock and awe* campaign. Each of these metaphors is now simply part of the English language.

In a 1942 message to the American Booksellers Association, Roosevelt said,

> People die, but books never die. No man and no force can abolish memory . . . In this war, we know, books are weapons.

The idea of books as weapons is a strong image, especially in a time when the entire world was involved in war and the average Jane Doe felt vulnerable. But metaphors don't always work well. They must remain fresh, have true depth, and a clarity. Barnes & Noble used a simple metaphor in one ad, but mixed it with others, so that while readers understand, the effect is tarnished:

> From coast to coast, we read hundreds of books every year to find the gems that might otherwise get lost in the shuffle.

Advertising Hides the Metaphor for a Reason

Aharon Appelfeld wrote these lines in a column, leaving no uncertainty about his reliance on this important language device to make his point:

> The Holocaust is a central event in many people's lives, but it has also become a metaphor for our century. There cannot be an end to speaking and writing about it.
>
> *New York Times*, November 15, 1986

Nor is there any uncertainty about metaphor in this line from *Physics as Metaphor*:

And what of the astronomer's black hole, the perfect metaphor for a bottomless well in space from which not even light may escape?

Physics as Metaphor, Roger S. Jones

Sometimes metaphor is more subtle, not as easy to extract from the reading, and yet the reader subconsciously knows that an unusual and indirect comparison is being made. "Taste the purity of nature. Buy only pure maple syrup." runs an ad by Maplemark. Immediately, the consumer thinks, "Yes, pure maple syrup; no artificial flavorings." But the ad is saying more; it's suggesting that to taste the syrup is to taste Mother Nature herself. This particular maple syrup, the ad says in essence, *is* nature—buy our product and taste the natural world. Advertisers spend large sums of money to guarantee sales. A sale is assured if the consumer believes he's buying an intangible that will enhance life.

An Esprit cosmetic ad is offering more than a new perfume when it names it *Life*. The Marlboro man metaphor suggested more than a cigarette; it suggested virility and a my-way-or-the-highway cowboy kind of attitude. In the same way, car and clothing ads don't merely advertise a specific vehicle or a pair of jeans. Companies spend millions to illustrate the glamorous, wealthy, serene, or lusty lifestyle that can be had for the purchase.

A special advertising section of the *New Yorker* (May 12, 2003) from independent booksellers preceded its list of book picks with this line, embedding two metaphors:

Literature can be a force of incandescent power not only for Americans but for cultures blanketed by oppression.

Linking *blanketed* with *oppression* deepens the idea of a dark, unilluminated society. Two apt images, one of which is based on a noun—force of incandescent power—and the other based on a verb—*blanketed* by oppression—join. While darkness isn't the first meaning of *to blanket*, when it becomes the active image here in connection to light, a strong metaphor forms.

These metaphors, chosen so carefully by their ad creators, etched both image and meaning into the consumer's mind. The comparison is indirect, but the motivation and results are very direct—sales. Novelists, too, want to hook a sale, a reader. Their

Exercise: Advertising Writing

Look for the subtle use of metaphors in five ads in which the product is being compared to a certain desired aspect of life.

Nouns that also act as verbs are good tools for metaphoric language. A short list of nouns that can also be verbs are: flower, telephone, bed, ship, corral, dance, catalogue, paint, button.

Choose one of these, or a noun of your own, and build a double metaphorical sentence around it, similar to the structure of the *New Yorker* ad discussed on page 55.

Examples: A cowboy can be a force of *unbridled* temperament not only for rodeo lovers but for Americans *corralled* by a president.

A fleet of oil freighters is a force of weighty proportion not only for oil companies but for countries left shipwrecked by the export.

usage of metaphor is no less compelling. Read on.

Metaphors in Literature

Metaphors appear in every possible venue and vehicle in literature. A metaphor can be large in scope—the foundation or theme of a story—as with Herman Melville's white whale or Miguel de Cervantes's windmills. These two metaphors and their stories have provided analysts with countless comparisons, layers, meanings, and images for interpretation.

Metaphors are also the base for shorter works, like the forked path in Robert Frost's poem, "The Road Not Taken." The title, the whole of the poem, and its single metaphor speak of the choices we make in life and how they affect our journey.

Two roads diverged in a yellow
  wood,
And sorry I could not travel both
And be one traveler, long I stood
And looked down one as far as I
  could
To where it bent in the under-
  growth;

Then took the other, as just as
  fair, . . .

Although Frost speaks only of the forked path in the woods, he's suggesting through indirect comparison that a forked path appears before us on a regular basis. Which will we choose? Which is the best choice? Will we regret the choice not taken? Clearly, Frost's use of such a fitting metaphor resonates.

Jeffrey Eugenides, in his Pulitzer-winning novel, *Middlesex*, extends a single metaphor through multiple lines when he has his narrator describe a certain character. He chose a single feature (freckles) and compared it to something totally outlandish (stars during the creation of the universe), and yet, it works beautifully, delightfully. Note his fine use of strong verbs and nouns, each of which amplifies the metaphor further, forcing the reader to stretch, too. It's the metaphor that makes the passage unforgettable:

Exercise: Extensions

Compose metaphors with correlating extensions.

F. Scott Fitzgerald said that "All writing is swimming underwater, holding your breath." Imitate that literary sentence by providing a different metaphor, and extending it a tad further.

Example: All writing is jumping off a cliff, hoping for an updraft.

> I'd never seen a creature with so many freckles before. A Big Bang had occurred, originating at the bridge of her nose, and the force of this explosion had sent galaxies of freckles hurtling and drifting to every end of her curved warm-blooded universe. There were clusters of freckles on her forearms and wrists, an entire Milky Way spreading across her forehead, even a few sputtering quasars flung into the wormholes of her ears.

Literature also provides a smorgasbord of metaphors beautifully placed in single sentences:

> ‣ Each hour in choir was a desert to be crossed on her knees.
> ‣ His voice was a rich sienna, the color of reassurance.

These metaphors in Mark Salzman's novel *Lying Awake* are compelling because of their unique comparisons. Likening a voice to a color, then giving that color a characteristic? If one compared an hour of choir practice to torture, the comment would not be memorable. In equating choir practice with crossing a hot, dry desert, an image and a feeling arise. By extending the metaphor (and the torture) with *on her knees*, the image becomes memorable. At the same time, the image resonates with history, conjuring ancient monks at desert hermitages.

In the same book, Salzman describes how his primary character reacts to her life's passion:

> Sister John emptied herself for the voice of the Holy Spirit, letting it resonate within her, turning her heart into a cathedral.

The idea of a cathedral—with its high, arched ceilings, stained glass windows, vast space filled with music from a huge pipe organ— gives power, size, and imagination to a heart. And of course, a cathedral implies sacredness. Salzman leaves no doubts for the reader that Sister John is in the right vocation. A strong image layered in meaning is the direct result of a well-crafted metaphor.

Charles Dickens loved the simple metaphor:

- "She's the ornament of her sex." *The Old Curiosity Shop*
- "In came Mrs. Fezziwig, one vast substantial smile." *A Christmas Carol*
- "I wear the chain I forged in life." *A Christmas Carol*
- "Let sleeping dogs lie—who wants to rouse 'em?" *David Copperfield*

Dickens describes a woman as an ornament, as though she were the epitome of femininity, and Mrs. Fezziwig as one huge smile: Can't you imagine a large, plumpish woman with a beaming round face? The ghost of Jacob Marley appears with a chain around his neck, a metaphor for the heavy burden of his former life. Letting sleeping dogs lie is a subtler image because of its implied relationship to old stories and secrets, where they are—in the past—or they could awaken to bite back.

Combining two related metaphors, building on each other, Martin Luther King, Jr., created an image of the power of the early Christian church, in 1963's "Letter from Birmingham Jail."

> In those days the church was not merely a thermometer that recorded the ideas and principles of popular opinion; it was a thermostat that transformed the mores of society.

Metaphors can have particularly strong impacts in historical contexts. Esther Forbes's classic children's novel *Johnny Tremain*, the 1944 Newbery Medal winner about the American Revolution, includes an economical description of the main character by one of his master's daughters. It speaks of his value to the family:

> Johnny worth-his-weight-in-gold Tremain.

A morning scene in the book has one sister brushing the golden hair of a younger sister:

> Very carefully she began to tie the child's halo of pure curls.

The rarity and value of gold to the modest characters in that time period escalate the value of the metaphor. The religious environment of the times is similarly used when the mistress of the house tries to rouse the apprentices who sleep in the attic. The reader immediately understands her attitude about the boys through metaphor:

> Frustrated, she shook the ladder she was too heavy to climb. She wished she could shake "them limbs of Satan."

Metaphors in fiction can be less direct than the typical Dickensian example, ranging in subtlety and levels of meaning. Nevada Barr, in her short story "Beneath the Lilacs," a mystery from the collection edited by Sara Paretsky, *Women on the Case,* writes of her main character:

> The heady scent of the lilacs wrapped around her in a gauzy cloak.

Scent is being compared to a lightweight fabric, which in turn has been woven into a cloak. Smells can't really wrap a person in a garment, but that's metaphor for you.

In the same story, Barr writes this line from her character's thoughts:

> [T]oo many years had passed since the death of a father she had never known for the lash of his murder to cut too deep.

Exercise: Similarity Among Differences

"The world is a ticking powder keg of nails and fear." So wrote Mark Morford in the *San Francisco Gate,* in a piece titled "Please Write More about Rape" (May 14, 2004). *World* and *powder keg* are two dissimilar ideas or things from which a connection has been made.

Choose two such dissimilar words from the list below. Determine whether a thread exists that could connect them. Create a metaphor that has some meaning for you. Beware of the bizarre pairing; a metaphor that is ill-chosen weakens a good piece of writing. Amplify the metaphor for more clarity if needed.

Eyes, lighthouse, canoe, mud, college degree, child, water bottle, storm, victory, failure, wallpaper, robin, croissant, sky, arms, stapler, notebook, journey, blemish, grapefruit, berries, walnut, sail, clothes-line, doorway, home

Examples:
- A college degree is my failure made concrete.
- Alisha's notebook was her sky, a place to let her imagination soar.
- I could see the storm in his dark eyes.

No obvious metaphor is present. And yet, *lash* and *cut too deep* stand out. What is being compared? These words are not referring to the father's murder by a whip, but to the daughter's reaction. The sudden revelation that her father was murdered is not as shocking as it might have been because she had never known him. Shocking news (*whiplash*) is being compared to its effect (a shallow laceration).

Sometimes nonfiction, too, couches the metaphor in rhetoric for specific reasons. When King wrote the long, carefully constructed, well-reasoned "Letter from Birmingham Jail," he hid his strong words among polite and humble rhetoric, including this metaphor to describe the white who is politically moderate:

I have almost reached the regrettable conclusion that the Negro's great stumbling block in his stride toward freedom is not the White

Citizen's Counciler or the Ku Klux Klanner, but the white moderate, who is more devoted to order than to justice, who prefers a negative peace which is the absence of tension to a positive peace which is the presence of justice, who . . .

King has chosen a metaphor for its indirect comparison rather than a simile, a direct comparison. He weaves the truth of the situation: if a large enough stumbling block (*the white moderate*) is placed in a pathway (*the Negro's*), the destination (*freedom*) will not be reached.

Mixing Metaphors Makes a Mess

The idea of mixing one's metaphors may be familiar, but perhaps it's not clear. A *mixed metaphor* combines multiple images or phrases that are unrelated, and that don't work well together. A reader would have to think long and hard about a line that combines these two images:

Old Bill Bailey has been made a sacrificial lamb for taking the lid off a can of worms.

As the sentence stands, *sacrificial lamb* and *a can of worms* have no correlation. What's the picture in your mind when you read that sentence? The power of the two metaphors is lost because they don't connect. If Old Bill Bailey had been described as a sacrificial lamb because of his naiveté about something he witnessed, the sentence would probably work. But applying the can of worms metaphor to the sacrificial lamb leaves, well, another can of worms.

A mixed metaphor is an inconsistent metaphor that mixes several images rather than completing one. "It's the silver lining at the end of the tunnel" might be a sentence the reader understands, but the mixed metaphors aren't related; a long dark tunnel never has a silver lining at its end. On the other hand, "A light at the end of the tunnel" may be clichéd, but it's a cliché in which two metaphors work together to create a single image.

"I've gone the extra mile by leaps and bounds" is a *double metaphor* that works. This one, with mixed metaphors, doesn't: "My brother is a bearcat, simmering for hours before he erupts." A bearcat doesn't

Exercise: Save the Metaphor

"My brother is a bearcat, simmering for hours before he erupts" is a mixed metaphor. Can you repair the damage by creating two completely different sentences, each with its own metaphor? Keep one-half of the original sentence:

1. My brother is a bearcat, _____ for hours before he _____.
2. _____ is _____, simmering for hours before ____ erupts.

simmer, and there's the jarring additional image of a volcano.

A humorous exchange in *A Confederacy of Dunces,* by Pulitzer Prize-winning author John Kennedy Toole, provides an illustration in which one character (who owns a Levi Pants company) tells another not to mix her metaphors:

> "It's a real tragedy, Gus, a real tragedy."
> "Don't try to make a big Arthur Miller play out of Levi Pants."

Metonymy (me-*ton*-a-me) substitutes one word or phrase for another. It's a quiet form of metaphor. In Greek, metonymy means *to change the name.* In this case, the substitution is another thing that bears the same meaning. So, rather than saying that a man is a *priest,* he's described as *a man of the cloth.* Rather than wondering whether a man asked a woman to marry him, metonymy is wondering "Did he give her a diamond ring?" Rather than suggesting that diplomacy is better than military action, "the pen is mightier than the sword."

In *A Confederacy of Dunces,* a character named Jones appears frequently; he is never without sunglasses and is a heavy smoker. In these four excerpts (within 60 pages), note how the author uses metaphor, especially, metonymy to describe the man's trademark characteristics in new and interesting ways, negating the chance of redundancy. Quiet metaphor is at work.

- The sunglasses blew smoke all over the old man's cards.
- A new cloud floated up.
- "Okay," Jones said brightly and blew a great thundercloud of smoke.
- Jones blew out a cumulus formation.

A Metaphor or Not?

Very often, a metaphor is formed with the *to be* verb: *All the world is a stage. He's a little devil. She was a slave-driver. Their voices were sound bytes from heaven. We'll be in the dog house if we do that.* But the *to be* verb is often used to describe something or someone and no metaphor is present:

He is an honorable, obstinate, truthful, high-spirited, intensely prejudiced, perfectly reasonable man.
Bleak House, Charles Dickens

Benjamin Franklin is the founding father who winks at us.
Time, July 7, 2003

Exercise: Fresh Choices

Metonymy substitutes a word or phrase for another fresher choice. When a student fails an exam or a course, he is often said to have *flunked* the class. Use a metaphor or metonymy to relate the idea in a new and different way.

Example: On the final exam, Elwood went down in flames.

And why aren't these two excerpts metaphors? Because two things are not being compared; the author and narrator have simply offered their analysis of these men.

Sometimes a newspaper headline will seem to be metaphoric, like this one: "Moving Mountains." Mountains don't move, do they? But this article's subject is the Black Hills where, literally, mountains have been removed to create Mount Rushmore and the Crazy Horse Monument. Granted, it took decades to move the mountains, but the fact remains that tons of the mountains' sides were removed.

An ad may have the appearance of metaphor, but in fact the line may be exactly true, as is this one by a company that builds communities:

A sense of place.
It's balmy breezes.
It's deep-green forests.
It's friendly neighbors.
It's Arvida.

Rarely, because it certainly appears otherwise, a negative *to be* statement is actually a metaphor. The difference between a negative metaphor and a plain negative statement is the author's motivation. Here's one that's a metaphor by Bernard Darwin, an English writer and golfer:

> Golf is not a funeral, though both can be very sad affairs.

A sentence from a story may have the feel and set-up of a metaphor, but in truth, it may be another form of figurative language, as in this line from *James and the Giant Peach,* by Roald Dahl:

> Below them, the sea is deep and cold and hungry.

Most seas are deep and cold, but the idea of hungry is interesting and seemingly metaphoric, a comparison. Instead, Dahl has made use of personification, a device that gives an inanimate object or abstract idea human attributes, the subject of another chapter.

And So . . .

- A metaphor is an indirect comparison that refers to or describes one thing as if it were the other. (The world is a stage.)
- A metaphor often creates a striking image or a surprising but engaging idea. (The landlady sharpened her claws.)
- A metaphor is a vivid and original means of expressing a comparison, which in turn clarifies. (The train cars jackknifed across the track.)
- An image may seem metaphoric, but the description is actually factual, or another figurative language device is in use.
- Beware of the clichéd metaphor; its overuse has diminished its freshness. (Her heart was broken.)
- Beware of the mixed metaphor that blends two unrelated images. It's jarring, if not downright silly, and almost always ineffective: (In coal mines, canaries are used as human guinea pigs.)

Nothing Like a Simile

The most common of rhetorical devices—the most easily recognized—is the simile. This short artistic figure of speech delights and clarifies by offering a surprising contrast about the idea being presented. The image of a well-done simile is interesting—even striking:

> She stood in front of the altar, shaking like a freshly caught trout.
> *I Know Why the Caged Bird Sings,* Maya Angelou

But similes, like metaphors, don't merely decorate writing. They are functional, substantive comparison devices that enable the reader to see, feel, or understand the scene or point. Yet a simile is different from a metaphor. This chapter will give you a clear picture of the many options for simile-making, as well as the reasons for forming them. The chapter will also illustrate the difference between the simile and the analogy, another form of comparison.

The Makeup of a Simile

A *simile* is the direct comparison of two dissimilar objects or actions in which a word of comparison is used; in contrast, a metaphor is indirect. The most familiar apparel for a simile are *like* or *as:* "He sang like a sick bullfrog" or "His voice was smooth as honey." These examples, though not particularly unique, are similes because the comparisons are dissimilar: Voices are being compared to a bullfrog and to honey. A simile can also be negative: "Her voice was not like honey at all; it was like sandpaper, gritty and rough."

Similes arrive in other dressings, too. *So,* often accompanied by *as,* can be a word of comparison in a simile. This form is often lengthier. Here are biblical examples:

> ▸ As a dog returneth to his vomit, so a fool returneth to his folly.
> *Proverbs* 26:11
> ▸ As cold waters to a thirsty soul, so is good news from a far country.
> *Proverbs* 25:25

A simile can also wear the comparative terminology of mathematics, such as *less than, more than, is as,* and *is similar to*:

> ▸ The truth is more obvious than the sun.
> ▸ He stalked out the door, looking as relentless as a guided missile.
> ▸ The row of houses was similar to a lineup of cardboard cookie cutter boxes.

Shows, resembles, remind are also comparative words that can be shaped into similes. But always, the key to whether or not a simile is present is the dissimilarity between the things being compared and the directness of the comparison: "She reminds me of a blue heron, tall and still, ready to strike."

Sometimes, no word of comparison is needed at all, but the simile is very much present:

> But [the Supreme Court] also has a chance to be an oasis of common sense on the most combustible legal question of the day.
> *New York Times,* op-ed, October 6, 2003

A **simile word** is often used as an adjective: flower-like symmetry, cathedral-like ceiling. But this device is not truly a simile unless a comparison is being drawn between two dissimilar things. So, a pinwheel or a brooch with its flower-like symmetry works, whereas the same symmetry description for a daisy doesn't because *daisy* and *flower* are in essence the same, not compared.

The portrait [three California scientists] got of this nuclear light bulb is a science fiction illustrator's dream, resembling a small city on Earth jammed with incandescent vibrating towers several times taller than any skyscraper.

Charles Petit, "Pulsing Stars,"
U.S. News and World Report, Special Edition, 2003

The second example has numerous similes and a metaphor (nuclear light bulb). *Portrait* is being compared to a *science fiction illustrator's dream* in a simile without a comparative word. The author might have said that the portrait was *like a dream*, but made the comparison even more direct: The portrait *is* a dream. He then extends the comparison by saying the portrait resembles a small city and that the city's lighted towers are taller than skyscrapers. On first glance, this final comparison may not seem to be a simile at all since towers and skyscrapers are often one and the same, but when the *towers* are in space, 30,000 light years away, then the comparison is indeed of dissimilar objects, and thus, a simile.

The Clichéd Simile

One of the reasons the simile is the most readily identified of rhetorical devices is that the same ones are used again and again and become ingrained in everyday speech. Clichés pepper our language: happy as a clam, eat like a pig, hungry as a bear, cool as a cucumber, deaf/dumb as a post. Even Robert Burns's eighteenth-century poetic line—"my luve is like a red, red rose"—might be today's cliché.

Sometimes an expression sounds like a cliché and yet it works for the kind of writing in which it's being used. Detective novels, for example, occasionally resort to a certain lingo. Here's that kind of expression used by interviewer Colin Covert in a newspaper article about a film director who exuded nervous energy:

Director James Foley is a pretty wired guy. Over a cheeseburger-hold-the-bun lunch in Minneapolis last week, his eyes cased the room like a stoolie on the lookout for a triggerman.

"Director Foley a Talent Magnet," *Star Tribune*, April 25, 2003

Exercise: Making New

Give your writing and your readers a lift. Brainstorm a new, interesting comparison from each of these overused similes. Pretend that your story's setting is contemporary urban:

) Hair, black as coal:
) Face, red as a beet:
) Personality, cold as ice:
) Garage mechanic, gentle as a kitten:
) Teacher, mad as a wet hen:
) Teen, smart as a whip:

The simile *good as gold* is a cliché, but in Charles Dickens's day, the expression was fresh and original. When Mrs. Cratchit in *A Christmas Carol* asks her husband how Tiny Tim behaved at church, Bob Cratchit replies,

As good as gold and better.

The significance of gold—wealth of pocket or soul—is carried by the comparison, adding depth and brilliance to a simple expression. Bob Cratchit clarifies, which moves the comment toward an analogy: Tiny Tim "gets thoughtful sitting by himself so much, and thinks the strangest things you ever heard." At church, young Tim had hoped that the people *would* see him as a cripple and "it might be pleasant to them to remember upon Christmas Day, who made lame beggars walk and blind men see." Indeed, Tiny Tim was better than gold.

The comparative images Dickens evoked in *A Christmas Carol* were original in his day, and some still are today:

) In came a fiddler . . . and tuned like fifty stomach aches.
) There were ruddy brown-faced, broad-girthed Spanish onions shining in the fatness of their growth like Spanish Friars.
) Old Marley was as dead as a doornail.

Doornails were large-headed nails—big, bold, brassy—and, of course, lifeless. Dickens applies another device, alliteration, by repeating a consonant sound—*d*. The comparison of the dead Marley to a doornail, becomes even more absolute.

[Scrooge was] hard and sharp as flint, from which no steel had ever struck out generous fire; secret, and self-contained, and solitary as an oyster.

In comparing Scrooge's penny-pinching ways to flint, Dickens extends the comparison, making an old expression fresher. *Flint and steel* describe Scrooge's rigid, cantankerous personality and are tools used in the making of fire. Such hardness brings generosity neither to his heart nor his hearth. Notice the alliteration once again: steel, struck, secret, self-contained, solitary. No passage in Dickens's capable hands is ever unclear. His writing is beautifully detailed and carefully fine-tuned, with fresh figurative language that propelled his work into the classics. The writing is as delicious today as it was a century and a half ago.

It's fun to know where or how our clichés originated, but, if used today, *good as gold* and *dead as a doornail* are just banal truisms. A fresh, original simile, used sparingly, is the goal.

Fresh, Original Comparisons

So, what do fresh, original similes look like? Since the first example in this chapter was one from Maya Angelou, let's take a look at more of her writing. In a chapter entitled "Uncle Willie" from *I Know Why the Caged Bird Sings*, a crippled man is described:

Uncle Willie used to sit, like a giant black Z.

Exercise: A Mystery

Detective novels often use similes, analogies, and metaphors that reference matters of death, thievery, police chiefs, etc. With "the boss is tough as nails," a writer could freshen the cliché with "the boss is tough as an ax blade" or create a metaphor with "the boss ate nails for lunch."

Below are three examples, one of which is a metaphor, one a simile, and one an analogy. Decide which is which. Then recreate the device in your own words. Try it once again, this time using a different kind of comparison.

1. The thief shook himself free of his lies as a dog rids its fur of raindrops.

2. The ax blade came down on the secretary's incompetence.

3. His voice sounded dead as a graveyard.

An analogy is applied for the reader's clarity in the article, "Pulsing Stars":

The bubbles, inflated with pure electromagnetic energy, occasionally move in sync like fans at a ballpark doing the wave.

Pretend that you're explaining something from your job or line of work to an audience unfamiliar with it. Further clarity is needed. Offer an analogy that would be familiar to your audience.

That's about as simple and visual a verbal illustration as a writer can paint. The simile offers so much more than a line like "Uncle Willie sat hunched over in his chair." Angelou goes on to describe how this fierce, complex man oversaw the schoolwork of his nieces and nephews. If the homework wasn't going well,

. . . his big overgrown right hand would catch one of us behind the collar, and in the same moment would thrust the culprit toward the dull red heater, which throbbed like a devil's toothache.

The simile associates Uncle Willie's actions with the devil and adds to the children's, and the reader's, impression of him as a threatening, scary taskmaster.

Later in the same chapter, the author visits her Uncle Willie's store and senses "a wrongness" in the place, like an alarm clock that had gone off without being set. The comparison of the store scene to a ringing alarm clock elevates the tension. The niece is alarmed. Something is askew. She soon realizes that her uncle is standing oddly erect, waiting on customers without his cane, pretending that he is whole, not crippled. The author comments:

He must have tired of being a cripple, as prisoners tire of penitentiary bars and the guilty tire of blame.

The double simile is especially effective here. Willie undoubtedly felt like a prisoner in his crippled body from time to time and his sister often informed customers and acquaintances that he'd been crippled as a child, that he wasn't born this way. Finally, Angelou shows Uncle Willie walking back toward his cane, hidden in the store's aisle:

Uncle Willie was making his own way down the long shadowed aisle between the shelves and the counter—hand over hand, like a man climbing out of a dream.

This fresh, effective simile provides not only a visual image, but a more profound glimpse of what the previous scene had been about, Willie living his dream of being whole. And now he is clumsily moving—hand over hand—back to reality.

The Difference Between Simile & Analogy

A *simile* and an *analogy* are similar but different. Both compare two different things, but an analogy compares the unknown to a known in order to explain further or deeper. The weatherman, for example, talks about *golfball-sized hail*—an analogy, because it substantiates or clarifies a point by offering a comparison that has several similar points of reference (in this case, the size and the color of golf balls and the hail are the same). A simile, on the other hand, creates a single, interesting, or surprising image: "Less hail fell than a pail of marbles."

One of the great rhetoricians of the last century, Winston Churchill once remarked,

Politics are almost as exciting as war, and quite as dangerous. In war you can only be killed once, but in politics many times.

Exercise: Extending Simile

A short story by Madison Smartt Bell is told from the perspective of the bird from Poe's poem "The Raven." He begins the story:

First of all, I am not a raven. A stately raven, with a four-foot wing spread and a beak like a samurai sword, probably wouldn't have fit in the room.
"Small Blue Thing," *Harper's*, June 2000

Bell doesn't extend the simile of the sword, so do it for him. Think about how to amplify the image of the raven's mighty swordlike beak or use the samurai sword to compare it to the beak of the narrator, actually a small crow. Add one sentence to the lines above.

Exercise: Simile Recognition

"The Lady Saddle," by Mary Carroll, in the children's magazine *Cricket* (July 1, 2003), is a story about a Quaker girl who must learn to ride a horse sidesaddle. Before reading the explanation that follows, decide in which sentences similes are triggered. Where they are not, come up with your own.

1. "Oh, Mama," I protested. "I want to ride brave and bold like the cavalry."
2. He yelped as I eased off the boot.
3. He seemed part of his saddle, while I sagged on my saddle like a bag of oats.
4. The snake slithered away as fast as it could.

The first and third examples are similes because they compare two dissimilar ideas or objects for clarification purposes. The narrator compares her riding to that of the cavalry and she contrasts her sidesaddle posture to that of a sagging bag of oats. Each of these similes relates to the story's historic setting. The *as* of the second example is a conjunction connecting two independent clauses. The final sentence seems to contain a simile, but note the absence of a second dissimilar thing.

The same magazine offers a nonfiction science story about foot-long fish called sea dragons ("Dragons Down Under," by Linda Herman). Again, which of these sentences have similes and which do not?

1. Mobility is limited even further because they don't have scales like most fish. As you would expect from a dragon, armor-like plates cover their bodies.
2. The slightest variation in water temperature will kill them, as can a sudden change in light.
3. Dragons can be identified by their white facial markings—as with fingerprints, no two patterns are the same.
4. When a tiny shrimp swims near, dragons use their long, narrow snouts like straws to suck up their meals.

(continued)

In example one, the first sentence does not use a simile; *like* is a simple preposition. In the second sentence in the same example, *as* suggests an upcoming comparison: *Armor-like* is the simile comparing the bodies of dragons to fish. The *as* in the second example is not part of a simile; it's a conjunction. In the final two examples, the markings of a sea dragon are being compared to the individual markings on a fingerprint and the narrow snouts are likened to straws. These comparisons are analogies rather than similes, aptly chosen for the audience they're addressing; kids will make an immediate connection to fingerprints and straws.

By comparing politics to war, the listener is assured of a better understanding of both the excitement and danger of politics. That's analogy.

In E. B. White's *Charlotte's Web,* the spider applies an analogy for her own benefit. The comparison of one thing to another provides a solution that gives her solace. At the same time, the analogy offers the young reader a clear life lesson: a part of one's life might aid in another part:

> Charlotte was naturally patient. She knew from experience that if she waited long enough, a fly would come to her web; and she felt sure that if she thought long enough about Wilbur's problem, an idea would come to her mind.

Analogies can be as subtle as metaphors. Louise Erdrich's skillful analogizing of fire to the anger between a man and a woman is implied, not stated, in *The Last Report on the Miracles at Little No Horse.* Erdrich continues to clarify the comparison so that by the time the analogy ends, the reader feels singed, too.

> When this happened, they fought. Stinging flames of words blistered their tongues. Silence was worse. Beneath its slow-burning weight their black looks singed. After a few days, their minds shriveled into dead coals. Some speechless nights, they lay together like logs turned completely to ash.

In another of her books, *The Master Butchers Singing Club,*

Erdrich uses weather and a landscape to describe a town, furthering the description with an analogy that would resonate with readers (at least with readers from the Midwest, where the story is centered):

> Snow is a blessing when it softens the edges of the world . . . This snow was the opposite—it outlined the edges of things and made the town look meaner, bereft, merely tedious, like a mistake set down upon the earth and only half erased.

Martin Luther King Jr. ends his "Letter from Birmingham Jail" with an extended analogy that compares and contrasts weather conditions to his hope for the future:

> Let us all hope that the dark clouds of racial prejudice will soon pass away and the deep fog of misunderstanding will be lifted from our fear-drenched communities, and in some not too distant tomorrow the radiant stars of love and brotherhood will shine over our great nation with all their scintillating beauty.

Extend the Simile to Provide More Clarity

A simile clarifies through comparison, but the image is often a leap. Sometimes the likeness isn't quite clear enough. Consider the sandpaper cited at the beginning of this chapter: "Her voice . . . was like sandpaper, gritty and rough." Adding *gritty and rough* extends and amplifies.

The Dickens example about why Tiny Tim is as *good as gold* extends simile, but it doesn't return to the image of gold. A true extended simile keeps the comparison going, as in this quirky example by Mark Salzman in *Lying Awake:*

> Sister Elizabeth looked like a can of soda that had been shaken hard, then opened. She popped up from her chair, clapped her hands, and asked . . .

Another example of an extended simile describes Sister John in a holy trance:

> She tried to obey but was frozen in beauty, like a fly trapped in amber. She could not move.

The first sentence has an artistic comparison, *frozen in beauty,* and it suggests a loveliness. That image is amplified with a second comparison that defines the scene with a harsher reality—a fly, trapped, timeless but dead, spiritless. Despite the dissimilarity of the two, the fly and the robed nun are both black, *winged,* and caught in the same awful predicament.

In *Crossing to Safety,* Wallace Stegner extends a simile through his narrator this way:

> Floating upward through a confusion of dreams and memory, curving like a trout through the rings of previous risings, I surface.

An even longer simile can imply many more levels. "The Things They Carried," by Tim O'Brien, first appeared in *Esquire* and then in the author's own book of the same title. In this piece, he lists the items in the packs and pockets of each Vietnam soldier. Here's a passage that extends one simile—one simple comparison of soldiers to mules—through an entire paragraph. O'Brien first suggests that the foot soldier carries the sky, the whole atmosphere, the humidity, the gravity of Vietnam, and then he writes:

> They moved like mules. By daylight they took sniper fire, at night they were mortared, but it was not battle, it was just the endless march, village to village, without purpose, nothing won or lost. They marched for the sake of the march. They plodded along slowly, dumbly, leaning forward against the heat, unthinking, all blood and bone, simple grunts, soldiering with their legs, toiling up the hills and down into the paddies and across the rivers and up again and down, just humping, one step and then the next and then another, but no volition, no matter of posture and carriage, the hump was everything, a kind of inertia, a kind of emptiness, a dullness of desire and intellect and conscience and hope and human sensibility. Their principles were in their feet. . . . and for all the ambiguities of Vietnam, all the mysteries and unknowns, there was at least the single abiding certainty that they would never be at a loss for things to carry.

Does this passage not describe the life of a mule? Could O'Brien have been any clearer in his description? By extending the simile through the characteristics of a mule—plodding beasts of burden—

the reader becomes as burdened with the weight of war as the soldier himself. O'Brien's word choice and apt simile is no accident; the author has deliberately helped the reader feel the weightiness of what was carried.

Avoid Overusing & Mixing Similes

Besides avoiding the prosaic simile, avoid sprinkling similes liberally throughout the same piece of writing. Similes that come in rapid order are distracting, not illuminating. Frankly, everything can't and shouldn't be compared to something else or the effect is diluted. The overused simile, like the cliché, results in trite, fake, or over-the-top ornamentation.

Comparisons must also be appropriate to the setting, the time period, the subject matter, and the simile itself—don't mix those similes or metaphors. If the color of a character's hair is likened to snow but the setting is Mexico, then the simile doesn't work. If the young sleuth of a contemporary children's story is compared to Dick Tracy, then the simile doesn't work; the connection isn't relevant to a young reader's world. If Lucy can sing like a canary, but is ousted from the chorale like an old shoe, then the simile is mixed and loses its effect.

And So . . .

‣ A simile is a kind of figurative language that compares two dissimilar things and—unlike the metaphor—does so in a direct way, with a comparison word such as like, as, similar to, resembles, more/than, less/than, as/as, so. Sometimes the comparative word is missing, but if so, it's implied. A simile offers a surprising comparison that clarifies, decorates and always delights. That is, unless it's overused or not apt to the subject.

‣ An analogy, on the other hand, is a comparison of two things for the purposes of explaining an unknown. Two or more aspects of the ideas or things are brought to light to illuminate the correlation.

‣ Remember that the short, surprising simile can elevate any line of writing, from titles like Ernest Hemingway's short story "Hills Like White Elephants" to M.E. Abbey's 1891 song lyrics "Life is like a mountain railroad" to a nonfiction paragraph by historian Barbara Tuchman:

> When it comes to language, nothing is more satisfying than to write a good sentence. It is no fun to write lumpishly, dully, in prose the reader must plod through like wet sand. But it is a pleasure to achieve, if one can, a clear running prose that is simple yet full of surprises.

Chapter 7

Personification: Making Images Live

A goal of a good writer, whether writing fiction or nonfiction, is to create vivid or memorable images. The previous chapters on metaphors and similes examined comparisons that enliven a scene or paragraph. This chapter offers yet another way of comparing and contrasting: personification.

What Is Personification?

... I hear the iron horse make the hills echo with his snort like thunder, shaking the earth with his feet, and breathing fire and smoke from his nostrils.   *Walden*, Henry David Thoreau

Personification is figurative language that clarifies, emphasizes, and enchants by comparing two different things, asserting that one *is* the other, even though it is not. But—you say—that also defines metaphor. More specifically then: When an object, a force of nature, or an abstract idea is given human characteristics, then the speaker or writer has created personification. When we make the wind whisper or shadows dance or an engine die, we are using personification. When a cartoonist shows Superman trying to budge a boulder and writes the caption "The rock stubbornly refused to move," he has created personification.

The word comes from the Greek word *prosopopeia*, meaning *a face or mask* or *to make a person*. The extra effort of creating personification gives the audience something familiar and uniquely human to hold on to.

Nouns & Verbs Become Forces to Be Reckoned With

Time and weather are well suited to personification because they already seem to show off human emotions, like anger (*a mighty gale, lightning, March*), gentleness or love (*a breeze, sun-beams, June*), renewal or appreciation of beauty (*snowflakes, rain-drops, spring*), violence (*tornado, hurricane, winter*). The secret is to get inside a whirling black cloud or the month of August and extract its human potential to illuminate a passage.

Children's writer Jerry Spinelli is fond of personifying months, as in *Maniac Magee*, where instead of stating that a boy is cold, he writes:

January slipped an icy finger under his collar and down his back.

Notice how Spinelli chooses a single noun, *finger*, and puts it into motion via the verb *slipped* and prepositional phrases, *under his collar* and *down his back*. All of these images give the month human form and personality. Here's another example, using the same process, in which he casts March and April as fighting foes:

Exercise: Monthly Humanity

Children's author Jerry Spinelli personified March and April as enemies in *Maniac Magee*.

Try the same thing, but put two consecutive months on friendlier terms, perhaps as school buddies (September and October) or holiday shoppers (November and December).

During the night, March doubled back and grabbed April by the scruff of the neck and flung it another week or two down the road.

Dylan Thomas personified snow and trees in *A Child's Christmas in Wales*. Note how the nouns and verbs accomplish the task:

Our snow . . . came shawling out of the ground and swam and drifted out of the arms and hands and bodies of the trees . . .

Fiction isn't the only place to use

nature personification, of course. Jonathan Franzen uses the device in a June 2003 *New Yorker* article, "Caught," to describe the sky, as if its dirty face of bad weather, could be washed off. This time, a single verb, *scrubbed*, does the job:

> It often happened on my birthday that the first fall cold front of summer came blowing through. The next afternoon, when my parents and I drove east to a wedding in Fort Wayne, the sky was scrubbed clean.
> "Caught," *New Yorker*, June 16/23, 2003

Inanimate Objects Come Alive through Shape or Movement

How about personifying something even more inanimate than time and weather, something in which not even a hint of movement is present to spark the writer's imagination? Food is rarely personified, unless it's a gingerbread boy. But Charles Dickens manages to do it, inducing giggles at the same time:

> [Peter Cratchit] blew the fire, until the slow potatoes bubbled up, and knocked loudly at the saucepan lid to be let out and peeled.
> *A Christmas Carol*

He also personifies chestnuts and onions:

> There were great, round, pot-bellied baskets of chestnuts, shaped like the waistcoats of jolly old gentlemen, lolling at the doors, and tumbling out into the street in their apoplectic opulence. There were ruddy, brown-faced, broad-girthed Spanish Onions shining in the fatness of their growth like Spanish Friars.

Exercise: Humanizing Things

Choose something from the first list below and assign it a human attribute from this list. Complete the sentence.

List 1: window, columbine, cave, tree branch, car engine, wind, rain, fence.

List 2: beckons, kisses, bends, stretches, sways, winks, coughs, belches, sings, yawns, nods, dances.

Example: The columbine nod their heads in the breeze.

Dickens has compared two round edibles to two rounded stereotypes of people, in a *parallel construction*. The Spanish Friars comparison is actually a simile, but the rest of the sentence and paragraph is alive with personification, this time with the help of nouns and adjectives.

Stick with *A Christmas Carol* a few seconds longer and be treated to the personification of a bell tower. Here Dickens has made full use of a person's upper torso—voice, eyes, teeth, head—to create this image:

> The ancient tower of a church, whose gruff old bell was always peeping slyly down at Scrooge out of a gothic window in the wall, became invisible, and struck . . . with tremulous vibrations after-wards, as if its teeth were chattering in its frozen head up there.

Dickens's church is personified as an old man, while Sylvia Townsend Warner personifies a church as a younger character in her memoir, *Scenes of Childhood*:

> It had a high-shouldered, asthmatic appearance, but wasn't tall enough to . . .

On a more somber note, even a knife can be personified, as it is in a murder scene in Alice Sebold's *The Lovely Bones,* a scene that would not have been as bone-chilling (excuse the pun) without the personification. The story is told from the victim's first-person viewpoint:

> He leaned to the side and felt, over his head, across the ledge where his razor and shaving cream sat. He brought back a knife. Unsheathed, it smiled at me, curving up in a grin.

Even Topography Can Be Personified

Mountains, valleys, sea, and land all carry substantial potential for personification. A nonfiction article on Theodore Roosevelt National Park describes the spectacular vista near a rest stop in North Dakota. It's at this point that the flat land of the plains suddenly drops into an amazing valley of rugged buttes. In one word, *yawns*, the author personifies the scene:

A colorful, crumbling bad-lands terrain yawns below at the edge of the prairie.

> "Theodore Roosevelt: Dakota Adventure," *National Geographic Park Profiles*

A subject as mundane as a road can be played with, making it more interesting than it naturally is. Natalie Babbitt does this in *Tuck Everlasting,* creating a mood shift along with the description. The verbs are the worker bees here:

> It wandered along in curves and easy angles, swayed off and up in a pleasant tangent to the top of a small hill, ambled down again between fringes of bee-hung clover, and then cut sideways across a meadow. Here its edges blurred . . . But on reaching the shadows of the first trees, it veered sharply, swung out in a wide arc, as if, for the first time, it had reason to think where it was going, and passed around.

Roald Dahl, in *James and the Giant Peach,* personifies the sea, giving it a different image with the final modifier:

Exercise: Mechanical Life

Let your imagination have some fun personifying a mechanical object. Here's how Richard Peck created a memorable image of a train in his children's novel *Fair Weather:*

> We sensed the locomotive pawing the track, mad to move on . . . but then the train lit out running and flung itself down the tracks.

Use some of Peck's words to personify different mechanisms:

- a computer
- an airplane
- a Model-T
- a puppet

Each of these suggestions already has a human attribute in place: movement through an energy source.

Below them, the sea is deep and cold and hungry.

Exercise: Personify an Emotion

Mystery writer Nevada Barr wrote of one of her characters in the short story "Beneath the Lilacs":

> Anger plucked her from the bed like a giant hand. She snatched up the phone.

Get your own character out of bed with an emotion. Watch the verb and adjective choices. Barr's choices of plucked and snatched and giant work well with anger. What word choices would you use if *love* replaced *anger*? What about *fear*? Or *pain*?

Animals Gain Personalities

Let's leap from the inanimate to the animate. Because they're living creatures already, animals provide an easy way into personification. Kate DiCamillo's dog in *Because of Winn-Dixie* is described through the eyes of the story's young protagonist, who sees friendliness, interest, and comprehension in her new four-footed companion:

> I went outside and untied Winn-Dixie and brought him inside, and he sat down beside me and smiled up at the preacher, and the preacher couldn't help it; he smiles back. . . . And so the preacher started in preaching again. Winn-Dixie sat there listening to it, wiggling his ears this way and that, trying to catch all the words.

In the world of J.R.R. Tolkien and *The Lord of the Rings,* animals, elves, and hobbits portray a mix of human traits. Here's one:

> A fox passing through the wood on business of his own stopped several minutes and sniffed.

Anthropomorphism—the attribution of human form or personality to nonhuman things—is different from personification, in that it's a story line and character decision rather than a specific figurative language decision. Thus, a story in which animal characters speak, think, walk, or dress like humans is anthropomorphic. *The Tale of Peter Rabbit* and *The Wizard of Oz* use anthropomorphism.

Animals, of course, follow their own paths, but the wording here is clearly human in its intention—foxes don't have *business*. Sure enough, in the next paragraph, the fox comments about the habits of hobbits.

How about the frog in Mark Twain's "The Celebrated Jumping Frog of Calaveras County"? The frog in question has a certain readiness for education, a human attribute, although the edifying has to do with froglike attributes such as jumping and fly-catching. The narrator is clearly impressed with this particular frog:

> You never see a frog so modest and straight for'ard as he was, for all he was so gifted.

Personifying Abstract Ideas & Concepts

Birth, life, and death are difficult concepts to define in a few words. Yet when an abstract concept is given a human face, the unwieldy subject is given shape, form, and personality. Notice how that happens with this simple personification from Jane Resh Thomas's biography of Elizabeth I, *Behind the Mask*:

> During the sixteenth century, death was everyone's companion.

Poet Emily Dickinson famously used personification to illuminate death and immortality:

> Because I could not stop for Death
> He kindly stopped for me.

Exercise: Personify the Expression of an Emotion

An abstract, like an emotion, becomes more concrete and interesting when given human characteristics. Stephen King in *Hearts in Atlantis* does that to laughter:

> You can't deny laughter; when it comes, it plops down in your favorite chair and stays as long as it wants.

How do you see giggles? Or angry fits? Or tears? How do they visit you? Do they creep up from the basement and surprise you? Or do you open the door and invite them to stay?

Exercise: Truly Alive

Here's a personification of a road that doesn't work very well, taken from "The Ones Who May Kill You in the Morning," by Marc Nesbitt, *Harper's*, August 2000.

> This is the road the wealthy live on—just gray rocks dead in their own dust, running past us, in front of us, winding through the woods.

Dead gray rocks don't strike a *running* pose very well. How can you improve the line? Think about making the road a river, instead, or the edge of a golf course, or a gray ribbon.

> This is the road the wealthy live on—

> The carriage held but just ourselves
> And Immortality.
> We slowly drove, he knew no haste,
> And I had put away
> My labor, and my leisure, too,
> For his civility.

Another poet, Naomi Shihab Nye, treats a different abstract concept similarly. In "Kindness," in *The Words Under the Words,* Nye casts the concept as a fully realized personality:

> . . . it is only kindness that makes
>   any sense anymore,
> only kindness that ties your shoes
> and sends you out into the day
> to mail letters and purchase
>   bread,
> only kindness that raises its head
> from the crowd of the world to
>   say
> It is I you have been looking for,
> and then goes with you every-
>   where
> like a shadow or a friend.

Hal Clifford, in his memoir of a mountaintop rescue, could have written quite simply that fear crept in at night. Instead, he used metaphor and a stronger personification to give this important emotion more substance:

In the abyss of the night, the fears I had pushed away returned to nestle beside me.

"Nightfall over the Deadly Bells,"
National Geographic Adventure, Winter 1999

Beware the Pathetic Fallacy

As with any figurative device, a writer must avoid overusing personification in any given passage. But a stronger point of concern may be its tortured usage: *the hateful sky, angry clouds, cruel sea, friendly sun.* Each of these examples is a *pathetic fallacy,* a term coined by nineteenth-century English thinker, writer, and art critic John Ruskin. Ruskin suggested that these kinds of personifications are a sign of the writer's or speaker's "morbid state of mind" because they attribute to the natural world a person's strong emotions or motivations. Charlotte Bronte's *Jane Eyre,* for instance, talks about *lonely fields,* indicating the speaker's own sense of loneliness, not that of the fields. *Pathetic* comes from the Greek word *pathos,* which means sympathetic pity; a *fallacy* is a false or invalid reference.

Yet, in the hands of a skilled writer, pathetic fallacy can work. Although the following example from a book review demonstrates an analogy more than a personification, it gives you the idea of what Ruskin was talking about.

A good metaphor should never be missed, and Hardie, a poet before she was a novelist, is alert, in a labored sort of way, to the possibilities of some fine pathetic fallacy. One passage, after a pointless bout of cruelty by Hannie, describes her black mood: "She felt rudderless and directionless, like the dead sheep the November rains had carried down the river. Day after day it had drifted up and down, up and down, moving swiftly away with the pull of the sea's ebbing tide, pushing back again as it rose. Bloated, a perch for the gulls until it snagged on some drowned tree and left off its journeying."

"Green Unpleasant Land," Catherine Lockerbie,
New York Times Book Review, December 22, 2002

And So . . .

The house slept. Houses don't sleep, but most readers immediately understand this short personification. The lights are out, the shutters are closed, all is quiet. This house is resting after a day of activity, laughter, ringing phones, doors opening and shutting. This house is alive.

A personification is a comparative device that gives human characteristics not only to inanimate objects, but to nature, abstract ideas, and animals. A personification can even bring death to life through the use of vivid verbs, specific nouns, and modifiers bearing human characteristics. The goal, as it is with similes and metaphors, is to bring clarity, imagery, or emphasis to a scene through the use of a comparison. Images come alive.

Devices of Contrast, Exaggeration, & Emphasis

Opposites Attract: From Paradox to Antithesis

A t least four writing devices are based on opposites. Each has its unique place and properties in speeches, literature, periodicals, conversation. You've used them time and again. Comedians, statesmen, journalists, and religious scholars, too, have all made good use of paradox, oxymoron, irony, and antithesis.

A Paradox, Both Contradictory & True

Since these four devices all deal with contradictions, we'll begin with *paradox* because its definition aids in the understanding of the other three. Ralph Waldo Emerson said, "A man may love a paradox without losing his wit or his honesty." Rooted in the Greek word *paradoxon*—meaning contrary to expectations or belief—a paradox is a statement opposed to common sense and yet containing truth. Someone or something with seemingly contradictory qualities is a paradox.

A person can live a paradoxical life by being both a poor student and a genius, as Einstein was, or by being both the author of the Declaration of Independence and a slave owner all his life, like Thomas Jefferson. A *Time* article says of Christopher Columbus:

> It was the people who came to the new world he discovered who made him a perpetual paradox, a symbol of pride and contention. . . .
> "Johann Gutenberg," Paul Gray, *Time*, December 31, 1999

Don't confuse **parody** with **paradox**. When an author or fictional character imitates another author's work or an action for either comic effect or ridicule's sake, parody has been created. *Saturday Night Live* skits are parodies of real life. Dr. Seuss's rhymes are often parodied.

But paradoxes also dwell in the expression of concepts. Because it is full of complexity, humanity is a ripe subject for paradox.

- Not to decide is to decide. Harvey Cox, Harvard professor and author
- Cowards die many times before their death. *Julius Caesar,* William Shakespeare
- He is an honorable, obstinate, truthful, high-spirited intensely prejudiced, perfectly reasonable man. *Bleak House,* Charles Dickens

Spiritual teachings through the centuries have often made good use of paradox, which in turn—because of its use of contradiction—perpetuates debate among scholars and followers:

- "When the people of the world all know beauty as beauty, there arises the recognition of ugliness. When they all know the good as good, there arises the recognition of evil." *The Way,* Lao-tsu
- The softest things in the world overcome the hardest things in the world. *The Way,* Lao-tsu
- Many that are first shall be last; and the last shall be first. *Matthew,* 19:30
- In the midst of life we are in death. *Book of Common Prayer,* Burial of the Dead

John Donne and the seventeenth-century Metaphysical poets carried paradox to extremes in their *conceits,* elaborate and inventive metaphorical images around which they build poems. Donne used paradox in his poems about divine love and physical love. Here, the poet speaks to God:

> Divorce me, untie, or break that knot again,
> Take me to you, imprison me, for I,
> Except you enthrall me, never shall be free,
> Nor ever chaste, except you ravish me.
> "Holy Sonnet XIV"

A **conceit** is an extravagant figure of speech: a contrasting of dissimilar images, an incongruous joining. In simpler terms, a conceit is a far-fetched metaphor or simile or analogy that is often extravagant or bizarre. This language device could be placed in the last unit with comparative devices and it could also be placed in the next chapter, with devices of exaggeration.

Donne moves back and forth, from one concept to its opposite—from divorce to 'taking me to you,' from untying to imprisonment, from chastity to ravishment. The yin-yang effect of this number of contrasts in a single love sonnet is elaborate paradox.

Paradox is used in every genre and venue. Here is the final paragraph of an essay, "English Is a Crazy Language," from *Crazy English: The Ultimate Joy Ride through Our Language,* in which Richard Lederer talks of the many eccentricities of the English language. A final paradox is, of course, the perfect way to end such a piece, providing a snug summary:

> Why is it that when the sun or the moon or the stars are out, they are visible, but when the lights are out, they are invisible, and that when I wind up my watch, I start it, but when I wind up this essay, I shall end it? English is a crazy language.

Newspaper headlines sometimes use paradox to force readers to pause, think, take note. A *New York Times* headline from July 1, 2003, illustrates a contradiction: "Under the Arctic Ice, a Seabed Yields Some Fiery Secrets." The article's subject is volcanic action below the Arctic Circle.

Exercise: A Paradoxical Theme for Your Writing

Writer and scholar Oliver Wendell Holmes said that "The world's great men have not commonly been great scholars, nor its great scholars great men."

This quote is a fine jumping off spot for an article about someone you know, someone who defies the usual. Write one page about this paradoxical person who has achieved a great thing despite his or her impoverished background. Or about someone who—despite the best education and richest provisions—has wound up in prison.

Exercise: A Paradox for a Maxim

A maxim about education might be: "One goes to school to learn that one doesn't know anything." A maxim about investment might be: "Money can't be saved by hiding it."

What kind of maxim can you create about *love* (give and take) or about *winter* (life and death)? Take your maxim a step further: Use it as an opener for an essay or place it in the dialogue of one of your characters.

Advertising is often shaped by paradox because the contradiction grabs customers' attention, forcing them to pause and think. An ad for State Farm Insurance says about Flight Director Gene Kranz, who helped 12 Americans walk on the moon: "He's a pilot most famous for the missions he never flew."

An Oxymoron Is a Two-Word Paradox

If a coach tells his team that their game was a "good loss," then he has used an oxymoron. If the subject of a classroom debate is "mercy killings," then an oxymoron is on the table. If the United Nations orders "peace-keeping forces," then news reports will repeat an oxymoron. When you eat "jumbo shrimp," comedian George Carlin famously has joked, you may be eating an oxymoron. When Simon and Garfunkel sing "Sounds of Silence," they're singing an oxymoron.

An oxymoron is a two-word paradox, a short phrase that seemingly contradicts itself. In fact, the two Greek words from which the word comes—*oxys* and *moros*—contradict themselves: One means sharp and the other, dull. The duo commonly arrives in the form of an adjective-noun, as in the examples above, or more rarely, as an adjective-adverb, such as *inertly strong*. This interesting

An **oxymoron** should not be confused with a **pleonasm**, which is also a two- or three-word phrase. Instead of a contradiction, however, a pleoplasm is a superfluity, a word or two too long: *true facts, shared consensus, advance reservations, past history, mental telepathy, 9 AM in the morning, the reason why.* A pleonasm is also an excess of words when a single different word would do: *at this point in time* (now) or *in the immediate vicinity* (near).

and entertaining device is used for effect, for emphasis, for wit, even for complexity.

As always, Shakespeare provides luminous examples of a figure of speech. Here are some of his oxymorons, both comedic and tragic:

A tedious brief scene of young Pyramus
And his love Thisby; very tragical mirth.
Merry and tragical! tedious and brief!
That is hot ice and wondrous strange snow.
Midsummer Night's Dream, Act V, Scene I, 56-59.

Why then, O brawling love! O loving hate!
O heavy lightness, serious vanity;
Misshapen chaos of well-seeming forms!
Feather of lead, bright smoke, cold fire, sick health
Still-waking sleep, that is not what it is!
Romeo and Juliet, Act 1, Scene I, 176-181

Think about the last time you heard an excellent speaker give a tribute. The poignant words may have been followed by the tribute of an audience's eloquent silence. Since *eloquence* is usually associated with words, an *eloquent silence* is the opposite, a successful contradictory wordplay, an oxymoron.

Exercise: Food for Thought

Tea and coffee, once considered only hot beverages, now have counterparts, as iced tea and iced coffee. Are these oxymorons? Probably not in today's culture. Other than jumbo shrimp, can you think of another oxymoron that you eat or drink?

Oxymorons can have a particularly striking effect in book titles, as in *Simple Abundance* or *Minor Monuments, Selected Essays*. William Styron called his memoir *Darkness Visible*, taken from John Milton's description of hell. In other literary uses, Jonathan Swift in "A Modest Proposal" makes "humbly bold" a certain account. In an 1842 lecture, Oliver Wendell Holmes, a physician, scholar, and writer, once described homeopathy as a "mingled mass of perverse ingenuity, of tinsel erudition, of imbecile credulity and of artful misrepresentation." Four consecutive oxymorons, no less!

In more modern usage, *expensive economy* is a recent oxymoron ascribed to the current times by a news commentator. Elaine Sciolino wrote in "The New Next-Door Neighbors" *(The International Herald Tribune*, April 14, 2003), "During the war next door, in fact, the official policy has been one of 'active neutrality' . . . ." Then there is Andy Warhol's, "I am a deeply superficial person." For effect, fun, or complexity, a good oxymoron enriches a piece of writing by offering an interesting little contradiction.

Oxymorons aren't always successful, which is why a writer needs to be on guard when using them. Readers, too. Jokesters like to talk about *honest lawyers, smart blondes, military intelligence, classic rock,* as if each of these bindings were oxymorons, which they are not. An unsuccessful oxymoron is unintentional, although a *sublimely bad steak* or an *unseen vision* or a *definite maybe* could work if used in the right situations. The device is most effective when the oxymoron is uniquely yours and when it's appropriate to the context.

Irony: The Discrepancy between Appearance & Reality

If a certain statement or idea is ironic, then once again we've entered the world of contradictions. Irony has a similar meaning to paradox, but with a twist. Think of irony as having a subtle attacker and a victim; there's a gap between what is stated and what is meant, often resulting in a scornful jab, an insult, a sarcasm, a humorous moment at someone's expense. A teen might say, "Sure Mom, a cross-country trip sitting in the backseat between two little brothers for six hours will be an immense amount of fun." The word *irony* comes from the Greek word *eironia*, meaning *dissembler*. Humorists, satirists, politicians, and witty folk all make use of irony.

Irony takes several forms. *Situational irony* involves a discrepancy

As with any contrasting device, a writer can get carried away with the idea and misuse it. Singer Alanis Morissette's song "Ironic" does that: An old man turning 98, winning the lottery ticket, and dying the next day is a fine example of situational irony, but there's nothing very ironic about rain on your wedding day or a black fly in the chardonnay or a no-smoking sign on your cigarette break. That's simply reading more into the cards than is there.

between what actually happens and what we expect to happen, whether we're readers or observers. "The Necklace," by Guy de Maupassant, is a carefully crafted story of irony. Maupassant draws the reader into the life of the beautiful Madame Loisel, a poor woman whose longing for riches leads to even greater poverty. Her dreams of fame and glory come true for one night, when she borrows a friend's diamond necklace. Its theft turns the rest of her life into an even more wretched reality as she scrapes together the money—year after year—to repay the debt. It's the situation she got herself into that is ironic. In Maupassant's capable hands, the reader doesn't see the full irony—the ultimate twist—until the very end of the story, when Madame Loisel discovers that the original necklace was only paste.

Dramatic irony occurs in a theater production, and is different from situational irony in that the audience knows the meaning of what's happening, but the characters do not.

Socratic irony is one's own admission of ignorance about something while exposing someone else's inconsistencies through questioning. It is based on the method of teaching Socrates used, as demonstrated in his student Plato's *Dialogues*.

Verbal irony is language that points to a discrepancy between two different levels of meaning. Language is sometimes used to express something other than—and especially the opposite of—the literal meaning. When writer Sylvia Plath spoke of her celebrated husband as "the clear beacon of devotion and

Exercise: Situational Irony

Think about the plot line for Guy de Maupassant's short story "The Necklace": A woman mistakes a paste necklace for real jewels and spends her life paying for its loss.

What kind of similar situation can you come up with for a story line? What kind of mistake could a certain character unintentionally make?

Make a short list. What event happens to set the mistaken judgment in motion? Make another list.

Now decide which mix of character, mistaken judgment, and event could most easily be played out all the way to the end, when the truth is finally revealed to both the character and the reader. Start writing!

support . . . that gem of perfection," she was speaking with irony for, in truth, her husband was the "most selfish and self-centered man I'd ever met." (*New York Times,* July 5, 2003)

Jonathan Swift's essay, "A Modest Proposal," is an exceedingly sharp-edged illustration of verbal and situational irony. As a fierce advocate of the Irish people in their struggles under British rule, he wrote his essay during the height of a terrible famine, a time when the British were proposing a major tax on the already impoverished Irish. "A Modest Proposal" was his bitterly ironic solution: He proposed the eating of starving children as a solution for the country's overpopulation and starvation. Here's a sample paragraph. Notice the specific detail Swift used to create images and the overall tone of logic.

I shall now therefore humbly propose my own thoughts, which I hope will not be liable to the least objection. I have been assured by a very knowing American of my acquaintance in London, that a young healthy child well nursed is at a year old a most delicious, nourishing, and wholesome food, whether stewed, roasted, baked, or boiled; and I make no doubt that it will equally serve in fricassee or a ragout.

Exercise: A Modest Proposal

Find and read Jonathan Swift's essay "A Modest Proposal." What contemporary political problem or issue do you feel passionate about? What wild scheme (e.g., one that involves the removal of children) can you dream up to "solve" the problem. Using Swift's essay as a model, mimic his ironic style and create your own modest proposal in a one-page essay.

Did Swift mean for this long and carefully crafted essay to be taken seriously? No and yes. Was his solution a modest proposal? He "humbly offers it to public consideration," so his tone was modest, but the apparent substance of the essay suggested the wholesale butchery of Ireland's babies. The proposal itself was not modest, so the title is as ironic as the essay. Swift's proposal was severe, biting, satiric irony at its best—the extreme opposite of the author's true beliefs; as reasonable in presentation as unreasonable in concept; and it made its political and humanitarian point with such potency that "A Modest Proposal" remains one of the most effective and well-known political and sociological commentaries today, 275 years after it was composed.

The use of irony allows an author to make a point without going straight at the point, which too often can be predictable and unmemorable. Imitate Swift and make your modest proposal so memorable that it stands the test of time or be a Winston Churchill and use irony to make a strong point without direct confrontation, as in this remark:

> I do not at all resent criticism, even when, for the sake of emphasis, it for a time parts company with reality.

The endings of essays, editorials, articles, speeches are often the best spots for authors to nail the irony they've been building. In a *Minneapolis Star Tribune* editorial about the 40-year anniversary of the 1963 March on Washington, author Syl Jones details the history and aspirations of the men behind that memorable event in the history of civil rights. He ends his serious commentary with these lines, which exemplify both a paradox—in the first line—and situational irony, in the second:

> For too many Americans, the "I Have a Dream" speech signaled both the arrival and the conclusion of the civil rights movement. . . .

Exercise: In a Word

Antiphrasis is a one-word irony, in which the speaker or author—with tongue-in-cheek—states the opposite of the truth. Which word in each of these two sentences is the antiphrasis?

> "Hello, Shrimp," she said to the large man.
> The thermometer registered a cool 110 degrees in the shade.

Create a greeting in which a character is talking to a short man. How about a calm man or a frazzled man? Write a line of description about a frigidly cold day or a windy knock-your-socks-off day. Remember, an antiphrasis is a single contrasting word that lends some fun or sarcasm to the situation.

How ironic, how sad, that King's dream, shared with the nation and the world out of a longing for justice 40 years ago today, has plunged so many into such a deep and bedarkened sleep.

Jones alerted his audience to the irony of his comments. But sometimes irony is signalled only through tone or style or clear exaggeration. A newspaper article extolled the virtues and follies of the retiring Concorde jet, and the announcement that Boeing scrapped its planned Sonic Cruiser. The article's final clause stated the contradiction—not humorously, not seriously, but with irony:

Almost a half-century after it was conceived—at a time when people assumed there would be passenger flights to the moon in the early 21st century—the Concorde will remain the plane of tomorrow, even in retirement.

"Farewell, Concorde,"
International Herald Tribune, April 14, 2003

Antithesis, an Opposing Theme

"We shall nobly save, or meanly lose, the last best hope of Earth," wrote Abraham Lincoln in his 1862 message to Congress, which dealt with emancipation. Doris Kearns Goodwin wrote in "Franklin Delano Roosevelt" (*Time,* December 31, 1999):"Paralysis crippled his body but expanded his sensibilities." In his inaugural address, John F. Kennedy said, "Ask not what your country can do for you; ask what you can do for your country." All are examples of *antithesis.*

This fourth device that deals in opposites or contradictions juxtaposes contrasting ideas or themes, usually in the same sentence and often with a parallel construction. Antithesis is especially beloved by statesmen, theologians, literary authors, or those seeking to compose a profound thought in a unique situation. Neil Armstrong, for example, used antithesis when he stepped onto the Moon: "That's one small step for man, one giant leap for mankind."

Perhaps Henry Adams was using antithesis in *The Education of Henry Adams,* when he wrote, in his third-person kind of way,

From earliest childhood the boy was accustomed to feel that, for him, life was double. Winter and summer, town and country, law and liberty, were hostile . . . .

Yet, a true antithesis shows a clear, contrasting relationship between two opposing themes by joining them together. The human mind has a natural inclination to systemize and categorize, so the idea of antithesis is not foreign, nor necessarily hostile. John Gray's book of antithesis *Men Are From Mars, Women Are From Venus,* is a clear example in its very premise of relationship.

In one movie review of *Laurel Canyon*, the critiquer juxtaposed the main character's personality with that of her son: "The story starts with her son, Sam. As straitlaced as Jane is freewheeling, ..." (*Minneapolis Star Tribune,* April 25, 2003). As simple as the antithesis appears in this statement, the conflict of the entire movie is premised on the antithesis of contrasting personalities.

Parallel structure fits naturally with antithesis because the construction provides a visual and aural balance. In an article, Simon Schama quotes Rudyard Kipling's *American Notes* to describe the United States as:

> a muscular republic on the verge of its imperial awakening . . .
> both ethnically primitive and technologically advanced.
>> "The Unloved American," Simon Schama,
>> *The New Yorker,* March 10, 2003

The adverbs and the adjectives are opposing but their relationship merges in one country. The parallel arrangement can appear in the form of single words, phrases, clauses, or sentences. Here are samples from a variety of sources, beginning with single-word and phrase contrasts and moving to full sentences:

- To be or not to be . . . *Hamlet,* William Shakespeare
- For this my son was dead, and is alive again; he was lost and is found. *Luke* 15:24
- He is the first and the last, the manifest and the hidden. The Koran
- Not that I loved Caesar less, but that I loved Rome more. *Julius Caesar,* William Shakespeare
- Mankind must put an end to war, or war will put an end to mankind. Address to the United Nations, 1961, John F. Kennedy
- It was the best of times, it was the worst of times; it was the age of wisdom, it was the age of foolishness . . . *A Tale of Two Cities,* Charles Dickens

And So . . .

Whether you choose to poke fun or make a profound point in a contrasting way, you have four devices in your tool box at your disposal. Two of them—paradox and irony—are larger in scope while oxymoron and antithesis are shorter in delivery. All four deal with opposites.

Here's a statement of contrast, made by John F. Kennedy:

Washington is a city of southern efficiency and northern charm.

Is it a paradox? Like a paradox, the statement is rather witty and certainly honest, but the idea is not opposed to common sense; the qualities aren't necessarily contradictory.

Is it an oxymoron? The two-word expressions— southern efficiency and northern charm—are not contradictory within themselves, though the flipping of the adjectives would seem more realistic to some.

Is the sentence an ironical remark? There's no twist of contradiction here.

It is an antithesis, a parallel construction that illustrates two halves of the country with quite different cultures coming together in one relationship—Washington D.C.

Excessively Extravagant Exaggeration

We are a culture of excess: supermarkets; sale extravaganzas; multilevel department stores; malls the length of several football fields, with shelves of options that seem infinite; new houses with four-car garages; farmers with bonanza farms; stadiums for tens of thousands.

Our language speaks of the same excess. Everyday language, advertising campaigns, news bulletins, and even literature make use of exaggeration, the language of excess. This chapter defines some of the literary terms of exaggeration, which either overstate or understate the case. You'll discover that these writing devices hold great power, unless, of course, they're overused.

Hyperbole, a Deliberate Exaggeration

The most overdone rhetorical device in the English language is *hyperbole*, and that's no hyperbole. Hyperbole is a deliberate exaggeration, an extravagant overstatement, often to the point of the ridiculous. From the Greek word *hyperballein*, it means *to throw beyond* or *to exceed*. For unrestrained or unaware writers and speakers, hyperbole is as overused as the exclamation point. Whether a note, a comment over the back fence, a compliment, an ad for a car or a sports news flash, word choice is often hyperbolic:

▸ There are a thousand reasons why I won't go out with him.

103

- Wow, that box weighs a ton!
- You make the best pies in the country.
- Columbian Coffee: The richest coffee in the world.
- The Cubs's collapse at home is complete.

If an astute writer uses hyperbole once in a great while—for effect, emphasis, or humor—it can be a mighty tool. Shaped as comparison or allusion or simile or metaphor, hyperbole can find a perfect home in various genres, each for its own reason. Here are two:

He was a large man with eyebrows that patrolled his forehead like gray battleships, ready to meet any threat to his parishoners' souls.

Lying Awake, Mark Salzman

Tuesday 3 January: 130 #s (terrifying slide into obesity—Why? Why?)

Bridget Jones's Diary,
Helen Fielding

Exercise: Hyperbolic Description

Create your own metaphoric hyperbole by mimicking part of this wonderful line from a short story, Dicey Scroggins Jackson's "Dreams of Home," in *Women on the Case*:

Even after she finally decided that it was safe, that this was not some kind of trap, she waddle-walked into the living room sweeping for land mines.

Example: She eyed the air ducts, x-raying for microphones.

A choice detail is underscored in both examples. *Eyebrows like gray battleships* is a simile, but the comparison is so outlandish that it is also hyperbole. This single detail tells the reader everything needed about the man, emphasizing a feature that represents his whole persona. In the same way in the second example, a single diary detail (130 pounds equated to a terrifying slide into obesity) informs the reader about a narrator's worst fear. Obsession about weight carries through the entire diary.

Hyperbole can be used for humor to embellish to the point of the ridiculous. Here are two excerpts from a lengthy article: The hyperbole in the first excerpt opens the article, serving as an attention-getter:

One morning, three days into a throbbing toothache that even a few silos of Advil could not muzzle, I realized I had no choice but to inflict myself on a dentist.

"Roots and All: A History of Teeth," Natalie Angier, *New York Times*, August 5, 2003

Later in the article, Angier inserts another hyperbole that underscores her long history with dentists. In this case, the hyperbole not only evokes humor, but accentuates her feelings about the topic:

As an adult, I have been fitted with more crowns than the Hapsburg dynasty, and I have celebrated many a wondrous event—my 30th birthday, the day I won a big journalism prize, the morning of my honeymoon—by getting a root canal.

It's the allusion to the Hapsburg dynasty that is the boldest hyperbole, of course—to a family that ruled Austria from the twelfth to the twentieth centuries and Spain from the sixteenth to the eighteenth centuries and much of the Holy Roman Empire. That's *a lot* of crowns! The idea that the author *celebrated* events with root canals is also hyperbolic, don't you think?

Even poets use hyperbole to illicit humor, as Carl Sandburg did in "The People, Yes," with a line that

Exercise: Tall Tales

Tall tales, like those about Paul Bunyan, provide classic examples of hyperbole, again used to evoke humor and awe, this time for the youngest reader:

At three weeks Paul Bunyan got his family into a bit of trouble kicking around his little tootsies and knocking down something like four miles of standing timber.

So, if you're the next Sid Fleischman, you might write a tall tale with a narrator that says something like this:

I hadn't seen anything that wouldn't grow on our wonderful one-acre farm. That trifling patch of earth is so amazingly rich we could plant and harvest two-three crops a day—with time left over for a game of horseshoes.

"McBroom Tells a Lie," *Cricket*, September 2003

Go ahead. Let your brain expand and try your hand at some hyperbolic tall-taling.

105

sounds like it could have been said by W. C. Fields: "It's a slow burg—I spent a couple of weeks there one day."

Marketers adore hyperbole. Circus impresario P. T. Barnum may not have started the trend, but he escalated it. Here's one handbill that advertised a wizened blind woman with fingernails six to eight inches long. Hyperbole permeates this advertisement:

> The Greatest Natural and National Curiosity in the World, Joice Heth, nurse to General George Washington . . . Joice Heth . . . was the slave of Augustine Washington and was the first person who put clothes on the unconscious infant, who, in after days, led our heroic fathers on to glory, to victory and freedom. To use her own language when speaking of the illustrious Father of This Country, "she raised him." Joice Heth was born in the year 1674, and has consequently now arrived at the astonishing age of 161 years.

Hyperbole is also used to accentuate a point, to underscore the author's feelings about the topic on which he is expounding. In a report on the behavior of one John Bolton, the Undersecretary of State for Arms Control and International Security, at a conference in Italy, Richard Cohen wrote:

> [A]fter having vindicated every European caricature of the arrogant American, he left this resort on Lake Como carrying a suitcase in one hand, a briefcase in the other—and a chip on his shoulder so big I feared he would exceed the weight limit for his flight home.
>
> ". . . But Still Rustling Feathers," Richard Cohen,
> *Washington Post*, June 17, 2003

When Apparent Exaggeration Is Not Hyperbole

Sometimes a statement is not an exaggeration or a hyperbole at all, but simply the truth. The effect of *apparent exaggeration* is that it mimics hyperbole but has the double punch of both attracting attention and being true. These few lines from the biography of a racehorse, Laura Hillenbrand's *Seabiscuit*, seem hyperbolic, but aren't:

> In contrast, Strub's purse was staggering: $100,000, plus a few thousand dollars in entry revenue, to the winner. It was the biggest purse in the world.

In *Coal, A Human History,* author Barbara Freese writes about a boiler she observed at an Xcel Energy plant. It's not hyperbolic, but accurate:

> It was hard to believe that on the other side was a 3,000-degree Fahrenheit fireball some forty-five feet across and ten stories high devouring up to five hundred tons of powdered coal.

A sentence later, she uses an apt, although difficult to imagine, simile. It provides readers with a comparative detail that we can almost see.

> But then Jack nonchalantly opened a tiny door in the boiler's side, just a crack. We shielded our eyes as a blinding white light poured out, like sunshine held captive underground for millions of years and finally set free.

The idea of sunshine being held underground for millions of years certainly seems hyperbolic. But in this case, the simile is an analogy that helps the reader visualize such a blinding intensity.

Understatement, the Counterpoint of Hyperbole

When Mark Twain wrote a note to the London correspondent who had reported his death, he said, "The report of my death was an exaggeration." Even though Twain must have felt the report was hyperbolic (since he was very much alive), the reporter thought it was true. Twain used understatement to stop the rumor mill.

Where hyperbole jumps into the excessive and egoistic to make a point, understatement moves into the ultra modest, also to make a point. Understatement is the deliberate expression of an idea as less important than it actually is. Why use such a device? The reasons are usually twofold. One is for ironic emphasis: "Scott was a little upset about flunking the term." The other is for politeness and tact: A pharmacist may say she knows "a little about drugs," an understatement, rather than saying that she's "an expert on pharmaceuticals." Both statements are true, but the former sounds less self-aggrandizing.

The goal of good writing is often to persuade rather than offend, especially if the readership is hostile or takes a different viewpoint.

Exercise: Understated Humor

Woody Allen tells the story of purchasing a small brownstone on Manhattan's Upper West Side in his short story, "On a Bad Day You Can See Forever." The following excerpt contains two examples of *hyperbole*, two of *understatement*, and one of *litotes*. Woody gives the clue for one, but can you find the others?

Miss Wilpong, of Mengele Realtors, promised us it was the buy of a lifetime, priced modestly at a figure no higher than the cost of a stealth-bomber. "It's a challenge," my wife said, breaking the women's indoor record for understatement.

Hyperbole: buy of a lifetime, breaking women's indoor record.
Litotes: priced modestly
Understatement: Mengele, an allusion to a Nazi death camp leader. "It's a challenge."

Martin Luther King, Jr.'s "Letter from Birmingham Jail," is addressed to white clergy. It uses understatement as it slowly builds the well-reasoned case for his actions in demonstrations in Birmingham, Alabama. Here's one example:

I must make two honest confessions to you, my Christian and Jewish brothers. First, I must confess that over the past few years I have been gravely disappointed with the white moderate. I have almost reached the regrettable conclusion that the Negro's great stumbling block in his stride toward freedom is not the White Citizens Counciler [*sic*] or the Ku Klux Klanner, but the white moderate, who is more devoted to "order" than to justice; who prefers a negative peace which is the absence of tension to a positive peace . . .

William Safire, in a column in which he talks about spinelessness in some of the commentators in Washington, D.C., shares this story about Winston Churchill, a man noted for his apt use of language to bedevil those he disdained. As Safire makes clear, at no point did Churchill directly accuse his victim of spinelessness or cowardliness; his understatement is far more powerful:

"I remember, when I was a child," said Winston Churchill in the 30s, directing his Commons oratory at J. Ramsey MacDonald's Labor government, "being taken to the celebrated Barnum's Circus, which contained an exhibition of freaks and monstrosities, but the exhibit which I most desired to see was the one described as 'The Boneless Wonder.' My parents judged that the spectacle would be too revolting and demoralizing for my youthful eyes," said Churchill, fixing a cherubic gaze at MacDonald, "and I have waited fifty years to see the Boneless Wonder sitting on the Treasury Bench."

"Invective's Comeback," William Safire,
New York Times, April 28, 2003

Time's July 2003 biography of Benjamin Franklin says that what Franklin modestly described as his "electrical amusements" made him the world's most famous scientist. In this case, Franklin is supplying the understatement, while the modern article may be headed toward hyperbole.

Litotes Denies Reality

What hyperbole does for exaggeration, *litotes* (*lie*-te-teez) does for understatement. It's a deliberate remark that denies the truth. In other words, it denies its opposite: "She's not too bright." Or in discussing war, a person may say, "A nuclear bomb can ruin a person's day." Or a neighbor says about a car accident: "Hitting that telephone pole certainly didn't do your car any good." Of course, a nuclear bomb causes permanent destruction, and a moving object hitting a stationary object often totals both. The speakers are each understating the obvious by deliberately denying the contrary. Their strong feelings are actually being moderately conveyed.

J. D. Salinger has his main character in *The Catcher in the Rye* use litotes when Holden says, "It isn't very serious. I have this tiny little tumor on the brain." Fiction makes good use of understatement for the purpose of showing the intense feelings of the character. Irony often plays a role. In fact, the use of irony goes hand-in-hand with both understatement and overstatement.

In "The Blood of the Martyrs," Stephen Vincent Benet tells the tale of a condemned man—a former teacher, bespectacled and small in stature. By extolling his tormentor's efficiency, the professor denies the intensity of his own vulnerability, with a litotes.

Professor Malzius stood, his fingers gripping the big, old-fashioned inkwell. It was full of ink. The servants of the Dictator were very efficient. They could shoot small people with the eyes of fox terriers for treason, but their trains arrived on time and their inkwells did not run dry.

Jonathan Swift, you may remember, wielded a sharp ironic sword when making his point about famine-stricken Ireland and British rule. His "A Modest Proposal" is an understated title for his ironic solution of using Irish children for food. Choosing simply to state, rather than describe in graphic detail, Swift makes a horrifying declaration than denies the truth, with litotes:

> Last week I saw a woman flayed, and you will hardly believe how much it altered her person for the worse.

Apophasis Pointedly Passes Over

Another form of understatement pointedly pretends to ignore or pass over something. It's called *apophasis* (a-*pof*-a-sis). The writer or speaker mentions something by saying it will not be mentioned. The effect, however, is that the subject *is* then on the table. Apophasis comes from the Greek word *apophanai* meaning *to say no*.

A writer or speaker can use this device to call attention to sensitive or inflammatory facts while remaining detached from them. This rhetorical trick is often used by lawyers, councilmen, board members. An example might be: "I won't bring up your racetrack gambling deals," or, "Let's pass over the rumors that he beats his wife and deals drugs because we will not allow personal matters to enter into our discussion."

Apophasis also supplies an interesting way to remind the listener or reader of something in a polite way. A teacher might say, "I don't need to remind you to bring several number two pencils to the test tomorrow."

Common phrases for apophasis include: *nothing need be said about, I pass over, I will not mention, we will overlook, I do not mean to suggest, you don't need to be reminded, no one would suggest.*

And So . . .

To emphasize, a writer might consider overstatement in the form of hyperbole or understatement in the forms of litotes or apophasis. Both directions can be used to create irony. Hyperbole tends to exaggerate to the point of the ridiculous, and can appear as a simile, metaphor, allusion, comparison. Overuse of this device shows up most often in over-the-top compliments or bombastic marketing. But hyperbole is also an effective and powerful tool in writing, especially when used to make a single point. Understatement is an even more powerful tool, for it persuades rather than offends. If a writer wants to deny the harsh reality of a situation, but express his strong feelings, litotes is the tool to use (Churchill was not a man to underestimate). If a writer or speaker wants to remain detached about facts or wants to appear polite, yet make a statement, he will use apophasis, a device that pointedly pretends not to mention.

More Writing Devices for Your Magic Toolbox

Dozens of rhetorical devices are ours for the taking. Earlier chapters have illustrated the power and possibilities of the more common ones. This chapter touches on more devices that you may have noticed in your reading or that might intrigue you and inspire your own writing. In fact, you may have already used some of them and simply not known their capabilities. Knowledge about how they work will empower your work and captivate you and your audience. As with any rhetorical devices, their strength emerges through spare usage.

A Missing Word: The Ellipsis

Ellipsis (el-*lip*-sis) comes from the Greek meaning *to come short*. That's exactly what happens in a sentence that incorporates an ellipsis: The sentence comes up short; a word or short phrase is missing because its omission is easily understood in the context. For example, "Jason loves Stella and Stella, Jethro" omits the word *loves* between Stella and Jethro. If used well, the omission of a repeated word not only enhances the flow of the sentence, but accentuates the relationship. An ellipsis can also add a touch of humor: "The average person thinks he isn't." In the first example, a verb is omitted; in the second, it's the adjective *average* that is omitted. (Did you note the omission of the noun *example* in the second part of the preceding sentence?)

The following is a quote from Winston Churchill. Which words have been omitted?

Use ellipsis to create a single strong sentence out of the cumbersome listing below:

Catherine will be attending the ceremony with Jason. Minnie will go with Matthew, while Rosa and Edward will be a couple.

Death and sorrow will be the companions of our journey; hardship our garment; constancy and valor our only shield. We must be united, we must be undaunted, we must be inflexible.

The ellipsis in Churchill's statement is powerful, for—paradoxically—the omission actually emphasizes his point. By omitting *will be,* Churchill demands that the reader or listener supply the words himself. Their omission accentuates the parallel between the most important words: *companionship, hardship, constancy, valor* and *journey, garment, shield.* Notice that he doesn't use ellipsis in the second sentence. There, the asyndeton and anaphora in a parallel construction (a triple *we must be*) give strength to his words in a different way. Did you also note the personification of death and sorrow in the first clause? The metaphors in the second and third clauses?

An ellipsis is also a form of punctuation—three spaced dots (. . .) that indicate an omission of words or a pause in dialogue.

An Interrupter: The Expletive

You probably think of an *expletive* as a curse or vulgarity, but it's also a literary term. Expletives are of two kinds: (1) a single word or short phrase that interrupts normal syntax in order to stress preceding or succeeding words, or (2) words such as *if, that,* and *there,* which are empty of meaning and used simply as filler. In fact, *expletive* comes from the Latin word *expletus,* meaning *to fill out* or *to plump up.*

Common expletives of the first kind include *indeed, in fact, without doubt, to be sure, of course, in short, it seems, after all, in brief, to tell the truth, at least, certainly, clearly.* An expletive serves as a signal that a particular part of a sentence or a whole sentence is especially important. Compare the difference in emphasis in these two sentences, the first without the expletive:

 ▸ But the house was not checked for mold.
 ▸ But the house was not, in fact, checked for mold.

Whether inserted at the sentence's onset, in mid-sentence, or at the end, the expletive is often offset with a comma or commas, which increase the stress on the surrounding words. Note in the excerpts below how the expletives direct the intent of the sentences, and why the authors thought their inclusion was important.

Exercise: An Expletive for Emphasis

Write a one-paragraph speech either for yourself in an essay or for a character in a story. Use two of the following expletives to emphasize specific points:

Indeed, in fact, without doubt, to be sure, of course, in short, it seems, after all, in brief, to tell the truth, at least, certainly, clearly, naturally, therefore, I trust.

Incredibly, Hale's proto-astronauts thrive in space and create a near-utopian society. Clearly, it takes the fertile mind of a fantasy writer to create . . .
"NASA Scales Back," Thomas Grose, *U.S. News & World Report,*
Mysteries of Outer Space, Special Edition, 2003

There were at least 240 Soviet agents who penetrated the U.S. government from 1935 to 1945—who were, in fact, spies, says David Major, former director of . . .
"The Power of Secrets," Anna Lulrine, *U.S. News & World Report,*
Spy Stories, Special Edition, 2003

But in truth, Sammy and Joe scarcely took note of their surroundings. It was just the clearing in which they had come to pitch the tent of their imaginations.
The Amazing Adventures of Kavalier and Clay, Michael Chabon

He ought, therefore, never to let his thoughts stray from the exercise of war; and in peace he ought to practice it more than in war . . .
Nor will I, I trust, be deemed presumptuous on the part of . . .

The Prince, Niccolo Machiavelli

"The Fosters have been waiting since yesterday morning," he
pointed out. "Naturally, they're very upset . . .."

Tuck Everlasting, Natalie Babbitt

Note that *at least* in the second example is not an expletive, but an
adjective. An expletive can also emphasize a phrase, so that the
audience is alerted to a certain topic: The Jileks, clearly a dysfunc-
tional family, live in an upper middle-class neighborhood.

The second kind of expletive is common to weak writing, and
often signals lack of specificity in thought. While our speech is full
of such expletive use—What's *it* to you? *There* is no reason for this.
Make *it* clear which you want. *There* were no cars in the driveway.
It's true that I love him. What's *that*?—good writing carefully avoids
such filler. In his poem *An Essay on Criticism,* Alexander Pope
made fun of poor poets who rely on filler, and their audiences,
who pay more attention to the number of syllables than to sense:

> But most by numbers judge a poet's song;
> And smooth or rough, with them is right or wrong:
> . . .
> Who haunt Parnassus but to please their ear,
> Not mend their minds; as some to church repair,
> Not for the doctrine, but the music there.
> These equal syllables alone require,
> Tho' oft the ear the open vowels tire,
> While expletives their feeble aid do join,
> And ten low words oft creep in one dull line . . .

Get this: Expletives are a part of contemporary casual speech, *you
know?*

An Interrupter That Explains: Parenthesis

Parenthesis is exactly what you think it is, and more. A word, a brief phrase, or even a sentence is inserted in a sentence or paragraph to serve as an aside offering a quick explanation or amplification of a point. This interrupter is usually set within a pair of punctuation marks (commas, parentheses, dashes—the dashes are a bit more forceful). An author chooses parenthesis to give the effect of immediacy, to add extemporaneity, and sometimes just to convey additional information most efficiently. (Of course, parentheses are also a set of punctuation marks that set off explanatory or additional material not needed in the main sentence.)

The examples that follow are from several articles in *U.S. News and World Report, Spy Stories,* Special Edition, 2003:

Exercise: Parenthetically

Toni Morrison uses a complicated set of parentheses in this excerpt from her Nobel Prize-winning novel *Beloved*. Find the five examples of the parenthetical.

The grandmother, Baby Suggs, was dead, and the sons, Howard and Buglar, had run away by the time they were thirteen years old—as soon as merely looking in a mirror shattered it (that was the signal for Buglar); as soon as two tiny hand prints appeared in the cake (that was it for Howard).

> The spy, code named Cato, based his opinion on . . .
> In a questionnaire, concealed in a microdot, they wanted details . . .
> He used his charm to woo women—including four wives—and to win the . . .
> Few believed that a man who would drink all night with Nazis and write all day for a Nazi-affiliated newspaper—an apparent mouthpiece for the regime, says Johnson—would even have time to be a Soviet sympathizer.

Remember that the parenthetical form gives a sentence further clarity, adds a fact, or puts a reference into context. A longer example, from Isabel Fonseca's *Bury Me Standing: The Gypsies and Their Journey,* shows off a parenthesis several sentences long:

All of these steps were complicated and protracted by the superstitions that had to be observed along the way. (Jeta spat on her broom. Why? Because she had swept under my feet. If I do not, she continued, seeing the first answer had not got through, your children will remain bald all their lives, stupid.)

Here's a double example from the children's classic, *The Lion, the Witch, and the Wardrobe,* by C. S. Lewis. In this case, the author uses parenthesis to interrupt and offer further explanation of his own story. While it isn't obvious in this excerpt, note that Lewis used the parenthesis as a style technique in another way: He's writing the story for a specific person, his goddaughter, Lucy, and the remark inside the parentheses is directed to her, although Lucy also represents the general reader.

> "This is not the point," he said. "But battles are ugly when women fight. And now"—here he suddenly looked less grave—"here is something for the moment for you all!" and he brought out (I suppose from the big bag at his back, but nobody quite saw him do it) a large tray containing five cups and saucers . . .

Pulitzer Prize winner Wallace Stegner does the same in *Crossing to Safety,* but this time the interruptions come from the story's narrator, not the author. The reasoning behind the parenthesis is the same—to offer the reader a clearer picture.

> But in our society (she means Cambridge), men (she means men of education and culture) no longer work with tools or use weapons.

Often set off by commas, an **appositive** is a noun, noun phrase, or noun clause that follows a noun or pronoun and renames it so as to clarify: *My sister, Ruth, lives in Texas.*

A **parenthesis** can sometimes appear to be an appositive: *The spy, code name Cato, based his opinion on . . .* , but is not. A parenthesis is an interruptor, an aside that offers information not needed in the sentence.

An appositive is not an interruptor but rather a clarifier that negates confusion.

An Interrupter That Vents: The Apostrophe

Not only do authors or narrators sometimes interrupt their stories to offer further explanation. In another rhetorical technique, an author, speaker, or character stops a story or discourse to address directly someone or something completely different. To take it further, the audience addressed may be present, absent, or inanimate. This rhetorical device, an *apostrophe*, is an effective way either to display sudden emotion or to stop the action for a particular purpose.

Antony addresses Caesar's corpse immediately following the assassination in Shakespeare's *Julius Caesar*. The apostrophe alerts the reader to his obvious emotion:

> O, pardon me, thou bleeding
>   piece of earth,
> That I am meek and gentle with
>   these butchers!
>   Act III, Scene I, 279-80

In the Newbery Award-winning fairy tale *Tale of Despereaux: Being the Story of a Mouse, a Princess, Some Soup, and a Spool of Thread*, author Kate DiCamillo periodically stops the story to address her young readers directly. Sometimes the apostrophe offers a question to ponder, sometimes a warning, sometimes a gentle reminder:

> Reader, as the teller of this tale, it is my duty from time to time to utter some hard and rather disagreeable truths. . . . I must inform you that . . .

Exercise: Apostrophe Addresses Another

An apostrophe is a literal *turning away* to address someone or something outside of the story. Sometimes a speaker departs from a speech to address someone from the audience, perhaps asking a question or making an example of the person.

1. You're the president of a company, giving a motivational speech. Interrupt your speech with this line: "Ms. Andrews here is a fine example of just what I've been talking about. She . . ."

2. Perhaps you're an essayist. Write a short piece about Mother's Day. Insert an apostrophe, asking your mother's forgiveness for the personal anecdote you're about to relate.

Reader, do you recall the word "perfidy"? As our story progresses, "perfidy" becomes an ever more appropriate word, doesn't it?

The narrator and main character in Alice Walker's *The Color Purple* addresses different audiences, namely God and her sister. But these addresses are not offered as asides or interruptions; they're the format of the entire book. *If on a Winter's Night a Traveler,* by Italo Calvino, speaks straight to the reader in every other chapter. This, too, is a format choice rather than apostrophe, although speaking to the reader often seems like an interruption.

Aporia to Express Doubt

A device that a speaker, an essayist, or even a fictional character might use when uncertain about what to say, do, or think is an *aporia* (a-*por*-ee-a). Aporia is an expression of doubt. The questioning may be a conscious response spoken to an audience, or to oneself. It may be a rhetorical question—one no one is truly being asked, but that remains a point of reflection. It is arguable whether the question is ultimately answered or not, but one of the most famous examples of aporia might be Hamlet's "To be or not to be." The intent of the aporia by the deliberator may be real or feigned.

Then the steward said within himself, "What shall I do?" *Luke* 16

You thought Pluto was a planet? It might be. But the ninth rock from the sun may also be a gigantic comet, the largest known member of the icy Kuiper Belt.

U.S. News & World Report, Mysteries of Outer Space,
Special Edition, 2003

"I've never forgotten you, Tillie. Oh my gosh, where are my manners? This is my daughter Mattie," she said.

Blue Shoe, Anne Lamott

If the right medication could bring Isa back to her old state, bright animated, bossy, and incredibly annoying, would Mattie want her? Would she want more years of the old Isa—to be talked to alternately as if she were the queen's eunuch and the Christ?

Mattie's interior monologue, *Blue Shoe,* Anne Lamott

Aporia, like any rhetorical question, can endear the narrator to the audience by adding an ethical dimension (as in the first and third examples) or it can serve as a way to develop an argument (second and fourth examples). In any case, aporia does not allow the audience to remain passive. It stirs feelings and often improves the credibility of the speaker.

An Interrupter That Summarizes: Sententia

Sometimes quoting a maxim or a wise saying brings a general truth to the passage or situation. *Sententia* concludes or sums up preceding material by offering a single, pithy statement. Your grandfather might lecture you that the early bird catches the worm. A speaker might conclude his speech with, "As Pascal reminds us, 'It is not good to have all your wants satisfied.'" Wallace Stegner provides an example in a mother's remarks:

> Nevertheless, let me give you a word of advice. It is neither decorous nor kind to mislead a boy in the condition you say he is in. Unless you're serious, or think you might be, don't encourage him. As the saying goes, I don't want his blood on the rug. Remember that.
>
> *Crossing to Safety*, Wallace Stegner

Sententia is related to the word *sentence*, and comes from the Latin for *to feel*.

An Interrupter That Clarifies: An Allusion

An *allusion*—an informal reference to a famous person, place, event, writing, fact—is a subtle interrupter in that it appears as part of the flow of the description or action.

Some of the best sources for allusion are literature, history, Greek myth, and the Bible. The most effective allusions are short, from a well-known reference, and provide an instant picture in a minimum of words:

 ⁃ The earthworm is the Hercules of the soil.
 ⁃ He could not be more eager to see the woods than if it hid the sources of the Nile.
 ⁃ Their blind date was the pairing of Einstein and Athena.

Exercise: Allusions, Allusions

Poet T. S. Eliot is the master of allusion, so much so that some critics have seen him as a referencer, more than a poet. His poem "The Hollow Men," for example, alludes to Joseph Conrad's *Heart of Darkness,* Shakespeare's *Julius Caesar,* the Bible, among others, and loosely follows Dante's *Divine Comedy.*

Can you think of films or movies that do the same thing—contain allusions to other movies or films?

▸ Her eyes blinked out hello in Morse Code.

▸ The child walked around in a crablike Quasimodo crouch.

Qualifiers are sometimes necessary in these allusions: Some people, characters, events, or works are famous for more than one attribute, and others aren't as well known. Solomon, for example, was famous for his wisdom, his many wives, his magnificent palaces and wealth. "She has the wisdom of Solomon" is a slightly amplified allusion. A *U.S. News & World Report* article titled "Nukes in Space" alludes to a 1960s movie and amplifies the allusion for the reader's sake by referencing a specific scene:

What's the first image that popped into your mind when you read the headline on this story? An outerspace version of *Dr. Strangelove,* with Slim Pickens riding an orbiting H-bomb, perhaps?

"Nukes in Space," by Thomas Hayden,
U.S. News & World Report, Mysteries of Outer Space,
Special Edition, 2003

Allusions may be made to scientific knowledge, sports, or any subject, of course. "Anthropologists dream of finding a Lucy." The allusion to *a Lucy* would not be effective if the reference were obscure or unknown by the audience, but if the audience remembers that Lucy refers to one of the most celebrated discoveries of the earliest human fossils, then the allusion is successful.

An allusion explains, clarifies, or enhances whatever subject is on the table, without sidetracking. It might help explain something difficult, offering a quick, reflective aside and is sometimes placed within commas, thus becoming parenthesis. An example of that kind of aside could appear like this reference from Stephen King's book *On Writing*. He's referring to one of the coauthors of *The Elements of Style,* by William Strunk and E. B. White:

> Even William Strunk Jr. that Mussolini of rhetoric, recognized the delicious pliability of language.

Because of the allusion to Mussolini and without having read *The Elements of Style*, King's reader will know that Strunk is a dictator about writing rules.

Dylan Thomas, in a scene in *A Child's Christmas in Wales,* uses an allusion in the midst of a simile:

> [S]moke was pouring out of the dining-room, and the gong was bombilating, and Mrs. Prothero was announcing ruin like a town crier in Pompeii.

An allusion to the ancient Italian city destroyed by the eruption of Mount Vesuvius gives Thomas's readers an idea of the agitation Mrs. Prothero is feeling and demonstrating. Thomas also makes use of polysyndeton (consecutive conjunctions that suggest much more is going on than is listed) and onomatopoeia (*bombilating* is similar to the actual sound of a gong).

In "The Last Word," an August 2000 *Harper's* article about constant change in the English language, author Earl Shorris says,

> The advent of another Shakespeare could vastly expand the vocabulary again.

Exercise: An Allusion for an Instant Image

You're writing a description of a man with sideburns. Using an allusion to create an instant image in an economy of words, you might say he has Elvis Presley sideburns. Think of an allusion that will bring an instant image to these descriptions:

1. a man's jolly countenance and girth
2. a palatial house with many gardens
3. an extremely tall athlete of incredible ability
4. someone who speaks with lyrical, thoughtful eloquence
5. a woman who trims too much of her boyfriend's hair (biblical)
6. a long arduous journey/adventure from youth to old age (literary)

The quick allusion to Shakespeare saves Shorris from having to explain how language grows and changes.

Even advertising uses allusions. The marketing team for Land Rover chose a famous set of explorers to highlight illustrations of their vehicles crossing rivers and climbing mountains: "Find your inner Lewis and Clark." The ad is also clever for its allusion to finding your inner child, an expression coined by modern psychoanalysts.

Eponym & Toponym: By Any Other Name

An allusion is different from an *eponym* or a *toponym*, which have become so common in usage that they are part of our everyday language. *Eponym* comes from the Greek word for *name*; a famous name is the source of a "new" word in the English language. Eponyms enrich our language, coming from every direction.

Eponyms may be the mythical or real ancestors that give a name to groups of people, or places. Examples include Rome, by legend named for Romulus; Colombia, named for Christopher Colombus; America for Amerigo Vespucci; even the Israelites, named after Israel, formerly Jacob, who was the son of Abraham.

Louis Pasteur, the microbiologist, is the source for the eponym *pasteurize*. Ludwig Doberman, a nineteenth-century dog-breeder, is the source for the eponym *Doberman*. *Teddy bear* comes from Theodore Roosevelt's name, a president and hunter who once saved a bear cub. If a man has a Vandyke, he's got a trim pointed beard, named after seventeenth-century Flemish portrait painter, Sir Anthony Vandyke or Van Dyck. Book titles that are the names of their main characters are also said to be eponymous: *Frankenstein, Silas Marner, Carrie.*

"Put your John Hancock there," someone tells you, and you proceed to sign your name. John Hancock's signature, if you remember, stood out prominently on the Declaration of Independence. John Hancock is both an allusion and an eponym, when used metaphorically.

Exercise: Eponyms

Eponymous words based on the names of real people include bloomer, bowdlerize, boycott, braille, diesel, guillotine, mausoleum, molotov, saxophone, vol and watt; and even a Mae West.

Look up several of the words to discover their origins. Can you think of others?

A *toponym* is like an eponym except that it's based on a place name rather than a person's name. Xanadu was the site of the summer home of Kublai Khan (grandson of Genghis Khan) during the Mongol dynasty in China. Marco Polo visited and marked it forever as a place of exotic luxury and magnificence. An example of this toponym in today's language:

> Although bachelor Gates is building a 37,000-square-foot Xanadu, he maintains that wealth loses all power to motivate once you have enough to be comfortable.
> "If People Complain," *People*, October 24, 1991

Eponyms and toponyms are similar to allusions in usage: They import an instant image in a word or two. The difference between and eponym or toponym and allusion is the difference between the common and the unique.The former has been used so often that it has become part of the vocabulary; the latter is more distinct, an association rather than an assimilation.

Partial to Synecdoche & Metonymy

Synecdoche (si-*neck*-duh-kee) means *to take on a share of* in Greek. In other words, this device is naming a part for the whole (her hand in marriage) or the whole for the part (he hit my body), the genus for the species (a cutthroat for an assassin), or the species for the genus (a rodent for a squirrel), the material for the thing made (steel for gun), and so on.

Synecdoche often gives language a sense of the colloquial. The Lord's Prayer uses synecdoche: "Give us this day our daily bread." Bread is a part of the whole—one's needs in daily life. If the United States wins a gold medal, the truth is that a team or an individual won that gold medal and the expression is an example of synecdoche. A literary example is a line from Samuel Taylor Coleridge's "The Rime of the Ancient Mariner." The substitution of *wave* for *sea* takes a share of the sea, a part for the whole.

> The western wave was all aflame, . . .

Metonymy, similar to synecdoche, comes from two Greek words meaning *to change the name*. Metonymy references the

Exercise: One for All and All for One

Metonymy and synecdoche are often confused; some rhetoricians simply lump them together. Yet their difference can be important. Both are metaphors, but metonymy is a bigger idea with more commentary, while synecdoche is more common, sometimes vague. Which two examples below are synecdoche, which two are metonymy, and which are simple artistic metaphors?

1. Their marriage is a bed of roses.

2. My brother borrowed my wheels.

3. I don't have two dimes to rub together.

4. Look at the mercury rising.

5. Put on Eric Clapton and turn up the volume.

6. She's the fabric and he's the glue in their relationship.

Key: Metaphor: 1, 6. Synecdoche: 2, 5; Metonymy: 3, 4.

relationship of the thing or person represented. It names an attribute of the thing, creating a bigger image. The *crown*, for example, represents the entire monarchy. Unlike synecdoche, the crown isn't part of the government or the whole of the government, but rather an image that is closely associated with it. Metonymy renames the thing, underlines it, gives it more emphasis.

"You can't fight city hall" is an example of metonymy; *city hall* is a metaphorical image representing the law or the government of the city. From the *Wall Street Journal Europe* (April 15, 2003) comes this line, talking about two governments, each represented by an image associated with it:

To be sure, the frost between the White House and Elysée Palace is still knee-deep.

The White House or the Elysée Palace, in this instance, is not a part of the whole or a whole of the part, as in synecdoche, but rather a representative image of its government—a metonymy. (Did you note that this line also contains an expletive, *to be sure,* and a metaphor, *knee-deep frost*?)

Euphemism for Delicacy

Euphemism comes from the Greek word meaning *to speak fair.*

Sometimes in writing or speaking, we wish to avoid saying something unpleasant, offensive, or harsh, so we use a euphemism instead. "Burned beyond recognition" is a euphemism for the graphic reality that could be detailed. Euphemisms about death abound: *passed on, passed over, asleep, gone away, gone to Heaven, with the angels.* An interesting euphemism about death is found in Shakespeare's *King Richard II,* in which the king asks about John of Gaunt:

> *King Richard:* What says he?
> *Northumberland:* Nay, nothing, all is said.
> His tongue is now a stringless instrument . . .

Euphemisms serve a character well, especially when a difference of opinion arises and tact must be observed. Here's a rather direct example in which the main character and her boyfriend's adult daughters are gauging each other:

> They looked at her suspiciously, as though she might be a gold digger or a floozie, searching, searching for their proper father's possible motives for involving himself with a broad-bosomed woman with tinted highlights in her hair, who opened her mouth wide to laugh and somehow did not seem—well . . . she knew a euphemism when she felt one coming up behind her—Texas.
>
> "The Widow Joy," Rosellen Brown,
> *Speakeasy*, March/April 2004

The Surprising Paraprosdokian

The unexpected or surprising ending to a story or even just a sentence or phrase is a *paraprosdokian,* something all writers love when it is done well. One of George Bernard Shaw's lines provides a good example: "What a pity that youth must be wasted on the young."

From *The No. 1 Ladies' Detective Agency* comes a line that doesn't seem too surprising because of its use of a cliché (*no point in beating about the bush*) except that the author, Alexander McCall Smith, doesn't stop there. He surprises the reader by adding to the cliché, making it fresh and unpredictable, especially because of the story's setting, which is Africa:

Exercise: Paraprosodokian Ending

Read a book of poems, noting the ones that have a surprising ending. Choose one of them as a model for your own poem. Or choose an everyday topic (e.g., a basketball, a dog's tail, a gopher hole, the red flag on a mailbox, the mole on your mother's face, a dandelion) and write a short poem. Turn the topic on its head to give it a final unusual twist.

"I'll get straight to the point," said Mr. Patel. "There's no point in beating about the bush and chasing all sorts of rabbits, is there? No, there isn't."

Nonfiction, too, uses paraprosdokian. Lewis Thomas in *The Lives of a Cell* begins one of his chapters with a long sentence that ends with a surprising final word, a paraprosdokian:

There was a quarter-page advertisement in the *London Observer* for a computer service that will enmesh your name in an electronic network of fifty thousand other names, sort out your tastes, preferences, habits, and deepest desires and match them up with opposite numbers, and retrieve for you, within a matter of seconds, and for a very small fee, friends.

Poetry, of course, is a great environment for paraprosdokian, for it usually houses a final nugget that surprises or delights. Pablo Neruda's love poem "Your Feet" rhapsodizes the feet of his lover, how they support the rest of the woman's beautiful body. Here's the final verse with its delightful ending line:

But I love your feet
only because they walked
upon the earth and upon
the wind and upon the waters,
until they found me.

Paronomasia for the Pun of It

Wordplay or *puns* are the more common terms for *paronomasia* (pa-ro-no-*may*-zee-a), the use of similar sounding words that differ in meaning. It plays on the sound or meaning of words. Parono-masia comes from the Greek *para*, meaning alongside, and *nomos*, name, and thus means *to alter slightly in naming*. Here's a success-ful and defining paronomasia: "A pun is its own reword."

Children love paronomasia in the form of knock, knock jokes and *daffynitions* (alarms = what an octopus is; pasteurize = too far to see) have entertained children for generations.

Two examples of punning paronomasia make great use of adverbs. A *wellerism*, which Charles Dickens's Sam Weller used in *The Pickwick Papers,* went like this:

> Out with it, as the father said to the child when he swallowed a farden (farthing).

A *Tom Swifty* also uses adverbs in a punny way and is also a form of paronomasia:

- ▸ "I've added vinegar to the dressing," he said, acidly.
- ▸ "I'm dying," he croaked.
- ▸ "The toilet works fine now," she said, flushing.

These were invented by Edward Stratemeyer, author of the Tom Swift and other book series.

Marketers and businesses could make good use of paronomasia. The sign over an antique shop might be "Remains to Be Seen" or a sign beside a brothel: "It's a business doing pleasure with you." The actual name of an herbal company is Good Thymes for You.

Headlines are a marvelous place to find or create paronomasia.

A *New York Times* sports article about golfing legend Arnold Palmer's final Masters tournament appearance and about the final score of new star, Justin Rose, is titled: "Rose Earns a Bow; Palmer Bows Out." The same newspaper titled an article about the shortage of seasonal workers with "The Butcher, The Baker, The Poultry Eviscer-ator." The first example is a **paraprosdokian**, and the second is a play on words, parodying an old nursery rhyme. Your newspaper's head-lines are excellent sources for puns, wordplay, allusions, zeugmas, alliterations.

Exercise: Double It with Zeugma

The headline of an article about the Botox injections that erase wrinkles is "What gives women a skin-deep approach to self-worth." The syllepsis or zeugma, of course, is *skin-deep* with its double meaning, one literal and one figurative.

Delight your reader with a headline or title that makes use of your own zeugma. Choose a word that can have two meanings. The trick, of course, is that the title must also have meaning for the context of the work.

Example: Suppose you've just written an information article on groundhogs. *Burrow* is an apt word with several meanings: a burrow in the ground or in the base of a tree (where groundhogs live), to burrow in for the winter, to burrow down deep. Create a title for your article.

"It's a Hughes Upset" rings a headliner about 16-year-old ice skater, Sarah Hughes, who wins the gold medal over favored skaters. "Langston's Hues" is the title of a poem by Langston Hughes about the colors of his life.

The Playful Zeugma or Syllepsis

A single word used both figuratively and literally at the same time is called a *syllepsis* (sil-*lep*-sis) or a *zeugma*. The same word, often a verb, has a double meaning:

> ▸ He missed his girlfriend and the train.
> ▸ She stole my heart and my wallet.
> ▸ The cat was put out.

One of Benjamin Franklin's political witticisms applies two different meanings to a single verb:

> We must all hang together or assuredly we will all hang separately.

Alexander Pope used the device in *The Rape of the Lock* when "black Omens" threaten the heroine with "dire disaster"; perhaps she will err in some respect,

> Or stain her honour, or her new brocade.

The zeugma doubles the reader's pleasure by providing two entirely different directions for the single verb.

A contemporary journalist selected two words used as a noun and a verb in the same sentence:

> An itch demands a scratch, but science has barely begun to
> scratch the surface of why an itch itches, and how to make it stop.
> "The Mystery of Itch, the Joy of Scratch," Abigail Zuger,
> *New York Times,* July 1, 2003

Advertising also shows off the zeugma. A line from ads for Purina One dog and cat food reads: How Great Relationships Are Fed. The syllepsis is *fed*, which figuratively refers to feeding a relationship and, literally, to feeding the pet. An advertisement for John Deere tractors provides a double image with "Runs like a Deere."

And So . . .

- *Allusion:* often a literary reference to a famous person, place, thing, or event to provide an instant image in an economy of words. (His difficult life was a pilgrim's progress of youth to old age.)
- *Aporia:* an interrupter that inserts a rhetorical question of doubt or uncertainty in order to establish argument or relationship. (Do you wonder about the effects of the ozone on our health?)
- *Apostrophe:* an interrupter that inserts an aside from the narrator or author for purposes of clarity or establishing relationship. (I must inform you, dear reader, that . . .)
- *Ellipsis:* a device of omission, eliminating words for smoother flow and more emphasis. (Kent's diet is gluten-free, Narisha's is low-carb, and Carrie's, high-protein.)
- *Eponym* and *Toponym:* names of people and places that have become part of our language (e.g., Braille, guillotine, Xanadu).
- *Euphemism:* a device of delicacy, lessening the stark reality with mild words. (My grandmother passed on.)
- *Expletive:* a device of interruption in which a certain word clues the audience to a statement of import. (Clearly, she doesn't know what she's doing.)
- *Paraprosdokian:* a final word or sentence that surprises and delights. (What a pity that youth is wasted on the young.)
- *Parenthesis:* an interruption or an aside, set apart by a pair of commas or dashes or parentheses, that offers new information or explanation. (He used his charm to woo women—including four wives—and to . . .)
- *Paronomasia:* a pun or play on words. (A pun is its own reword.)
- *Sententia:* an interrupter that inserts a maxim for purposes of summarizing. (The apple certainly doesn't fall far from the tree.)
- *Synecdoche* and *Metonomy:* light metaphors that exchange a part for a whole or vice versa (Those are nice threads you're wearing.) and renames an abstract with a concrete image (The Spanish throne is at risk.).
- *Zeugma* or *Syllepsis:* an entertaining double wordplay resulting in two meanings, literal and figurative. (He opened his door and his heart.)

Part II

Dazzling Word Choices & Techniques

Words & Pictures, Power & Grace

Hang Noodles on Your Ears: Vibrant Words for Vivid Images

"The difference between the almost right word and the right word is really a large matter—it's the difference between the lightning bug and the lightning," wrote Mark Twain in an 1888 letter.

A group of words may state what needs to be stated, but a passage must be shaped to ring with clarity or bring forth an image. Weak words simply do not engage the imagination.

What Are Weak Words?

"He ran home." A simple, clear sentence, is it not? Simple, yes. Clear, not really. Did *he* run with hesitancy or with determination? Did he run like a gazelle or a rhino? And who is he? What is home? More apt words would provide a clearer image and leave a more lasting impression. Here's how Jack London wrote that same sentence in *White Fang:*

White Fang trotted boldly into camp straight to Gray Beaver's tepee.

With more complexity, here's the way Kathryn Makris wrote it in her true story "On the Way Home":

The Goddess Athena, in Homer's tale, plucked Odysseus from his twenty years of travel and travail and dropped him on the shores of his home, "clear-shining" Ithaca.

The verbs in both examples suggest specific action and the nouns contain specific names. The naming of people, places, and actions are so much more intriguing than *he* and *ran* and *home*. Dull pronouns, overused verbs, and nonspecific nouns say nothing. Specifics create interest and image.

In the same book of stories from which the Makris example is taken, *Travelers' Tales, Greece,* Tara Austen Weaver writes this line:

> "Yamas," the brown-haired woman said to us as she held up a shot glass of ouzo, tinted pink.

The author might have used the word *cheers* and every English-speaking reader would understand. Instead, she chose the Greek word *yamas*, which accentuates the setting and makes the sentence and scene richer. In the same way, the shot glass of pink-tinted ouzo creates a much more interesting and specific image than a mere glass.

The single most effective way to make a sentence stronger is to seek and find the exact verb, the exact noun, the exact modifier that the passage or scene deserves.

In describing a walk down a path, the same author might have written: "The tree-lined path curved ahead of me." The sentence attempts personification but doesn't work all that well. It creates no clear image. Here's a passage Makris wrote in "On the Way Home":

> The path shot nearly straight up over jagged boulders. Tree branches and thorny bramble clawed at me with every step. . . . When at last the path leveled, it set me among the familiar arms of olive trees.

Makris chose active, vivid verbs and specific nouns to put across a distinct message, a clear image: This path is no passive ribbon of pavement. It's alive and wild with specific adjectives (*jagged, thorny, familiar, olive*) and personification (an athletic path and trees that claw and welcome with open arms).

Mark Twain had another good piece of advice in *Pudd'nhead Wilson:* "As to the adjective, when in doubt, strike it out." For new writers, who tend to overwrite, this statement is true. But for sure-

Exercise: Specifics Add Credibility

Specifics create interest. Details enliven a piece of writing. Highlight or activate the following dull details. Examples are included, but create your own.

- Blue (robin egg blue)
- The house (the squat one-story brick rambler)
- A tree (a fifteen-foot leafless crabapple)
- A highway (County Road 15)

footed writers like Makris, adjectives are critical. The trick is to choose them with discretion. Makris does not settle for using the word *colors* in her short story, nor is she content to name only the broad *red, blue,* and *gold,* each of which brings any number of hues to a reader's mind. Instead, she captures the color in a Byzantine chapel:

> Slowly my eyes adjusted to cowrie blue, wine red, and the glitter of gold leaf in a dozen somber icons.

With the aid of personification and alliteration, Makris brings the reader further into the building and opens the senses by detailing the smells; in making them personal for herself, they become more personal for the reader:

> Two scents—the bite of holy incense and the sweet, sad exhale of a decaying building—twinned in a perfume that took me back to childhood.

Makris does the reader the lovely favor of taking the time to re-create a setting that could so easily have been passed over with far fewer and far less interesting words. Instead, the reader is impelled to see the red wine and glittering gold and to ponder the idea of a sweet, sad smell. A realistic and honest scene has been recreated in a true story, and would have been as effective in fiction. But here in this true story of Greece, Makris's evocative use of detail echoes classic lines from Homer's *Odyssey,* in which vibrant adjectives and amplification are also key:

> Gray-eyed Athena sent them a favorable breeze, a fresh west wind, singing over the wine-dark sea.

Exercises in Vivid Verbs: Sports Writing & Beyond

One of the easiest and surest ways to beef up a writing passage is to exchange lifeless verbs for strong, active ones. To study vivid verbs, new writers might look to sports writers; they pepper their articles with strong action verbs. From the sports section of the *International Herald Tribune* (April 14, 2003) come these lines:

> Tiger Woods roared into the Masters picture like a train racing toward its appointed destination.

A strong verb and a simile make the line memorable. Another line from the same page is inserted into a story that isn't entirely action-driven:

> Paula Radcliffe shattered her own world marathon best time Sunday in the London Marathon when she sprinted . . . .

There's this one about rugby:

> Leicester's hopes of a third straight European Cup victory were dashed when it lost, 20-7, to Munster in a bruising quarterfinal Sunday. The Irish side avenged its defeat . . . .

It's the verbs in the sentences that give life to otherwise dry statistics—*dashed, avenged.*

Time and again, in her biography of a horse and its trainers, *Seabiscuit,* Laura Hillenbrand recreates historic scenes pumping with action, as much through vivid verbs as anything else:

> Seabiscuit slashed into the hole, disappeared between his two larger opponents, then burst into the lead. . . . He shook free and hurtled into the homestretch alone as the field fell away behind him.

Strong to the Hoop, by children's picture book author John Coy, uses the same active verbiage with sentences likes these:

> ‣ Zo glides down the lane, fakes a pass, then flips a finger roll with his left hand.

▶ I drive left, spin right, and soar to the hoop.

▶ His shot rattles off the rim. Zo rebounds, and we race the other way.

Active verbs aligned with alliteration (*flips a finger roll, rattles off the rim*) come part and parcel with children's picture books. The short punchy sentences are fun to read aloud.

Because their pages are limited and their audience is young, children's writers strive for image in every word. Restless readers (and not just the young) are engaged when stories fill their minds with images. Descriptive action verbs evoke reaction from readers. In this paragraph from the picture book *Jacob and the Polar Bears,* author Janet Graber shows Jacob discovering something unusual about his new polar bear pajamas:

Wood crackled in the potbellied stove, and a deep silence blew down from the hills and hugged the little house, but Jacob was wide awake. He twitched. He tickled. He itched. He threw off his blanket. Jacob's bed was full of tiny polar bears! They scampered, somersaulted, leapfrogged all over the sheets!

Exercise: Strong Verbs Activate a Scene

Remember the E. B. White paragraph in *Charlotte's Web* in which Templeton the Rat emphasizes his worries and wishes about being confined to a crate?

Kindly remember that I'm hiding down here in this crate and I don't want to be stepped on, or kicked in the face, or pummeled, or crushed in any way, or squashed, or buffeted about, or bruised, or lacerated, or scarred, or biffed.

Using this line as a model, tell someone what you don't want to have happen to you. Use a list of six vibrant verbs.

Kindly remember that I'm hiding behind the drapes and I don't want to be . . .

Active verbs bring the bears to life, not the other way around. Because of sound devices like alliteration and assonance, their careful placement creates a lyrical tone, making the story fun to read aloud.

139

Exercise: Exchange Dull for Sharp Contrasts

What would you exchange for the mediocre verbs and adverbs in these sentences? How would you revitalize these sentences? Think of ways to give image to sentences that begin with weak starters like *it* and *there*.

▸ Papa John called loudly, then inadvertently tripped over a tree root.

▸ It was an ugly building. There were no windows and it was long and low to the ground.

▸ It began to rain. The drops fell fast and sharp. It sounded like a pellet gun.

Every kind of writing benefits from strong, image-filled verbs, even science writing with its particular call for accuracy. From the science section of the *New York Times* come sentences with exacting verb choices that make the description a stand-out:

As Mr. Zienowicz's body sloughed off burned skin, the lining from his eye sockets and eyelids peeled away. Meanwhile, the disease eroded his corneas—a devastating journey.
"A New Lens Restores Vision,"
A. Moore, July 1, 2003

Dull adverbs and mediocre verbs can often be replaced by a single vibrant verb. Thus, *talked quietly* becomes *whispered* or *mumbled*. *Ran quickly* becomes *raced, sprinted, shot*. The following sentence is fairly clear: "Miriam bowed, then backed quietly away." But how much more interesting and memorable to write, "Sister Miriam bowed, then faded from the room," as Mark Salzman did in *Lying Awake*.

In "Franklin Delano Roosevelt" (*Time*, December 31, 1999), biographer Doris Kearns Goodwin uses an effective transitive verb more often used as a noun: "Roosevelt's critics were certain he would *straightjacket* the free-enterprise system once America began mobilizing for war."

To Be or Not to Be

The excerpts here employ very few *to be* verbs—*am, is, are, were, was, will be*—and as essential as *to be* is to our language, its forms are often weak and used thoughtlessly by writers. Strong active verbs create an image, leave an impression, and make a scene come alive; *to be* verbs rarely do. If not used sparingly, they'll deaden the scene. Below are three paragraphs from three different publications that have doused themselves into mediocrity (if not numbness) by the verb's overuse:

> The worst part is that most of us are not even aware that we are not free. There is something inside that whispers to us that we are not free, but we do not understand what it is, and why we are not free.
>
> *The Four Agreements,* Don Miguel Ruiz

If the first few words in each sentence were deleted—including the dull sentence starter *there is*—and if the paragraph could rid itself of some of its redundancy, the writing would be stronger:

> Most of us are not even aware that we are not free. Yet, something inside whispers that we lack freedom, but we do not understand how or why.

The next example uses *was* as the helping verb for two verbs that stand stronger alone. A commonly used but weak sentence-starter, *was* often has no reference, no clear identity. This overall scene would be better served with a construction that cuts out half or more of the dull *was* verbs, as indicated in the rewritten version:

> *Original:*
> His forearm was ripped open to the bone. The man was badly frightened. It was not so much the dog's ferocity as it was his silence that unnerved the groom.
>
> Jack London, *White Fang*

> *Rewrite:*
> His forearm ripped open to the bone, the frightened man was more unnerved by the dog's silence than by its ferocity.

Note that all truths have their exceptions, however. One of the most famous and powerful lines in English literature, the opening to Charles Dickens's *A Tale of Two Cities* uses *was* with great power, through its coupling with other rhetorical devices:

It was the best of times, it was the worst of times, it was the age of wisdom, it was the age of foolishness, it was the epoch of belief, it was the epoch of incredulity, it was the season of Light, it was the season of Darkness, it was the spring of hope, it was the winter of despair, we had everything before us . . .

The third example of the weak use of *to be* constructs suffers from two opening sentences in three short consecutive paragraphs using the same syntax—subject plus *to be* verb, the second of which is the weak *there was/it was* construct. A simple deletion of dull words plus a shifting in sentence structure helps.

Original:
 ▸ The surroundings were no longer quiet and deserted. There was a trickle of rudely dressed people, heading toward the castle. . . .
 ▸ Not surprisingly, it was misting heavily, but there was enough light to show a stone bridge, arching . . .
 ▸ The castle itself was blunt and solid. This was more like an enormous fortified house . . .

Outlander, Diana Gabaldon

Rewrite:
 ▸ The surroundings were no longer quiet and deserted. A trickle of rudely dressed people headed toward the castle . . .
 ▸ Not surprisingly, a heavy mist hung in the air, but it allowed enough light to show . . .
 ▸ The castle, blunt and solid, was more like an enormous fortified house . . . .

The peppering of *to be* verbs, and of helping verbs such as *do, have, can, may, might, must, ought, could, should, would* deadens a paragraph or a scene faster than hail on a tin roof deadens the senses. Action verbs activate a scene every time. In general, helping verbs create a passive tone. "The waves were crashing against the rocky shore" becomes noticeably stronger when the helper is eliminated: "The waves crashed against the rocky shore." The effect is more immediate, more action-driven. In the same way, "The women were coatless" or "The cat is spitting" or "The man was frightened" are more effective as *the coatless woman, the spitting cat, the frightened man,* followed by active verbs. Adverbs—as in *badly* frightened—become unnecessary when the rest of the sentence clarifies the man's fear.

Move from the General to the Specific by Naming

Move from a general description into the specific to create a stronger scene and elevate writing. The specifics come through not just via verbs, but in the chosen details. Take a look at a paragraph from Isabel Fonseca's *Bury Me Standing: The Gypsies and Their Journey:*

> Nicu slept in, and Nuzi sat moodily on the porch step, chewing an unlit Victory and patting his shoulder-length hair, waiting for Liliana to make his coffee. That was her job, and—ever since he lost his post at the Ministry of Vegetation—waiting for it was his.

The author begins by identifying the players—the three specific and unusual names make the scene believable. Fonseca doesn't show Nuzi simply and mundanely holding a cigarette; she zeroes in on the fact. His hair color isn't provided; what he does with it is, in a more unique detail. Nuzi doesn't just wait for Liliana, he waits for her to do something specific. Adding that detail to the job loss makes the end of the paragraph all the more meaningful and dramatic. Rather than simply stating that Nuzi has lost his job, Fonseca names the job site, which adds credibility. The details make all the difference in seeing and feeling the reality in the scene.

Naming comes part and parcel with biographies and profiles. It provides corroborating evidence. Whether people, places, or things, names make the scene real, the article believable. Alec Wilkinson profiled a guitar player named Mark Stewart in "An Instrumental Man." Wilkinson lists his subject's background, in part, like this:

> He has worked in the pit of several Broadway shows, and he is also a member of the Bang on a Can All-Stars, the Fred Frith Guitar Quartet, and Arnold Dreyblatt's Orchestra for Excited Strings, and with Rob Schwimmer, he performs as the brainy, downtown cabaret act Polygraph Lounge, in which many of his instruments find a place.
>
> "An Instrumental Man," Alec Wilkinson,
> *New Yorker,* May 12, 2003

If the article weren't about a real man, the reader would think Stewart's memberships were fictionalized. Specifics like this make the paragraph a standout. Ann Lamott makes this point as well in *Bird by Bird: Some Instructions on Writing and Life:*

> [Books] are full of all the things you don't get in real life—wonderful, lyrical language for instance, right off the bat. And quality of attention: we may notice amazing details during the course of a day, but we rarely let ourselves stop and really pay attention. An author makes you notice, makes you pay attention, and this is a great gift.

We've all read science articles that are as lifeless as dead grass. In contrast, science researcher Lewis Thomas built a reputation as a remarkable writer, in such works as *The Lives of a Cell: Notes of a Biology Watcher*. Lewis takes time in the details when he writes about the possibility of consciously directing the organs in his body, rather than letting the body take care of itself:

> If I were informed tomorrow that I was in direct communication with my liver, and could now take over, I would become deeply depressed. I'd sooner be told, forty thousand feet over Denver, that the 747 jet in which I had a coach seat was now mine to operate as I pleased; at least I would have the hope of bailing out, if I could find a parachute and discover quickly how to open a door.

Thomas has opted to create a very clear impression of how complex a machine the liver is by comparing it to a 747 jet. A medical researcher, he knows the intricacies of the body, and yet he states, unequivocally, that his expertise is no match for the liver's skills in doing its own work. Without this comparison, or analogy, the complexity of the liver's work would be lost on the reader. Thomas has placed the reader not only on a 747, but in the coach seat and at a specific height above a specific city. He has implanted the ideas of opening a plane's exit door, of locating a parachute and jumping at that ridiculous and fatal height. In this case, the specifics of something familiar not only heighten a reader's interest but place him in the jet, sensing the loss of control of an extremely complicated machine.
Here's Thomas again as he talks about directing the brain:

There are several things I would change, given the opportunity: certain memories that tend to slip away unrecorded, others I've had enough of and would prefer to delete, certain notions I'd just as soon didn't keep popping in, trains of thought that go round and round without getting anywhere, rather like this one.

A lesser writer might have used one noun, *thoughts*, to describe those things that run through our minds. Instead, Thomas chose three more exacting words: *memories, notions, trains of thought.* Notice the fine choice of active, vivid verbs and adverbs: *slip away, delete, pop, go round and round.* What a splendid juxtaposition, placing *trains of thoughts* next to *go round and round.*

Peter Mayle does a delicious job in *French Lessons: Adventures with Knife, Fork, and Corkscrew,* of naming items as he describes foods that will make a reader's mouth salivate:

First into the pan goes a generous knob of butter, followed by the chicken breasts and legs, a large onion cut into quarters, a dozen or so sliced champignons de Paris—those small, tightly capped white mushrooms—a couple of cloves of garlic en chemise, crushed but not peeled,

Exercise: Naming

The naming of things enriches the experience, giving the reader something concrete to hold onto. In moving from the general to the specific, exact names provide legitimacy, life, and meaning. In *The Lives of a Cell Notes of a Biology Watcher,* Lewis Thomas opens up our bodies and shows us the moving parts. We don't need illustrations; he paints the movement with words:

Our smooth-muscle cells are born with complete instructions, in need of no help from us, and they work away on their own schedules, modulating the lumen of blood vessels, moving things through intestines, opening and closing tubules. . . .

Mimicking Thomas's style, think about your own area of expertise. Use its vocabulary to name those parts for readers, providing them with an illustration.

Exercise: Food for Thought

In the style of Peter Mayle or E. B. White, list in exquisite detail the contents of a recipe or a holiday meal you enjoyed. You might begin with words like these:

The table groaned under the weight of its smorgasbord: light fluffy potatoes topped with melting butter and green scallions . . .

and a bouquet garni of herbs. When the color of the chicken has turned to deep gold, a large glass of white wine is poured into the pan and allowed to reduce before half a liter of crème fraiche is added.

Interesting, specific noun choices—a *knob* of butter, *champignons de Paris*, a *bouquet garni* —push the recipe, making it memorable. The author names foods and sprinkles in adjectives (*deep, sliced, generous, tightly capped white*) that deepen the meaning resulting in a recipe that makes the reader ready to bolt to the kitchen. Fried chicken has never sounded so good. Specificity is the key.

Food was on E. B. White's mind, too, when he created amazing lists of nouns, each of which multiplies the effect of the scene. Old Sheep succeeds in convincing the rat, Templeton, to go along to the fair, with this commentary:

A rat can creep out late at night and have a feast. In the trampled grass of the infield you will find old discarded lunch boxes containing the foul remains of peanut butter sandwiches, hard-boiled eggs, cracker crumbs, bits of doughnuts, and particles of cheese. In the hard-packed dirt of the midway . . . you will find a veritable treasure of popcorn fragments, frozen custard dribblings, candied apples abandoned by tired children, sugar fluff crystals, salted almonds, popsicles, partially gnawed ice cream cones, and the wooden sticks of lollypops.

White could so easily have had Old Sheep simply state that the fairgrounds are home to a good amount of edible litter that a rat would enjoy, but he has elevated the scene by listing, by naming these items. In fact, he not only names them, but attaches adjectives that activate the taste buds of both a rat and a young reader.

Once again, naming details moves a scene from the general to the specific, from the dull to the lively, from the barely credible to the realistic. The scene is rich and memorable.

Show, Don't Tell

An easy—but lazy—way to describe a boy might be this: "Hans is very tall." Height is relative, so the reader has no clear image. Specifics clarify: "Hans towers over his father and three brothers." The first example tells—states—that Hans is tall while the second example shows a clear image through the use of a strong verb and a comparison.

How much more intriguing to say, "a black-frocked man in angry, earnest conversation with my mother" than "a priest preaching at my mother"? How much more memorable to say "Her hair is a cotton-candy tangle in the wind" rather than "Her thin hair is messy." These two examples are excerpted from *Chocolat*, by Joanne Harris. The first of the two is a statement of fact, the second a metaphor. From the same book comes:

> I feel light, insubstantial as milkweed fluff. Ready for any wind to blow away.

Yes, the narrator is telling the reader that she feels light, but it doesn't mean a thing until she clarifies, until she shows or creates an image with a simile. She does the same thing in another scene:

> He brings my attention to a growth under Charly's chin, about the size of a hen's egg, gnarled like an elm burr.

What an image! Through amplification and simile, the author shows the priest in action, creating an image of tangled hair, offering a comparative sense of lightness, detailing the chin growth—all to dramatize or show the scenes of which these play a part.

Rosellen Brown details the final moments of a life in "The Widow Joy." Through a terrific analogy and a single word of dialogue, readers are treated to an instant image of the bedside scene. The final line of introspection shows Joy's resulting emotions, the details of which will resonate with any reader.

He blinked out gradually and silently, like a lightbulb dimming. And like a bulb, he flared once at the every end, another gift to her. Staring straight ahead where she was not, he cried out "Joy!" as if, astonished, he was calling out to show her something. As if Joy were an emotion, not a name. She had always thought her celebratory name silly, but she forgave her parents then and there for their hopefulness and prescience.

Speakeasy, March/April 2004

In *Where No Gods Came,* Sheila O'Connor does an equally successful job of illustrating a scene, this time a busy city street. Notice how she amplifies the first line by adding vibrant details that result in vivid images. She does this through strong active verbs and the specific naming of things, which adds reality and credibility to the scene.

I go back to Mission Boulevard, the sidewalks sizzling and edgy, as though the whole city is close to exploding. Girls with tangled hair panhandle; their bare bellies flash over the tops of their filthy hip-hugger jeans. Navy men bristle and spit at the hippies who hand out flowers. Most of the shops along the boulevard have changed their names. The Place, Magic, Carpet, Electric Avenue. They sell black lights, psychedelic posters, pipes for smoking grass. On the street corners, with their guitar cases propped open for donations, boys strum guitars and sing James Taylor, Cat Stevens or Crosby, Stills, Nash and Young. They sing off-key in high voices that . . .

Columnist Mark Morford created this concrete image (a metaphor) for his readers, one that is powerful enough to do exactly what he suggests. Note his use of polysyndeton (consecutive conjunctions) that extends the list of torturous adjectives:

If you saturate yourself with only one perspective, or you choose a path wherein you are blasted to the core every moment with the worst humanity has to offer, well, the world responds in kind and is nothing but bleak and sad and torturous, full of little tiny leeches with sharp jagged teeth . . . that devour your large intestine while you sleep.

"Please Write More About Rape,"
San Francisco Gate, May 14, 2004

F. Scott Fitzgerald wanted to capture the idea that writing is damn hard work. But those simple words don't offer a comparison or capture a sensation or image. So he worked hard at finding just the right words: "All writing is swimming underwater, holding your breath." Now the reader has an image to hold onto. Writing is not an easy crawl; it's not a floating on top of water; it's not a dive. It's constantly swimming underwater where one's vision is blurred, where the water's pressure is heavy, where one cannot breathe. Now, that's hard work. And that's showing, not telling.

And So . . .

> . . . a large man with eyebrows that patrolled his forehead like gray battleships, ready to meet any threat to his parishioners' souls.
>
> *Lying Awake,* Mark Salzman

- By choosing a single personal trait to describe in specific detail, a person or character becomes real, tangible, and memorable.
- Strong active verbs, descriptive specific nouns, and well-chosen modifiers each play a role in creating vivid writing.
- Careful word choices provide not only clarity, action, and image, but a scene that can be felt, smelled, heard, and seen. Move from the general to the specific.
- The *to be* verb—easily overused as a passive voice or a descriptor, and weak modifiers (e.g., *very, quietly, beautiful*) and dull sentence starters (e.g., *there is/are, It's/It was*) undermine the potential for a standout sentence or scene.
- Vivid words create vivid image, effectively illustrating a scene or personality, rather than simply describing it or telling about it.

More Words or Fewer?

H ow much specifying, detailing, naming should a writer do?
How many vivid modifiers does a piece of writing need? When
is enough enough? When is it too much? Should the writer's motto
always be *simplicity, clarity, specificity*? Should a writer stay away
from the decorative language that some writers and readers enjoy?
Through the excerpts and discussion provided in this chapter,
judge for yourself.

A Lengthier Accounting Can Clarify

The light-hearted paragraph below comes from an article titled
"Rediscovering Rhubarb." At first glance, the paragraph seems
overwritten; rhubarb doesn't deserve such a wordy soliloquy. On
second glance, the reader sees that the paragraph is straightforward: The government's definition is followed by the author's
humorous rebuttal.

Rhubarb is a vegetable, no matter what the government says: a
member of the buckwheat family of herbaceous plants including
buckwheat, dock and smartweed, which are characterized by having
swollen joints, simple leaves, small petalless flowers and small, dry,
indehiscent fruit. Indehiscent means 'not dehiscent,' not opening at
maturity to release the seed. So "indehiscent" means "hard, dry,
holding onto the seed," which actually describes Norwegians quite

Exercise: Add Detail to Heighten Interest

In *Bury Me Standing: The Gypsies and Their Journey,* Isabel Fonseca talks about a society steeped in tradition, myth, superstition. She inserts parentheses to clarify:

All of these steps were complicated and protracted by the superstitions that had to be observed along the way. (Jeta spat on her broom. Why? Because she had swept under my feet. If I do not, she continued, seeing that the first answer had not got through, your children will remain bald all their lives, stupid.)

Mimicking Fonseca's paragraph, add a parenthesis—an aside that clarifies or adds— about a different topic, your grandmother's recipe:

All of these steps were complicated and protracted by my grandmother's antiquated measuring system: a smidgen of salt, . . .

well. Most Norwegians consider dehiscence to be indecent. They hold the seed in. But rhubarb pie comes along in the spring, when we're half crazed from five months of winter—it's the first fresh vegetable we get, and it makes us dehisce.

"Rediscovering Rhubarb,"
Carol Stocker,
Boston Globe, May 16, 1996

The reader enjoys the paragraph because of the excellent specificity of the description, the playful verbal stab at Norwegians (among whom the author seems to count herself), and the conclusion that "we" want—we need—rhubarb pie in the spring. Could this conclusion have been reached without the set-up? No. Has rhubarb ever been more humorously yet grandly described? Probably not. In fact, this lengthy rhubarb paragraph is one a reader actually savors.

In *Bury Me Standing: The Gypsies and Their Journey,* Isabel Fonseca quotes Jan Yoors, who traveled with the nomadic Lovara Gypsies and fell in love with their language. Yoors stayed with them for six years, and when it came time to leave them in 1940, he despaired about the loss of this language from his daily life.

I would no longer express myself in the wild, archaic

'Romanes,' unfit for small talk. I would no longer use the forceful, poetic, plastic descriptions and ingenious parables of the Roma or indulge in the unrestrained intensity and fecundity of their language. Old Bidshika once told us the legend about the full moon's being dragged down to the earth by the sheer intensity, weight, and witchery of the Romany tongue. And it almost seemed that it could be true.

How could Yoors explain this gypsy language without the specifics he has included here? Nouns are his strongest tool in trying to define the language: *Romanes, descriptions, parables, intensity, fecundity, Bidshika, legend, weight, witchery, tongue.* When combined with well-chosen adjectives *(wild, archaic, forceful, poetic, plastic, ingenious, unrestrained, Romany)*, the explanation becomes even clearer. Each word of this description has weight. Each defines a bit more. Together, the paragraph becomes a tour de force.

A Lengthier Accounting Establishes Character

First published in 1905, *The House of Mirth* by Edith Wharton is written in a literary style now considered dated. Some readers may consider the following excerpt overwritten, but the word choice is delectable:

> Evie Van Osburgh and Percy Gryce? The names rang derisively through her brain. *Evie Van Osburgh?* The youngest, dumpiest, dullest of the four dull and dumpy daughters whom Mrs. Van Osburgh, with unsurpassed astuteness, had "placed" one by one in inenviable niches of existence!

Wharton carefully chose her words. The disdain of the viewpoint character is obvious, for the author has named names and repeated one of them in italics to highlight the character's distastefulness. Wharton also used alliteration to add ridicule, and the modifiers are fraught with contempt: *dumpy and dull, inenviable.* The narrator is not only unhappy about the union of these two acquaintances, Evie and Percy, she is contemptuous.

Earlier in the novel, Wharton described a scene in which the same Percy Gryce is admiring of Lily and the way she pours tea:

Exercise: Reveal through Monologue

Background information about a fictional character can be woven into a story through internal monologue. It's especially effective if the monologue pertains to ongoing action. Pretend that you've created a street scene in which the viewpoint character observes a pickpocket stealing a man's wallet. Reveal one thing about the narrator's own character as he watches the transaction.

Example: My heart raced as I realized what the man was doing. His fingers deftly lifted the wallet while his gait matched the victim's stride. His eyes gazed straight ahead. The audacity, the skill, the risk-taking by this man thrilled me.

When the tea came he watched her in silent fascination while her hands flitted above the tray, looking miraculously fine and slender in contrast to the coarse china and lumpy bread. It seemed wonderful to him that anyone should perform with such careless ease the difficult task of making tea in public in a lurching train. He would never have dared to order it for himself, lest he should attract the notice of his fellow-passengers; but, secure in the shelter of her conspicuousness, he sipped the inky draught with a delicious sense of exhilaration.

The details delineate a drama in which, by its end, the reader knows much about Percy: He's easily amused and bewitched. Not a risk-taker, he is unsure of himself, lacking social ease and graces. He knows the value of something when he sees it, whether it's Lily's hands, china, bread, or a service performed. It would comfort him to have someone take care of him. So much meaning is gracefully compacted in one well-written paragraph that goes out of its way to employ vivid descriptors, nouns, and verbs. Yes, more is better in this case.

In 1851, Herman Melville opened *Moby Dick* with the narrator, Ishmael, telling the reader why he is going to the sea. It's a wordy, involved, single-sentence explanation that nevertheless gets exactly to the bottom of his raging restlessness and, at the same time, speaks to a reader's own occasional disquiet:

> Whenever I find myself growing grim about the mouth; whenever it is a damp, drizzly November in my soul; whenever I find myself involuntarily pausing before coffin warehouses, and bringing up the rear of every funeral I meet; and especially whenever my hypos get such a upper hand of me that it requires a strong moral principle to prevent me from deliberately stepping into the street, and methodically knocking people's hats off—then I account it high time to get to sea as soon as I can.

Melville's repetition of the word *whenever* to multiply the effect (the device called *anaphora*) and convey Ishmael's mounting depression makes the sentence another fine example of more words being better than fewer. After this explanation, the reader, too, wants Ishmael to get to sea. Perhaps the reader takes the words to heart to explain his own occasional disease or odd behavior.

In "Honoring Our Hunger for the Ecstatic," Fred R. describes some of the same out-of-control behaviors as Ishmael, when he writes about his addiction. The wordy, involved, two-sentence explanation—also making good use of metaphor, anaphora and of asyndeton—once again serves to show the author's distress:

> I'm a recovering alcoholic and drug user who spent years and years in a sort of left-wing sandbox, screaming at the social system for not advancing me, at the economic system for not rewarding me, at God for not rescuing me from an unhappiness that was too blunt to even become anything as exciting as despair. It took a period of recovery before I realized that I drank and drugged because I wanted the effect that the drinks and drugs produced, and that by spending most of my time in bars or curled up in the fetal position in furnitureless studio apartments, I was omitting a key stage in my quest for social standing and economic security: action.
>
> *The Utne Reader,* October 2001

Lengthier Passages Establish Setting

Getting inside a character's head through first-person viewpoint, as the examples above show, needs pacing and effective wording to make a point and to introduce a character's personality. The introduction of a character can also take place through a third-person viewpoint. Jhumpa Lahiri's short story "A Real Durwan" from a collection called *Interpreter of Maladies* describes her main character with details that also begin to convey the setting:

> The only thing that appeared three-dimensional about Boori Ma was her voice: brittle with sorrows, as tart as curds, and shrill enough to grate meat from a coconut.

The author has chosen one feature to illustrate and then uses metaphors and similes to communicate specifics. Can't you hear the acrid, harsh tone? Yet, *brittle with sorrow* needs further clarification. Once again, *character* development also means *setting* development:

> It was with this voice that she enumerated, twice a day as she swept the stairwell, the details of her plight and losses suffered since her deportation to Calcutta after Partition. At that time, she maintained, the turmoil had separated her from a husband, four daughters, a two-story brick house, a rosewood almari, and a number of coffer boxes whose skeleton keys she still wore, along with her life savings, tied to the free end of her sari.

That voice is now speaking, spewing out its tortuous list of lost items, which—because they're named—become more real for the reader and weightier for Boori Ma. She's laden with these losses. They define the remainder of her life. Wordy? Yes. Overwritten? No. Each line adds another layer of understanding about this woman.

The delectably timeless story *Chocolat*, by Joanne Harris, percolates in its descriptions from the weather to chocolates. On the opening page, Harris has carefully selected her words to help the reader see, smell, taste, feel, and remember the setting:

> We came on the wind of the carnival. A warm wind for February, laden with the hot greasy scents of frying pancakes and sausages and powdery-sweet waffles cooked on the hot plate right there by the roadside, with the confetti sleeting down collars and cuffs and rolling in the gutters like an idiot antidote to winter. There is a febrile

excitement in the crowds that line the narrow main street, necks craning to catch sight of the crêpe-covered char with its trailing ribbons and paper rosettes. Anouk watches, eyes wide, a yellow balloon in one hand and a toy trumpet in the other, from between a shopping basket and a sad brown dog. We have seen carnivals before, she and I; a procession of two hundred and fifty of the decorated chars in Paris last Mardi Gras, a hundred and eighty in New York, two dozen marching bands in Vienna, clowns on stilts, the Grosses Tête with their lolling papier-maché heads, drum majorettes with batons spinning and sparkling. But at six the world retains a special luster.

The paragraph abounds with alliteration (*warm wind, confetti on collars and cuffs, crepe-covered char, ribbons and rosettes, toy trumpet, batons spinning and sparkling*) and metaphor (*on the wind of the carnival, confetti sleeting and rolling in the gutters, like an idiot antidote to winter*), and rich, sensory detail. One can smell the pancakes, sausages and waffles. One can feel the warm wind, the confetti slipping down into collars, the excitement. The sights are colorful and moving, sparkling, spinning. The verbs and nouns are strong and active. To make the idea of a carnival even stronger, Harris lists in detail other carnivals and parades she and her daughter have experienced. Somehow that sad brown dog and yellow balloon are standouts, aren't they? That's because their descriptors are common, ordinary. The paragraph continues, but the reader doesn't mind. In fact, this opening is only the appetizer for the feast that follows. In addition, one of the strengths of the paragraph is its rhythm and movement due to the careful placement and phrasing of specific words. The result: a *febrile excitement* that the reader actually feels.

Exercise: Details Lend Richness to a Common Setting

Think about the place you grew up and make it into a setting. Make a list of smells, sounds, textures, visuals, tastes that filled the landscape or cityscape. Then, be choosy. Weave some of those details into a rich tapestry—all in one paragraph—using either first- or third-person viewpoint.

Reread the carnival setting in Joanne Harris's *Chocolat*, excerpted on pages 156–157, to get you started.

Sometimes Less Is Best

> I have made this letter longer than usual, because I lack the time to make it short.
>
> *Blaise Pascal*

Taking the time to be choosy, to pare down lengthy passages and explanations or exposition with exactly the right word or combination of words, makes writing stronger. How, for example, would a writer describe a spider's web with a drop of dew on it? The easy, lazy way is to write simply that it's *a beautiful thing.* But that doesn't say a thing: Beauty is too broad, subjective. Exerting more creative effort might result in a description of a dewdrop shimmering in the spider's web as water sparkles in the sunlight. But that borders both on overwriting and on the predictable. Compare Mark Salzman's effective image in *Lying Awake*:

A dewdrop caught in a spider's web flashed like a prism.

The slightly surprising second verb, *flashed*, combines with the strong descriptive noun, *prism*, to form a simile that is perfect and simple. Less is more.

Pithy quotes abound in articles, on the radio, on billboards, on posters, in greeting cards, in books. "By necessity, by proclivity, and by delight, we all quote," said Ralph Waldo Emerson in an apt quote that demonstrates how a few well-chosen words can say it all. Why use more words when fewer words will do?

Edward Everett's oration at Gettysburg lasted two hours, while Abraham Lincoln's speech was only 270 words—lasting three minutes. Have you ever read or heard quotes from Everett's speech? Can you quote lines from Lincoln's Gettysburg address?

Winston Churchill, another man of many words and many books, said, "Short words are best and the old words when short are best of all." A case in point may be his own words when describing the relief felt when the bullet goes astray: "Nothing in life is so exhilarating as to be shot at without result." How succinctly put!

While a short retort to personal criticism is common and often effective, Churchill in one instance crafted a more eloquent, formal response, one recorded in the House of Commons. Note the understated irony, a polite tactic that makes this line memorable:

> I do not at all resent criticism, even when, for the sake of emphasis, it for a time parts company with reality.

The Styles of Spare Writing

Spare writing doesn't merely suggest a few vivid words. Spare writing also means style. The question may not be which details to describe, but how to describe them. Take a look at a few examples from *Chocolat*. "The wind plucks gleefully at my skirts" describes a single action and a single detail. Two perfectly selected words carry the weight—*plucks* and *gleefully*. The words are few, but the image is full and fresh. In another scene, Harris takes a commonplace action, walking, and uses a well-chosen analogy to create a picture and convey mood and character: "The feet dragged sullenly at the cobbles like the feet of children going to school." In this case, a few more words are much better.

Fragments are incomplete short statements that may technically be grammatically incorrect, but they sometimes convey an idea or seem more appropriate than a formally constructed explanation with excess words. Here, *Chocolat's* protagonist, Vianne Rocher, has cleaned a house that was not only filthy but full of evil spirits. She and her daughter have vanquished them with candles and songs:

Exercise: Word Type & Syntax Accentuate Character

In *Chocolat*, author Joanne Harris details a woman in short, staccato-like sentences. This time, the spare writing style accentuates the twitchy personality of the character:

> I was waiting for her. Tartan coat, hair scraped back in an unflattering style, hands deft and nervous as a gunslinger's. Josephine Muscat, the lady from the carnival.

Mimicking this staccato style, describe a CEO who is—not twitchy—but sure and abrupt in her mannerisms. Use asyndeton (a list without conjunctions) for your second line. Begin with:

> I was waiting for her . . .

And yet for the moment it is enough to know that the house welcomes us, as we welcome it. Rock salt and bread by the doorstep to placate any resident gods. Sandalwood on our pillow to sweeten our dreams.

Two fragments create the effect of a list (asyndeton). Vianne undoubtedly performed more tasks to make the house safe and welcoming, but this short list is enough to illustrate.

Short punctuates effect. Sometimes a spare writing style suggests a personality and sometimes it adds drama or emotion, as in these paragraph starters:

- The carnival is gone.
- My mother was a witch.
- It was cancer.

The spareness of these lines packs a wallop. In these cases, the *to be* verb is very effective. Less is best because less is strong.

Another effective use of a minimum of words occurs in *Chocolat* when Vianne stresses a point through an extended analogy. She is describing the town's powerful priest:

In a place like Lansquenet, it sometimes happens that one person—schoolteacher, café proprietor, or priest—forms the linchpin of the community. That this single individual is the essential core of the machinery that turns lives, like the central pin of a clock mechanism, sending wheels to turn wheels, hammers to strike, needles to point the hour. If the pin slips or is damaged, the clock stops. Lansquenet is like that clock, needles perpetually frozen at a minute to midnight, wheels and cogs turning uselessly behind the bland, blank face.

Set a church clock wrong to fool the devil, my mother always told me. But in this case I suspect the devil is not fooled.

Not for a minute.

What lasts in the readers mind is not the phrase but the effect the phrase created: laughter, tears, pain, joy. If the phrase is not affecting the reader, what's it doing there? Make it do its job or cut it without mercy or remorse.

Isaac Asimov

Vianne's final few words form their own paragraph and end the chapter, simple but packing a punch. The punch is more effective because Harris has taken the time to precede the sentence with well-chosen words that aptly detail a primary character. Besides the analogy to a clock, she has inserted her mother's pithy maxim (sententia), which effectively summarizes. The reader knows that these two characters have met their match.

Children's Books: Pure Forms of the Spare & Vibrant

Poetry, especially in the form of the haiku with its five-seven-five-syllables, uses the sparest language of all. If the audience is children, then the clearest, fewest and most lively of words is instilled in a single scene. Joyce Sidman, in her collection about pets, *The World According to Dog,* offers these haikus:

"Tag"
Dog and toad play tag
under the spring junipers.
I fear for the toad.

"Awakening"
I dream of deep-sea
fishing: awake to find dog
breathing in my face.

Exercise: Haiku

Image. Emotion. In haiku, it all arrives within a few syllables. The economy of words teaches again and again that the key to stand-out writing is the choice of word—the quality of word, not the quantity.

Create your own haiku. Think of a one-word theme with which to title it: toothpaste, January, sweetheart, mud, popcorn, cattail.

Another Sidman poem is "What Your Ears Remind Me Of." The lyricism and imagery of these poems work through spare, specific word choice, as well as with rhetorical devices like alliteration, assonance, and asyndeton.

Camouflaged entrances to
a secret underground cavern.
The beard of a Sikh warrior,
the tail of his steed.
The lazy fold of the sleeve

of some royal garment.
Grandma's antique bone-china
gilt-edged Wedgewood teacups.
    A windy beach, scored with
    ripples of sand and sea.
A conch shell, curled and pink,
waiting for whispers.
    A lap I used to press
    against while weeping.

Picture books host stellar examples of spare, vibrant language. As with a poem, every word must count in this genre. Yet detail matters, too. It becomes a question of which detail to highlight and which to eliminate. Here's the opening page to *Down at Angel's,* by Sharon Chmielarz:

My friend Angel lives in his cellar. In the dim light from the window his tabletop shines like his supper—hard-boiled eggs and Spanish onions in a bowl.

"So, you want a bar of chocolate or a bite of garlic?" Angel always asks when my little sister and I visit him. Angel has one good eye, nut-brown and merry. The other eye is like a milky star and fools me. "Do you help your mama now that your papa's passed on?" asks Angel.

I always nod, and the candy is ours.

The reader, young or old, knows much about the two primary characters by the end of these few words: where Angel lives, what he eats, what kind of housekeeper he is, what he looks like, and what kind of spirit he has. The single facial feature is not detailed as simply as it might be (Angel has one good eye and one bad one). Instead, Chmielarz adds color and emotion; one eye makes the young visitor merry and the other one fools her. Angel's questions reveal his humor, his awareness, and his generosity. Why choose those details? Because they feed the rest of the story. The table, the cellar, the milky eye, the chocolate, the visits, and the generous spirit show up again and again. So much in so little space!

And So . . .

Should a writer use a few words or many to engage an audience? Depending on who that audience is, either will work as long as the goal is clarity and image. Spare writing offers profundity, pithiness, and proclivity. A few well-chosen words will illustrate an action or person in a vivid, fresh way. A longer, well-crafted description will make a scene come alive. Well-crafted description helps a reader understand a character, see a personality, and sense a setting. The key is the choice of detail. Ultimately, a subject is more credible—more reliable—when its essence is qualified, not quantified.

An Eighth of an Iceberg: Implication

Exposition offers considerable explanation. It's the stuff of magazine articles, newspapers, and textbooks. *Implication*, on the other hand, is the hallmark of good fiction. Giving the reader credit for grasping the full meaning of a scene or situation is both powerful and efficient. Powerful, in that the writing is usually stronger for what has been deleted. Efficient, in that implication deletes the need for explanation. Powerful, in that the reader is trusted to extrapolate meaning. Efficient, in that the language is sparer and more acute.

> **The dignity of movement of an iceberg is due to only one-eighth of it being above water.**
>
> *Death in the Afternoon,* Ernest Hemingway

Ernest Hemingway's iceberg theory is at the base of this chapter. That eighth that is revealed above the water suggests the depth of the rest of the story. The seven-eighths not revealed is background material, all the details that are embedded but merely implied.

Imply Character through Action, Dialogue, Monologue

New writers often create large tedious blocks of background information because they believe the reader needs to know everything the author knows. When it comes to background information,

Exercise: Maxim-ize Implication

One can infer a great deal from old maxims. But most of them are today's clichés:

▸ A penny saved is a penny earned.
▸ Don't count your chickens before they hatch.
▸ The early bird catches the worm.

Create your own pithy maxim, a line that implies more than it says. If desired, use a metaphor.

the adage "less is best" is true. Much can be implied by a few carefully disclosed details.

Bud, Not Buddy, a Newbery Medal winner, is a story set in 1936 about a 10-year-old orphan boy who sets out to find his unknown father. Before he can do that, he must escape an abusive foster family that has locked him in a dark woodshed. Bud climbs on top of the woodpile to be near the window, which is covered in newspapers. Here's a line that follows:

After a while that got to be pretty boring, so I scraped at the paper with my fingernails so I could see outside, but I like to keep my nails bit down real low and the paper didn't budge.

Buried in that line is the seemingly inconsequential information about his fingernails. But the author, Christopher Paul Curtis, is saying more: Bud is often worried and scared. Nail chewing, fear, and worry go hand-in-hand. At no point does the author explain this statement. It simply stands there as is—off-handed evidence of a boy with far too many problems for his age.

A short story from the anthology *Interpreter of Maladies* often allows implication to speak for an entire background. In this passage, Boori Ma, "the sweeper of the stairwell," is commenting about her past life in India:

A man came to pick our dates and guavas. Another clipped hibiscus. Yes, there I tasted life. Here I eat my dinner from a rice pot . . . Have I mentioned that I crossed the border with just two bracelets on my wrist? Yet there was a day when my feet touched nothing but marble.

"A Real Durwan," Jhumpa Lahiri

The author has chosen only a few details to describe her character's former life. Notice how the senses come into play: taste, smell, glitter to catch the eye, the feel of marble underfoot. Dates, guavas, and hibiscus give the illusion of riches, especially when compared to rice. But her last comment tells it all. In a nanosecond, the reader understands that she was once a woman of wealth and privilege, perhaps of royalty. She was waited on, not the reverse, as her current life illustrates. Like Curtis, Lahiri allows the reader to infer this woman's background through spare detail provided through narration, and a subtle emphasis on action—picking, clipping, tasting, eating, crossing the border, touching.

Exercise: And Yet

In dialogue, imply a character's wealthy past. The use of *yet* (an expletive) adds emphasis to the rest of the sentence. First comes a quote from Jhumpa Lahiri, then an example. Create your own, with an expletive and a detail that implies.

Lahiri: "Yet there was a day when my feet touched nothing but marble."
Example: "After all, a time came when I slept only on satin sheets."

A natural place for character development is in internal monologue. Implication gives the viewpoint character insight and the reader a more efficient read. David Haynes's *Right by My Side* is a coming-of-age story about Marshall, who grapples with his own problems but also with those of two friends. Marshall has this to say about Todd, his friend from "the wrong side of even the wrong side of the tracks":

Often his clothes look clean. There's something rather homemade about them. You get the idea if you pulled a string, he'd unravel.

The implication is created through double meaning or *zeugma*, a single verb that has both a figurative and literal meaning. Todd

Implication is the action taken by the writer or speaker, whereas **inference** is the action taken by the audience. An author implies or enfolds a point; a reader infers or guesses.

himself might unravel if pulled or pushed. Sure enough, the reader later learns that Todd's father is a mean cuss and his mother, a timid mouse, unable to protect her son.

David LaRochelle's story of a teen that does everything he can to avoid the dawning realization that he is gay, *Absolutely, Positively, Not . . .* (scheduled for publication by Arthur Levine Books) makes use of internal monologue to reveal the main character's turmoil. The first line speaks volumes about what's left unsaid:

> What I like about square dancing is that there's never any doubt about what to do. A promenade is always the same: men on the inside of the circle, women on the outside, escort your partner until you come back to your home position. When we're all in perfect step with each other, it's like I'm part of a well-made machine. It's beautiful.

Imply Setting, Time, & Mood through Action

Have you ever noticed how long paragraphs, some that may even extend to pages, are devoted to details of setting, stopping all action in the process? Some writers are more successful at this than others. Henry James is known for his lengthy paragraphs and detailed descriptions, and yet he moved his story forward at an exquisite pace. James's style is formal and not always to modern tastes, but his rhetorical skill is superb. Consider this opening paragraph from *The Golden Bowl*:

Exercise: Imply Emotion through Gesture

Introduce a person with a handicap. Through a gesture, imply this character's state of mind.

Example: "How are you, then?"

Joe spun his wheelchair away and faced the wall.

The Prince had always liked his London, when it had come to him; he was one of the Modern Romans who find by the Thames a more convincing image of the truth of the ancient state than any they have left by the Tiber. . . . If it was a question of an *Imperium*, he said to himself, and if one wished, as a Roman, to recover a little the sense of that, the place to do so was on London Bridge, or even, on a fine afternoon in May, at Hyde

Park Corner. It was not indeed to either of those places that these grounds of his predilection, after all sufficiently vague, had, at the moment we are concerned with him, guided his steps; he had strayed simply enough into Bond Street, where his imagination, working at comparatively short range, caused him now and then to stop before a window in which objects massive and lumpish, in silver and gold, in the forms to which precious stones contribute, or in leather, steel, brass, applied to a hundred uses and abuses, were as tumbled together as if, in the insolence of the Empire, they had been the loot of far-off victories.

Exercise: Embed Setting into Action

Try your hand at embedding setting into action. An example in the text has Jhumpa Lahiri speaking of how news of a marriage "spread between our window bars, across our clotheslines, and over the pigeon droppings that plastered the parapets of our rooftops."

Imply your own home setting by providing three details while spreading news:

News spread between . . .

Writing is stronger when the setting is presented within the story movement. The need to explain or describe scene can be relinquished if the details are woven into the action. The implication is action, but setting is also served. A line in another of Lahiri's stories from *Interpreter of Maladies*, "The Treatment of Bibi Haldar," demonstrates:

News [of marriage] spread between our window bars, across our clotheslines, and over the pigeon droppings that plastered the parapets of our rooftops.

The passage of time affords another opportunity to integrate information, make implicit. In her picture book about family alcoholism, *Daddy Doesn't Have to be a Giant Anymore,* Jane Resh Thomas illustrates the passage of time by activities:

Daddy was gone for a long time. We ate five Sunday dinners without him. Five Saturdays I watched cartoons while Mommy did the

Exercise: Implied Allusions

Every year, new vocabulary drifts into our language from many venues: inventions, research, TV, films, travel, sports. Football, alone, has spawned dozens of words: *punt, tackle, huddle, game plan* arrived in the game's early years. Words like *jock, scramble, sudden death* were added in the last 40 years. Corporate America enjoyed football images enough to adopt some of them into their world: *game plan, team players, take the ball and run with it, Monday morning quarterback.* Corporations adopted this vocabulary because football was of interest to businessmen. The implication behind these idioms was enough for employees to catch on quickly; further explanation wasn't necessary. As more women climb the corporate ladder, future implications will undoubtedly come from a different direction.

▸ Think about the worlds of television or film. Which words have come into our language through this media? In reference to the analogy of football to the corporate world, how have allusions to the entertainment world been mainstreamed into your world? Or into other worlds? Can you think of mainstream expressions (e.g., *shock jock, couch potato, special effects*)?

▸ How about history? At the turn of the century, the Wright brothers' invention of a flying machine soon necessitated more words: *airplane, pilot, cockpit, takeoff, tailspin*. Think of more. What implications of these words are used today, in other venues, on other topics?

crossword puzzle. For old times' sake, she said, because Daddy wasn't there to do it.

Instead of writing "Daddy was gone five weeks," Thomas moves through a young child's mind, a mind that doesn't think in weeks but in generalities *(a long time)* and in specific family traditions *(Sunday dinner, crossword puzzles).* The word choice also allows young readers to infer that the little girl misses her father, as does her mother, who speaks of *old times' sake.*

A Newbery Honor book, Marion Dane Bauer's *On My Honor* is

the story of a boy who learns how to deal with the accidental death of his best friend. In Bauer's hands, Joel's tentativeness and conflicting feelings arrive through one tiny, common movement. He is asked about his friend's whereabouts:

> "Where is he then?"
> Joel gave a small shrug.

A detail, an action, an implication, Joel's gesture forces the reader and the other characters in the scene to infer that the protagonist either doesn't know his friend's whereabouts or doesn't have the words to express what has happened, and feels conflicted.

Exercise: Implication through Expression

The Westward expansion incited the gold rush and vocabulary that lives with us still. Build an implication around the expression *goldbrick* (something or someone that appears to have great value, but is worthless) or *golddigger* (a person who uses charm to extract gifts). Remember not to explain the meaning of the word.

Example: "Those stocks are a pile of goldbricks!"

Metaphors Imply

As the examples illustrate, implication can be as long as a paragraph or as short as a single comparison. In the following three examples, despite brevity, the reader immediately understands the author's meaning:

> • I'm afraid of the clerks, a cloud of perfume around them like a fortress. "Jane," Theresa Williams, *The Sun,* April 2004
> • [Books] are my failure made concrete. *Ibid*
> • How odd that I still distance myself from my feelings, as if sadness itself were my enemy, a smooth-talking terrorist with one foot in the door. "Sy Safransky's Notebook," Sy Safransky, *The Sun,* April 2004

Each line is weighty in meaning and each word judiciously selected for that purpose. No lengthy exposition is needed because an apt metaphor, simile, or personification, with its implication embedded, has been applied.

Bauer offers this line near the end of a scene in *On My Honor* in which Joel has confessed to his father his culpability in his friend's death: "The racking sobs flowed out of him like water." Flowing water is the perfect simile because Joel's friend has drowned. The implication is that Joel has also been drowning—in guilt, in loss, in remorse, in anger. This is no small descriptive detail about Joel.

Herman Melville had no problem writing long, involved sentences, as below in *Moby Dick,* but in their midst are subtle points that could easily have been expounded upon but are not:

> Whenever I find myself growing grim about the mouth; whenever it is a damp, drizzly November in my soul . . .

A *drizzly November in my soul* is a succinct metaphor to describe the most overcast and ominous of calendar months. Winter is coming, the season of death implied, not spelled out through exposition.

Implication through a Single Word

At times, a paragraph of information can be replaced by a single apt word or phrase. An allusion, analogy, or contemporary idiom skillfully used can imply much more than is said.

In 49 B.C., the Rubicon was a small river that formed the boundary between Gaul and Italy. Julius Caesar crossed the Rubicon that year with his army and the action signified a declaration of war with his former ally, the general Pompey. Today, this historic fact has become a phrase that implies a point of no return:

> The age-old Labour debate between universal and means-tested social benefits is being decisively resolved in favour of means-testing. Tony Blair's government has indeed crossed the Rubicon.
>
> "The Universal Means Test,"
> *The Economist,* March 6, 1999

The implication, of course, is that Tony Blair acted in a way that means no going back. The decision has been reached, he has declared war, and the outcome is yet to be determined.

A *silver bullet* means the quick solution to a thorny problem. A sentence that employs such a phrase deletes the need for lengthy explanation, as shown in this line from an article about the advent of the Internet.

172

Try fixing programming errors, known as bugs, and you often introduce new ones. So far he, [Stuart Feldman] laments, nobody has found a silver bullet to kill the beast of complexity.

"Survey: The Beast of Complexity," *The Economist,* April 2001

Bugs is a simple vocabulary word and part of contemporary idiom. *Silver bullet,"* on the other hand, carries its own meaning, its own implication. The phrase came from the belief that werewolves could be killed with a silver bullet, so it had a kind of magical power. The phrase can stand alone, without such an explanation. In this case, the analogy of computer viruses and computer programmers to the world of frightening creatures works beautifully.

Implication Can Build Subtle Humor

Humor is a commodity longed for by many editors—subtle humor particularly, for it fits into any genre.

Haynes's novel, *Right by My Side,* is not a funny book, but it has comedic moments scattered throughout the story. Lucille, Marshall's aunt, comes to live with him and his dad for a time. Marshall is anxious about this no-nonsense woman's decision to stay, and his ironic humor comes through in this initial description of her. The last line—with its zeugma or double meaning—implies that if his aunt had a husband, she would not have the time to take him to task:

Lucille is a widow woman, or that's what Sam calls her. In fact she has put three husbands in the ground in her fifty years and, also according to Big Sam, is not without a gentleman friend for too long, even these days. She must be between engagements at present.

"It Counts as Seeing," a short story by David Means, shows the development of the narrator's character when he attempts to help a blind man down a flight of stairs. When the man falls, the narrator tries to explain:

The blind man's face gave the impression that it might be cleaned up with a good scrubbing: just a nail brush and a bar of Lava soap. My desire was only to clean up this man, to move him toward someplace where he might be able to bathe, to rub his back with a brush, to scrub beneath his nails, to shave, to buff his feet with a pumice stone, to shampoo his scalp, to dab a cloth under the folds of his ears, to sprinkle aftershave across his face, to trim his nose hairs, to pluck his brows, to clip his nails, to exfoliate his skin, to brush his shiny hair . . .

"It Counts as Seeing," David Means, *Harper's*, September 2000

The narrator's obsessive-compulsive tendencies are implied. The list of what he would do for the blind man is excessive. The effect of multiplicity is achieved through *amplification* and *asyndeton*, which are set in a parallel construction of infinitives (*to* plus a verb). The long list and the vivid verbs begin to make a reader smile. Although the narrator leads the reader to believe that the man accidentally falls, by the end of the passage the reader infers that the narrator's compulsivity may have been the blind man's undoing.

LaRochelle's character in *Absolutely, Positively, Not . . .* is learning to drive. Through well-chosen verbs, a modifier, and specific detail, the passage builds in subtle humor. Can't you feel the main character's embarrassment, his exasperation, his frustration? Yet none of these emotions are explained; they're implied through the humor.

I slowly eased up on the gas pedal until my mother's death grip loosened. When she finally let go we were creeping along at 28 mph in a 40 mph zone.

"That's better," she said. "Don't you feel safer? Don't you feel as if you have more control of the car?"

I felt like I was going to be late for school.

We crawled past the city park and . . .

The humorist strives to elicit guffaws from his readership. And yet, a successful humorist often pokes fun at himself in the process, thus making him an Everyman. Here's a paragraph about humorist Dave Barry's hometown. Notice the innuendos. An outsider may miss some of the implications, but certainly not all, and that's why Barry has included more than one, building to a climax with the Castro clincher.

Miami loves to party. We party to celebrate when something good happens, such as winning the World Series, which we do, like clockwork, every six years. When something bad happens, we party to cheer ourselves up. When nothing is happening, we party because we are bored. If Fidel ever dies, Miami will not regain consciousness for decades.

Dave Barry, *Miami Herald,* December 6, 2003

One-liners are best for what they don't say. Succinct, apt words in a pithy sentence or two often become a *sententia,* a very quotable quote. Implication builds the humor. *Reader's Digest* magazine makes a point of collecting them; here are a few collected there and their original sources:

▸ The trick in eating crow is to pretend it tastes good. William Safire, *New York Times*
▸ One good thing about living in America is that there is no neurosis too insignificant to merit its own paperback. Deborah Solomon, *New York Times*
▸ Trying to run a Presidential campaign is a little like driving a freight train while you're still building the tracks. Steve Forbes, *A New Birth of Freedom*
▸ If you don't decide what your priorities are, someone else will. Harvey MacKay, in *SAM's Club Source*

And So . . .

Exposition is often a necessity with nonfiction, but successful fiction replaces exposition with implication. Some types of nonfiction benefit from implication, too. Background information, personality, moods, setting, humor can all be subtly woven into story through action, metaphor, analogy, allusion, and familiar expressions. Sometimes writers do this naturally, without awareness, but often—as usual— implication is a carefully crafted part of writing that requires intention and practice. Apply the iceberg theory. Is only a portion of your story revealed? Or is every facet of the entire unwieldy mass visible above water? If so, watch out. The mass will sink and the reader will be asea.

A Matter of Style

The word that encompasses the whole subject of word choice is *style*. Novelist Kurt Vonnegut answered the question about why one must write with style: "Do so, if for no other reason, out of respect for your readers." But what is style?

Writers and readers tend to throw around words like *genre, style, form, tone, and voice,* but their meaning is often unclear. For the sake of clarity, let's define them. Style is not *genre*, which is a broad term referring to types of literature, like historical romance or biography or science. Style is not *form*, which rather delineates a genre: Poetry can be written in the form of a sonnet or a haiku; an editorial may take the form of a full-circle essay or a theme-driven defense; a novel can be young adult, mystery, contemporary, pulp fiction. Style does comprise *voice* and *tone*, which are each author's individual stamp. Identifying style is like recognizing that this painting is a Vincent Van Gogh and that one a Rembrandt van Rijn, that this play sounds like Anton Chekhov and that one, Arthur Miller.

A fine suit of clothing has style. The cut, shape, length, fabric, buttons, zippers, and bows enhance the garment, giving it style. Fashion designer Yohji Yamamoto was written up in the fashion review section of the *New York Times* ("Wearing America on Their Sleeves," by Cathy Horyn, July 1, 2003) as someone who juxtaposes "ethnic skirts with street-inspired denim layered with flapping plaid skirts."Another designer, Paul Smith "showed stripes ultra wide and in classic seersucker jazzed up with poppy prints." These designers created distinct styles.

Most published writing has a certain style, though we've all read bland work that seems to have no style at all. The choice of words, the length and makeup of sentences and paragraphs, their shape and rhythm and ornamentation, enhances writing, giving it style. When style is lacking, the writing is dull. It may be choppy or monotonous, redundant, feeble or confusing. When style is present, the writing is lively or smooth, depending on its substance and purpose. It is well-paced, fluid, fresh, with a voice that can range from meditative to furious.

Preceding chapters have discussed lively writing styles and specific figurative devices a writer can employ to create original style (metaphor, alliteration, anaphora, irony). This chapter touches on originality and lively writing, but zeroes in on fluidity, pacing, rhythm—the overall tone of a work. It's this unique flavoring, beyond single lines, that gives the whole of writing personal authenticity.

The small, classic primer, *The Elements of Style*, by William Strunk Jr. and E. B. White, offers specific interpretations on this important piece of the writing craft called style.

Combine Ideas in a Long, Smooth Sentence

Even Ernest Hemingway, famous for his spare style, believed that easy writing makes hard reading. He was referring to the kind of language that dribbles out of our mouths every day without much thought or constraint, and is difficult to follow in print. Unless the writing demands such a colloquial style for a particular effect, consecutive short sentences sound choppy and uninteresting. A dull, bumpy construction is hardly fresh:

The house was small and square. Green grass surrounded it. A picket fence circles the grass.

How does a writer shape a passage without the same old dull and lazy structure of subject-verb, subject-verb, subject-verb-object, subject-verb-object? Exchange the dull, bumpy sentences for a longer, more fluid sentence, a sentence that contains several ideas. Use a variety of dependent and independent clauses, phrases, and punctuation. Show the relationship between ideas, giving a passage fluidity and contrast.

In the capable hands of Natalie Babbitt, the same material in the example above is woven instead into a single sentence with originality and style:

> On the left stood the first house, a square and solid cottage with a touch-me-not appearance, surrounded by grass cut painfully to the quick and enclosed by a capable iron fence some four-feet high which clearly said, "Move on—we don't want you here."

Exercise: Imitate Effectively

Select effective or well-crafted sentences you find in your reading. Study them: Does each sentence flow smoothly, incorporate effective descriptive words, use fresh figures of speech and rhetorical devices like alliteration and metaphor? Does it have interesting punctuation and a variety of clauses and phrases?

Imitate effective sentences.

Babbitt has conveyed emotion, a sense of reclusiveness, strength, and intrigue. The style in this sentence comes off through the use of meaningful modifiers—*touch-me-not, painfully, capable*—and a complex sentence structure—an introductory prepositional phrase, a triple verb structure, several modifying phrases, two dependent clauses, and one independent clause that breaks the statement of facts with an imperative command. Note, too, three personifications: the touch-me-not cottage, grass cut painfully, and the capable iron fence that speaks.

Speaking of a single complex sentence, read aloud this fluid, lyrical line by Dylan Thomas, from "Notes on the Art of Poetry":

> I could never have dreamt that there were such goings-on
> in the world between the covers of books,
> such sandstorms and ice blasts of words,
> such staggering peace, such enormous laughter,
> such and so many blinding bright lights,
> splashing all over the pages

Exercise: Clear up Confusing References

Besides clichés and redundancies, mis-referenced pronouns—those that don't agree with their subjects or those whose reference is questionable—is a common problem for beginning writers. *It* and *this* are often the culprits. Style breaks down when confusion reigns, as in this example:

A percentage of the population suffers from Alzheimer's. The cause of it is unknown. This reveals a mysterious shutting down of short-term memory, then long-term memory, and finally the memory of basic skills.

What do *it* and *this* refer to in the passage? *It* could refer to *percentage*, the subject of the preceding sentence. *This* doesn't appear to refer to anything at all. What nouns could be added or exchanged?

in a million bits and pieces
all of which were words, words, words,
and each of which were alive forever
in its own delight and glory and oddity and light.

Could the idea of books be more moving, more entertaining, more beautifully crafted than in this passage? That's style.

Short Effective Sentences Add Drama & Emphasis

Short, well-placed sentences can hold complex ideas, heighten tension, or highlight a point. In *The Tale of Despereaux*, a story about a mouse who saves a princess from the dungeon, Kate DiCamillo makes use of complex and simple sentences. The two-word sentence is even more emphatic when placed in its own solitary paragraph. The tension is heightened. Drama and effective pacing are present.

Despereaux pushed the spool of thread forward again, into the kitchen, where he saw, too late, that there was a light burning.
He froze.

Exercise: Undangle the Dangling Modifiers

A source of confusion that weakens writing and erases style is misrelated modifiers. You can add artistic complexity to your writing without adding unwanted complexity. Clarify the following embarrassments:

▸ Filled with chocolate and coconut, the baker frosted the cake. (It's not the baker who's filled with chocolate and coconut, is it?)
▸ The cloud had changed color since leaving home. (Who left home?)
▸ After trimming the crust, the bread can be cubed. (Can bread trim its own crust?)
▸ Looking through his field glasses, the bird flew away. (The bird owns field glasses?)
▸ Only nine miles in circumference, a person can walk around the lake in a day. (How big is that person!?)

The shortest sentence in the New Testament is "Jesus wept." DiCamillo echoes this passage and uses the repetition of a key word to impart Despereaux's despair in this scene, which follows his rescue from the dungeon and subsequent axing of his tail. The paragraph has a good variety of sentence structures and lengths, allowing for smooth, fluid reading. Then comes the four-word sentence and paragraph. The narrator turns directly to the reader in an *apostrophe,* a powerful device when used in this way, and then refers to Despereaux not by name, but as *the mouse,* almost as an Everymouse. The simplicity of the action—*he wept*—then tells all with force and subtlety both.

> So Despereaux wept with joy and with pain and with gratitude. He wept with exhaustion and despair and hope. He wept with all the emotions a young, small mouse who has been sent to his death and then been delivered from it in time to save his beloved can feel.
> Reader, the mouse wept.

Even fragments can be effective points of emphasis. As we've seen, in this book DiCamillo interjects the intermittent voice of the

Exercise: Create a Unique Image

Here's a sentence worthy of imitation by novelist Tom Wolfe: He has a thin face with sharp features and a couple of eyes burning with truth oil.

Example: She has a willowy body with a long back and a couple of legs tensing with ballet-bar dedication.

narrator, who soothes the heart of a young reader while telling a terrible tale. Here's another example of that technique, that style:

> Honestly, reader, what do you think the chances are of such a small mouse succeeding in his quest [to save a princess]?
> Zip. Zero. Nada.
> Goose Eggs.

These fragments—complete in their own paragraphs—add humor, punch, and pacing. The last two lines carry a fresh, interesting tone. That's style.

Sentence Variety Heightens Pacing and Style

Paragraphs often need as much help as single sentences. Bring emphasis, interest, and balance to a paragraph by using a variety of sentence types and structures. Change sentence lengths. Vary the arrangement of your material, the syntax. The right grouping of words and phrasings creates fluidity and liveliness, and a mix of sentences in a paragraph creates movement and pacing. Sentence variety helps a scene flow smoothly with a pacing that is as beautiful as a piece of music.

"In the Jungle," an essay from *Teaching a Stone to Talk,* by Annie Dillard, details the setting along the Napo River in the jungle at the headwaters of the Amazon. In this paragraph, note the complexity of the third sentence; each clause, phrase, and lone modifier adds more image, clarity, and depth. Note the personification of the stars and the song. Through anaphora, amplification, and climax, the final short lines offer a summation that drives home the point in an interesting, amplifying way.

Each breath of night smelled sweet, more moistened and sweet than any kitchen, or garden, or cradle. Each star in Orion seemed to tremble and stir with my breath. All at once, in the thatch house across the clearing behind us, one of the village's Jesuit priests began playing an alto recorder, playing a wordless song, lyrical, in a minor key, that twined over the village clearing, that caught in the big trees' canopies, muted our talk on the bank side, and wandered over the river, dissolving downstream.

This will do, I thought. This will do, for a weekend, or a season, or a home.

The pacing of this passage flows as smoothly as the river along which this scene is set. Note the differences in sentence complexity and length:

▸ Each breath of night smelled sweet, more moistened and sweet than any kitchen, or garden, or cradle. Declarative, complex, 17 words.
▸ Each star in Orion seemed to tremble and stir with my breath. Declarative, simple, 12 words.
▸ All at once, in the thatch house across the clearing behind us, one of the village's Jesuit priests began playing an alto recorder, playing a wordless song, lyrical, in a minor key, that twined over the village clearing, that caught in the big trees' canopies, muted our talk on the bank side, and wandered over the river, dissolving downstream. Declarative, complex with multiple dependent adverbial clauses, 60 words.
▸ This will do, I thought. Declarative, compound, 5 words.
▸ This will do, for a weekend, or a season, or a home. Declarative, 12 words.

Exercise: Change Sentence Lengths & Types

Take your time in deciding how to change this wordy sentence. Delete words, create several sentences, add complexity, and your own style. Your goal is to heighten the drama:

Unsteadily, she searched for the pistol in her saddlebag, eased her horse to a halt, then proceeded to aim and fire at the cougar.

Example: Her eyes glued to the cougar's tawny form, she reined in her horse. The pistol felt weighty, deadly, in her hand. Lifting her shaking hand, she aimed. Her finger massaged the trigger. She fired.

A completely different style and voice—not lyrical and not metaphorical or rich in description—is this one from a short story in the collection entitled *Women on the Case.* Here, the spare detail establishes a historical perspective. The paragraph brims with rhetorical devices and emotion. The variety of sentence types and lengths make for a paragraph equally interesting, if different from the paragraph above. Each does what it needs to do and does it well.

> Please, I beg you! Don't ask me to recount the story of that cruel night in 1892! As Shakespeare says, "On horror's head horrors accumulate." I have nightmares to this day! Besides, I was not the tragedy's heroine. I'm bound to admit that I was merely the comic relief. Or worse. But if you insist—
>
> "Parties Unknown by the Jury; or, The Valour of My Tongue,"
>
> P. M. Carlson

Here's a structural analysis of the sentences: Exclamatory, simple, 4 words. Imperative, simple, 13 words. Declarative, complex, with quote, 8 words. Declarative, simple, 6 words. Declarative, simple, 7 words. Declarative, compound, 11 words. Fragment, 2 words. Fragment, conditional, 4 words.

Sentence types are:

- declarative (statement)
- interrogative (question)
- imperative (command)
- exclamatory (strong emotion)

Sentence structures are:

- conditional (if. . . then),
- compound (2 independent clauses),
- complex (a combination of independent and dependent clauses).
- compound-complex (2 or more independent clauses and at least one dependent clause)

Voice and Style

Style often arrives in the form of tone or voice. The previous excerpt, for example, has a dramatic and frantic, but educated voice. Sportswriters sometimes write with a hyperactive and hyperbolic tone. Nonfiction books and articles are written with the friendly, but self-assured voice of the expert. Humor writing often carries an ironic tone, whereas inspirational writing carries a tone of reassurance.

A reader isn't always conscious of the viewpoint from which a story is told, but the voice is a different matter. The more authentic the voice—with its own tone, modus operandi, vocabulary, speech patterns—the more memorable the writing—whether fiction or nonfiction. Mark Twain's "The Celebrated Jumping Frog of Calaveras County" is written in the dialectical cadence of the story's narrator:

> Well, thish-yer Smiley had rat-tarriers, and chicken cocks, and tom-cats and all them kind of things, till you couldn't rest, and you couldn't fetch nothing for him to be on but he'd match you.

Despite the homespun tone, the sentence is compound in structure, with three independent clauses. The interesting structure, the effective choice of words, and the tone all translate as style.

Exercise: Sew Your Own Style

Write a five-sentence description of your bedroom or your home of origin. Incorporate your feelings about the place. Include a variety of sentence types, lengths and structural patterns.

Doublecheck your verbs and nouns: Are they vivid, active, strong, specific? Keep modifiers to a minimum, but make those few stand-outs.

A voice can portray so much about its owner. Think about your own voice, with its tone, speech patterns, cadence, vocabulary, and your modus operandi. Your voice may come across as authoritative, old-fashioned, intellectual, distant, funny, spunky, sarcastic, clipped, thoughtful, prosy, lyrical, angry, fearful, shy, fast-paced, quirky, impatient. Which voice will you adopt for your next essay? Novel? Speech? Op-ed? Letter? Poem?

Exercise: Identify a Tone, a Voice

Write several objective, dispassionate lines about a bog or a pasture being turned into a parking lot or a highway. Rewrite those sentences, instilling anger or fury. Write it yet again, this time with a tone of gentle persuasion.

A *Newsweek* commentary by Anna Quindlen included the following sentence about the reality of motherhood. The tone of the piece is harried and chaotic. The passage will take several readings to understand, but that's the point. The scene is chaotic; there is no order.

But there's another part of my mind, the part that remembers the end of a day in which the milk spilled phone rang one cried another hit a fever rose the medicine gone the car sputtered another cried the cable out *Sesame Street* gone all cried stomach upset full diaper no more diapers Mommy I want water Mommy my throat hurt Mommy I don't feel good.

"Playing God on No Sleep,"
Anna Quindlen,
Newsweek, July 2, 2001

Thank goodness the entire column is not written in this particular style or the reader wouldn't endure it. But despite its appearance, Quindlen's sentence is a controlled, intentional, compelling and ultimately clarifying collection of words. It is style.

"Gone" is the mesmerizing account of the kidnapping of three Americans in the Ecuadorian jungle in 2000. Tom Junod wrote the piece for *Esquire* with a furious, sardonic voice. Here's the opening:

The first American they met when they came out of the jungle? That's easy. It was a shrink. Of course it was. They spent 141 days with guns stuck up their asses. They were in dire and sweltering and abject captivity. They ate practically nothing but cat food and rice unless the occasional rat or snake happened by. They all lost significant percentages of their own precious mass, starting with body fat and eating into muscle. They all grew these huge, luxuriant beards. They had pieces of their flesh rotting away. They itched to the point of insanity. They all stunk to high heaven . . .

Exercise: Try on Someone Else's Style

Novelist Sheila O'Connor uses the first-person and present tense viewpoint to create a clipped, measured tone for the adolescent main character in *Where No Gods Came*. Realistic details, multiple verbal clauses, and word omissions (ellipsis) are important to this author's unique style. Finish the next paragraph, mimicking O'Connor's style:

> At home, Lenore sleeps. When I slip inside her dark bedroom, she opens her eyes, lazily, then returns to her dreams. "Wake me for supper," she murmurs. "I'm glad to see you're home." I empty her overflowing ashtray, crumple the empty packs of Salems, pick up her half-eaten serving of cottage cheese and canned peaches, dried into a heap on the china plate. Then I carry it all to the kitchen to wash up the few dishes left from the morning: my cereal bowl with the crust of milk, my crystal goblet of orange juice, Lenore's coffee cup. I wash them in scalding water, leave them to air dry in the wire rack.
>
> In my bedroom, I . . .

Besides the ferocity of the tone, the author wields his sentences well: Types and lengths and complexities vary, word choices are graphic, and a repetitious parallelism pointedly contrasts the three men (*they*) and the shrink. The short sentences and syntactical repetition create a kind of listing that amplifies the men's primary needs for nutrition, clean water, and medical attention, versus a psychiatric exam. This short-sentence format helps create tone, by adding tension and heightening drama. All these components spell style.

Op-ed columns, the venue for passionate opinion-makers, are fertile ground for language devices. The result is added emphasis, interesting tone and pacing, an editorialist voice that is compelling:

> Hey, it happens. I understand your sentiment. I know its impetus. It all follows the same rule: If all you have is a hammer, everything looks like a nail. If all you have is a narrow media-saturated tragedy-thick anger-ravaged abuse-drenched worldview, everything looks like

a crime against the spirit and everything is something meant to induce peril and everything is something that will completely piss you off, somehow.

"Please Write More About Rape," by Mark Morford,
San Francisco Gate, May 14, 2004

The unique maxim, or sententia (*If all you have is a hammer, everything looks like a nail*) makes a bold, pithy point that underscores the sentences that follow. *Each and everything* (anaphora and polysyndeton) emphasizes the idea of a longer list of vitriol that the author finally punctuates with *piss you off*. He has used anaphora to amplify the sententia, too, but it's the second *if all you have* that is so powerful with its furious list of adjectives, each of which drives home the hammer metaphor.

The tone of a piece of writing should be determined before writing. Ask:

- Who is the audience?
- Am I writing to sway, entertain, educate, reassure, inspire?

Choose Your Own Words, Be Original

Before ending this chapter on style, let's take a quick look at some classic boulders that stop style in its tracks. As mentioned in earlier chapters, clichés and common phrasing are used so often in speaking and writing that they no longer offer anything new or surprising. Neither the reader nor the writer is stretched with descriptions like *a face as red as a beet, food for thought, in the thick of the night, flat as a pancake*. The reader skims over the words. Too many skimmed sentences and the audience will be missing, too. Delete or replace clichés and old expressions with synonyms and fresher images and writing is stronger: *a crimson face, a compelling commentary, at the night's heart, flat as a French crepe*.

In her picture book, *One Dog Canoe,* author Mary Casanova could simply have written "I paddled down the river." Instead, she wrote "I dipped my paddle into ribbons of blue." The use of a strong verb and a fresh description of the lake give this passage movement and rhythm; the reader feels the water and wants more.

Casanova then made use of repetition, something children look for, especially when it appears at key points throughout the story. *One Dog Canoe* repeats the question "Can I come, too?" seven times, along with the response, "It's a one-dog canoe." Carefully placed, the refrain amplifies the tension and unifies the story form. The lyrical repetition provides pacing and rhythm, all integral to the book's style.

It's easy to describe August as hot, dry, and still. Babbitt chose a denser, but oh-so-much-more interesting, description in *Tuck Everlasting:*

> The first week of August hangs at the very top of summer, the top of the live-long year, like the highest seat of a Ferris Wheel when it pauses in its turning. It is curiously silent, too, with blank white dawns and glaring noons, and sunsets smeared with too much color. Often at night there is lightning, but it quivers all alone.

The writing demonstrates style with its use of metaphors, alliterations, vivid verbs, lively modifiers, and complex sentence structure. The writing is original. The word choice stretches the reader's mind and no doubt stretched the author's. That's Babbitt's style.

Avoid Redundancy

Like clichés, redundancies often pepper early drafts. Only through revision or oral reading does a beginning writer, and even a seasoned writer, catch the overused words. Style is lacking when redundancy rules.

Redundancies appear in many forms. Sometimes they are found in dull, unobtrusive pronouns and verbs, as in this piece from a regional magazine:

> He had a wide nose and a large head. He had a thick chest and stick legs. He was a big kid.

The same subject-verb construction and dull verbs spell redundancy of sentence structure and common words—a lack of style. Even today's primers wouldn't inflict this kind of writing on its young readers.

Overuse of prepositions creates another kind of redundancy.

Note the number in this passage taken from a text manual:

> The solution to the problems of journalism is the recovery of a sense of authority, not necessarily a recovery of superiority to its readers, but a recovery of equality to its readers who make up the journalists' peer group.

How much smoother and more interesting the style becomes when most of the prepositions—*to, of*—and redundant words are dropped while weaving more complexity into the sentence structure:

> Journalists need to recover a sense of authority; they need a sense—not of superiority—but of equality to their peer group.

But don't confuse redundancy with intentional repetition, which can be an effective style of writing, especially for purposes of rhythm, emphasis, pacing, and unity. Martin Luther King, Jr., said in Montgomery, Alabama:

> The urgency of the hour calls for leaders of wise judgment and sound integrity—leaders not in love with money, but in love with justice; leaders not in love with publicity, but in love with humanity; leaders who can subject their particular egos to the greatness of the cause.
>
> "Facing the Challenge of a New Age," 1956 speech

Opening with a strong word such as *urgency*, the use of anaphora, and parallel construction all make this passage stand out. King used repetition to emphasize and amplify; the passage has movement and rhythm. That was his style.

Repetition of a key word, for the purpose of sarcasm, irony, or parody, is an effective style technique. Here's a passage from the first chapter of *Hard Times*, by Charles Dickens, in which the narrator pounds home a point about getting back to a basic education. The capitalization of the repeated key word further emphasizes. In the last line, note Dickens's use of metaphor and the double meaning behind the final verb, *root*, a zeugma.

> Now, what I want is Facts. Teach these boys and girls nothing but

Facts. Facts alone are wanted in life. Plant nothing else, and root out everything else.

The Perfect Nest, by Catherine Friend, is a picture book that not only makes great use of repetition in the form of three different fowls, each with its own language, but also in its rhythm and pacing. The title of the book and the point of the story is often repeated, as you'll soon see. But the three kinds of fowl, adult or baby, and their special-language expressions reappear time and again, too. The entertaining repetition is as fun as the story's perfect plot:

> Soon enough a chicken came along. "Caramba!" she cried. "A perfect nest." She hopped up and laid a small egg.
> Then a duck waddled by. "Sacre bleu," she cried. "Zee perfect nest." She pushed the chicken out, hopped up, and laid a medium egg.
> Then a goose lumbered up. "Great balls of fire," she cried. "A perfect nest." She pushed the duck out, hopped up, and laid a large egg.

Review picture books for their rhythm, pacing, repetition, and spare writing style. The text of a children's picture book is never redundant; every word is chosen with attention and intention. Successful picture books—as with any genre—have their own style, their own voice. Not unlike song lyrics, if the pacing and rhythm are well crafted, the reader will want to read the words aloud again and again.

And So . . .

Style means interesting writing, and that means making use of:

- metaphors and figures of speech for rhythm, emphasis, interest
- vivid fresh word choices and phrasing for originality
- a variety of sentence types and sentence lengths for fluidity
- a tone or voice that conveys your mission to a specific audience

To avoid dull writing that lacks style, stay away from:

- clichés and tired phrasing
- redundancies
- confusing pronouns
- the same consecutive syntax

Paying attention to pacing, tone or voice, fluidity and flexibility, rhythm and emphasis—matters of style—will not only elevate your writing, but will expand your brain cells. But "if for no other reason, do so, out of respect for your readers."

Hooking the Audience

Chapter 15

Attention Grabbers: Titles & Headlines

So many titles, so little space. Walk down any bookstore or library aisle and note the titles that fly out at you: *Disobedience, The Other Mozart, The Left Hand of Darkness, Trouble After School, Strong to the Hoop, Maniac Magee, Holes, Angels and Demons, The Tears of the Giraffe, Was It Beautiful?, The Master Butchers Singing Club, I Fatty, Big Mama Makes the World, What a Woman Must Do, Ten Serious Illnesses Doctors Often Miss, Who Moved My Cheese?, Eureka!, Eat the Rich, How to Win Friends and Influence People, Behind the Mask.* Because of the word choice, each title tugs at a reader's attention. Whether these titles and the thousands of others worthy of discussion are good or poor choices for a buyer's library is another story. That a title can hook a reader into reading further is the subject of this chapter.

What Makes a Title Stand out in the Crowd?

Hooking a reader into a story or article via a well-chosen title is not much different than businesses using billboards to lure a client to the doors of True Value Hardware or Best Buy. Particular combinations of words attract customers. An impactful title may, in fact, not even consist of words. In 1948, George Orwell wrote *1984*. His *Animal Farm* had been successful two years earlier and may have helped sell the book, but Orwell's dystopian novel had a title that became part of the popular culture. In the 1950s, 60s, and 70s,

Successful titles work in three ways:

> ▸ easy recall
> ▸ provocative
> ▸ provide a glimpse of book's contents

Nonfiction books often carry a primary title and a subtitle. One title attracts attention and the other zeros in on the subject matter.

1984 was memorable for three reasons: It was easy to recall and so could easily generate word-of-mouth sales. It was provocative, in bringing to mind a single, specific future year; the normal reaction is to react to the foreignness of the future. And, it suggested an answer to the wondering, a glimpse of a story within. These three ingredients give a title an edge.

Nathaniel Hawthorne's *The Scarlet Letter* sold 4,000 copies in just 10 days, in part, because of the title. A scarlet letter had a shaming, undermining meaning in 1850, although less than it did in the book's time period a century earlier. The title provoked, perhaps titillated, its readers into buying the book. Both *1984* and *The Scarlet Letter* became classics not because of their titles, but because of their contents. Yet it is readers who make books endure and titles are readers' enticements.

Another classic, *Charlotte's Web,* has been a beloved children's book for half a century. In 1952, spiders were not named nor beloved nor wise. Instead, they were scary, hairy, and classified. For E. B. White to give a spider—of all creatures—a beautiful name like Charlotte was a bold move. *Spider* is not a part of the title; the author went a step beyond, allowing the reader to infer Charlotte's identity. *Web* has its own draw; it captures insects just as this title captures readers.

A contemporary work on its way to becoming a classic, *The Poisonwood Bible* by Barbara Kingsolver hooks the reader with its startling title—definitely an easy recall. Linking *poison* and *bible* has a tinge of heresy to it, making the title choice a somewhat courageous decision on Kingsolver's part. The title forces the book shelf passerby into wondering what the author has to say about religion, what the story might be, and so a reader reaches out to open a cover.

Key Words Suggest or Describe

A key word like *poison, princess, trouble, adventure, death, murder,* often attracts attention. Thousands of titles bear the words *power* or *secret.*

A key word either *denotes* (directly states) or *connotes* (implies) an idea. A title containing the word *mystery* carries the suggestion of a secret to uncover, as in *The Mystery of Marriage: Meditations on the Miracle* or "Mystery Money Men" or *Mystery of Witches Hollow.* The first two titles are especially memorable because they employ alliteration, which plays on a single consonant sound. Key words that imply are often more provocative or tantalizing than those that are more direct.

A title with *how* denotes a specific idea. It divulges contents: *Rules for Corporate Warriors: How to Fight and Survive Attack Group Shakedowns* and *How to Survive and Prosper As an Artist: Selling Yourself Without Selling Your Soul.* Both titles indicate—even promise—that the pages within will teach survival skills for a particular world. Words like *warrior, fight, survive, attack, prosper* all suggest winning a war, and the reader is excited. The second title is decorated with alliteration, parallelism, and double meaning (selling self, not soul), all of which add balance, beauty, easy recall, and motivation.

Secrets, whether in a modern seller like J. K. Rowling's *Harry Potter and the Chamber of Secrets* or Frances Hodgson Burnett's classic *The Secret Garden* or the Nancy Drew book, *The Secret of the Old Clock,* have enticed untold numbers of young readers. In the adult fiction world, James Thurber promises to divulge the unknown in *The Secret Life of Walter Mitty* and Sue Monk Kidd in *The Secret Life of Bees.* Nonfiction books promise the same: *The Secret Gardens of Paris, Secrets of the Baby Whisperers, 10 Insider Secrets.* Magazine readers love secrets, too, whether titillating or mysterious or character-building: "The Sex Secret Every Woman Must Try," "Real Boys Spill Guy Secrets," "The Secrets of Cartooning," "Secrets to Finding Strength, Peace and Limitless Potential," "Italian Comfort Secrets."

Power dominates the contemporary adult nonfiction market. Today's ego seems to need, demand, power of some ilk. From self-help to history, nonfiction authors offer studies on the effects of power. Eckhart Tolle's *The Power of Now* suggests the untapped potential in the present moment and the subtitle, *A Guide to Spiritual Enlightenment*, attracts the reader by *enlightenment*, which Tolle says conjures the idea of a superhuman accomplishment, a goal sought by many.

As the title suggests, *Hidden Power: Presidential Marriages That Shaped History* offers a glimpse into the effect, for good or naught, of presidents' strong wives on their husbands. From the opposite direction, *Abuse of Power: The New Nixon Tapes* denotes a study of one man with a power problem. A handful of other power titles are equally alluring: *The Power of Full Engagement, The Power Elite, The 48 Laws of Power*.

A word like *story* doesn't attract much attention today. Although it's an important word, it is a common one. But *legend*, which suggests extensive history and even universal Truth, has a more substantial yet alluring connotation. A *tale* elicits yet another kind of appeal. Whether coming from the tradition of *Grimms' Fairy Tales*, Geoffrey Chaucer's *Canterbury Tales*, or J. R. R. Tolkien's *Lost Tales*, tales evoke a sense of fantasy or tantalizing entanglement. Charles Dickens's *A Tale of Two Cities* captures the reader even before its famous first sentence because it's a tale, a story that promises to weave a spell on the reader. The same promise is suggested in contemporary titles such as Margaret Atwood's *The Handmaid's Tale*, Stephen King's *Everything's Eventual: 14 Dark Tales,* or Judy Blume's *Tales of a Fourth Grade Nothing*. Even a political news magazine like *Newsweek* uses the word for its news features in titles like "Tale of an American Taliban" (December 2001).

Adventure attracts readers in

Exercise: Secret Knowledge

Secrets are divulged in every genre, for every audience, on every subject. Magazines attract readers with the idea of power, in articles such as those titled "The Healing Power of Yoga" or "Coffee's Hidden Health Power" and, as with books, suggest an article's content while evoking a response from the reader.

▸ Incorporate *power* into a title for a magazine article on a topic that you find powerful.

▸ Divulge your own *secrets* in titles for articles.

Exercise: Recall

While titles are attractive because of their easy recall, their hint of the story to come, and their provocative word correlation that either suggests or nails the topic, the downfall of key words is the word's eventual overuse. The first title of the Magic School Bus series was *Ms. Chipps Class Trips.* Did the key word, *magic*, make all the difference in the excellent sales of this children's series? What key words pop out at you from your own bookshelves? Why?

Romance titles run the gamut, often with no telling key word (though certainly a cover illustration) to define its genre: from the classics *Pride and Prejudice, Jane Eyre, Gone With the Wind*—to today's *The Last Hellion, The Burning Point, Sunrise Song, Heart of the Sea, The Gamble, The Bridges of Madison County.* What would your romance be titled?

Create some easy recall titles with key words for these books:

- A story about a flying horse that takes its master to fantastical places
- A coffee table book on historical French castle gardens
- A children's story about a boy who loves basketball
- A historical western about a courageous woman named Buckskin Annie
- An article on how to teach your dog simple tricks
- The mystery of a library theft by sleuth Prescott Wiles
- A biography on singer Elvis Presley

principle and title. It has the pull of perils and grand feats, whether of former or contemporary times. Think of *The Merry Adventures of Robin Hood, The Adventures of Huckleberry Finn, Alice's Adventures in Wonderland.* From recent years come *The Amazing Adventures of Kavalier and Clay, The True and Outstanding Adventures of the Hunt Sisters: A Novel, Adventure Capitalist: The Ultimate Road Trip, Adventures Beyond the Body: How to Experience Out-of-Body Travel, The Idiot Girls' Action-Adventure Club: True Tales from a Magnificent and Clumsy Life.*

Katherine Tegen, Editor at HarperCollins, edited *Animals Who*

Have Won Our Hearts, by Jean Craighead George. When the book went into paperback, the marketing department wisely decided to change the title to *Incredible Animal Adventures,* which has much more appeal to kids, making the book more accessible.

Death is a key word that can either offer a suggestion, as in *A French Kiss with Death* (a mystery), or be a factual subject, as in *The Death Penalty: An American History* or *The Life and Death of Rudolf Valentino/Adolf Hitler/Great American Cities.* We're all acquainted with titles like Willa Cather's *Death Comes for the Archbishop,* Arthur Miller's *Death of a Salesman,* Robert Frost's "Death of a Hired Man," and Elisabeth Kubler-Ross's *On Death and Dying.* A provocative word, *death* is mesmerizing for some, abhorrent to others, but dismissed by none. Thousands of authors have made use of this attention grabber for their books or articles. Adult magazines offer it up in many categories: "Death of a Chef" (*The New Yorker*), "Death of a Nation" (*Harper's*) and "The Death of the Hired Poem" (*Harper's*).

Magic is another word that lures readers because of its implication of enchantment and secrets revealed. Thousands of books, from gardening to music entice readers by using the word in their titles: *The Magic Gourd, The Magic of Ordinary Days, The Magic of Thinking Big, Dime Store Magic: Women of the Otherworld, The Magic Mountain, Practical Magic, Classic Disney: 60 Years of Musical Magic.* Although secrets are revealed within its pages, it's no secret why this book you are reading has *magic* in its title.

Sequences Lure Readers

The A to Z Mysteries for children by Ron Roy *(Missing Mummy, Runaway Racehorse, Quicksand Question),* Sue Grafton's adult alphabet mysteries *(A Is for Alibi, K Is for Killer),* and Janet Evanovich's series of mysteries *(One for the Money, Two for the Dough, Three to Get Deadly)* each use a letter or number as hooks, an audience attraction. A mystery reader becomes a book collector not just because of a main character (Sherlock Holmes) or the author (Agatha Christie), but also because of a sequence. The word choice of these titles is a mnemonic device, as well as a mysterious lure.

In the consumer periodical world, numbers count; magazine readers are regularly in for the quick fix. At any given time, a magazine stand overflows with numbered headlines and article titles. Here's a sampling from the front covers of a variety of magazines: "Five Pretty Women Talk Beauty," "Pasta with Bacon & Cheese and 8 Other Homey Baked Dishes," "4 Tips: Wake Up a Winter Face," "22 Ways to Fight Cancer," "60-Minute Splurge," "How to Lose 266 Pounds (or Even Just 20)," "4 Scenarios for the Future of Google," "10 Things I Wish I'd Known Before I Bought My Cabin," "Bigger Biceps in 7 Minutes," "His 240 Sexiest Secrets," "50 Timesavers to Try Now," "105 Satisfying Comfort Food Recipes," "10 Most Outrageous Fetishes," "10 Surefire Ways to Bag a Buck This Season," "25 Greatest Stock Picks of All Times." The list goes on and on, but in magazines, title power is in the numbers.

American consumers aren't the only ones that are drawn into the numbers at a magazine stand. Here are a couple of headlines from the front covers of German magazines at a Frankfurt newsstand: "350 Top-Weine," "60 neue Rezepte," "100 Wochen Urlaub," and "150 Gebrauchte im Test."

Plenty of numbered book titles are on the shelves, too, and are equally provocative and memorable. *Ten Stupid Things Couples Do to Mess Up Their Relationship,* by Laura Schlessinger, is not a short title, but it plugs the book's theme in a simple, straightforward, unforgettable manner. *Ten* also has the hint of manageability. *8789 Words of Wisdom,* on the other hand, would be over the top, although the audacity of the number and the desire for *wisdom* might hook some readers into taking a closer look. Isaac Asimov's *100 Malicious Little Mysteries* invites the reader into numerous nights of entertainment. But Wayne Dyer's *Ten Secrets for Success and Inner Peace* also suggests some profitable reading time in a manageable way.

Exercise: The Secret Is in the Numbers

Patricia Schultz, in *1,000 Places to See Before You Die,* used both the power of numbers and a key word, *die,* to attract attention, evoking a sense of urgency. Create titles that use the following:

- *1,000* and *survive.*
- *dozen* and *cats*
- *192* and *tales*
- *16* and *secrets*

Exercise: One-Word Titles

One-word titles are rare, but are definitely easy to recall, especially if the word holds meaning or an image: *Blind, Girlfriends, Scandalous! Hope, Houdini, Tracks, Balls.*

Brainstorm several one-word titles that would capture your interest.

The Four Agreements, by Don Miguel Ruiz, may have even more pulling power. The small number—a doable, understandable number—and the curiosity aroused by *agreements,* are all economical and enticing, especially when augmented by the subtitle, *A Practical Guide to Personal Freedom.* Whether fiction or nonfiction, *A Is for America* and *101 Dalmations* and *30 Days to a More Powerful Vocabulary* attract readers by their appeal to a specific scope, a certain manageability. The concreteness of their numbers or letters appeals to the right side of the brain. A reader also feels attracted to the unveiling of the specific sequence. Consequently, titles like these are easy to recall.

Alluring or Humorous Partnerships

Creating a title that attracts an audience and provides a glimpse of the story's contents takes brainstorming. But sometimes it's right there inside the story, ready for the taking. A case in point is *The Man Who Mistook His Wife for a Hat,* written by Oliver Sachs, a professor of clinical neurology at Albert Einstein College of Medicine. The memorable title first sold as an article in a periodical and then as the title of this best-selling collection of fascinating case histories. The title is easy to remember because, of course, the reader thinks the idea preposterous. More important, the word selection creates an unusual image. It adds an element of surprise or humor.

A standout title in a recent edition of *The Best American Short Stories* catches the eye with its unusual word choice and strange imagery, "Jealous Husband Returns in Form of Parrot." True to its title, the story of a relationship struggle proves to be both humorous and poignant. A children's story in *Cricket* was titled "In General (You Can't Wear Underwear on Your Head)." Of course, any mention to kids of a word like *underwear* sets off laughter and invites interest, but the whole phrase is the magic.

Art and Fear, seemingly a conceptual antithesis, provides an alluring word-positioning that speaks volumes to those working in the arts. A two- or three-word title is always easy to recall, especially if the words add an element of surprise. *One Flew Over the Cuckoo's Nest. Whale Talk. A Dangerous Woman. The Grapes of Wrath.* Interesting juxtapositions of words abound on bookshelves. Their word choice speaks of thought, image, provocation, and sometimes wit.

Jane Resh Thomas's working title for her children's story about a historic English princess who leaps forward in time and lands in a pigpen was *A Splinter of Sunlight,* a line straight out of the text. Her editor suggested that children would identify more quickly with *Princess in the Pigpen.* Indeed, the imagery evoked by such a strange juxtaposition of words and ideas not only attracts a young reader's attention but suggests the story within more strongly.

Wordplay and Copycat Titles Attract Readers

Newspapers are great places to study titles that attract attention, yet speak of the story to come. A Minnesota newspaper article, "On Thin Ice: Lessons Learned and Lives Lost," is memorable not only for its compelling theme of danger and death, and the alliteration newspaper headlines often use, but also for its play on words (a zeugma)—thin ice is both literal and figurative.

Not long after she died, "Katharine the Great" headlined a profile about Katharine Hepburn. The play on words, an allusion, works for the "feisty, formidable, fiercely independent" 96-year-old movie star.

Headlining a newspaper review of a book entitled *Coal: A Human History* is "Old King Coal." If the author spotted the review, she may have wished she could throw out her rather dull title and replace it with this wonderful allusion. "A Master Work" headlines a review of Louise Erdrich's book *The Master Butchers Singing Club.* Like the previous examples, it plays on words and, in this case, indicates not only the book as mastery, but the author as a master. Though they're newspaper headlines, these easy-to-remember titles capture a reader's attention by key words that provoke a response and suggest the article's contents.

"Zen in the Art of Writing," an essay (and later, a book) by Ray Bradbury and *Zen and the Art of Motorcycle Maintenance,* by Robert Pirsig, were both published in the early 1970s. Pirsig's book quite brilliantly put together two unlikely ideas, of which he freely

Exercise: Collect Titles

An issue of a local newspaper headlined three articles this way:

- "Lofty Ideals" (an article on loft living)
- "Relish the Radish" (from the cooking section)
- "Yes, Virginia, There is a Media Double Standard"

This pun, zeugma, and allusion give a reader pause. Word play is the neon light of headlines. Check out your own newspaper and magazine collection. Clip titles that make you pause, think, or laugh . . . not because of the article's contents, but because of the title's play on words.

admits little association to either in his subject matter (a philosophical explanation of quality of life). Bradbury says he chose the word *zen* for its shock value; he was referring to its unexpected association with writing. Dozens of others have since taken the same success route: *Zen and the Art of Making a Living, Zen in the Art of Archery, Zen in the Art of Stand-Up Comedy.*

Copycat titles will bring to mind the *for Dummies* phenomenon that has sold millions of titles on every possible topic in 39 languages around the world. But in 1987, frustrated computer customers were simply trying to adapt to new technologies by studying manuals that were dull and difficult to understand. At first, bookstores vetoed *DOS for Dummies,* saying their customers would be insulted. But some tried it, of course, and the Dummies phenomenon began. Today, customers can find a reader-friendly Dummies book on everything from Shakespeare to national parks to Japanese to dating. Riding the coattail of this publisher's success came another publisher's Idiot's Guides. Will these overused titles eventually lose their effect?

More recent parodies of classic familiar titles are *How to Lose Friends and Alienate People* (a takeoff on *How to Win Friends and Influence People)* and *The Wind Done Gone,* both of which grab the attention of a passerby by its audacious remake of a classic title.

Shocking Titles

An author's or publishing house's choice of a shocking title is a risk, and can prove to be either a bold marketing move or a poor one. The same title can both attract readers and repel them. Alice Randall's *The Wind Done Gone* is a parody of the 1936 classic, *Gone With the Wind,* and told from the mulatto perspective. In 2001, it became the single most talked-about book of the year as it fought its way through the court system in a copyright lawsuit brought by the Mitchell estate. The injunction was subsequently lifted and the book remained on the bestseller's list for weeks. The title is easy to recall, hints at the story to come, and is definitely provocative.

As mentioned earlier, *The Poisonwood Bible* title might be shocking to one reader, but prove to be an excellent choice for another. Either way, it creates interest. *Nigger*, written by Harvard Law School professor Randall Kennedy, provides the history and analytical study of a troublesome word. The bold white lettered title on a dark brown background—shocking to both black and white Americans—is successful: it's easy to recall, it's provocative, and it provides a hint of the story to come. *How to Succeed in Business Without a Penis: Secrets and Strategies for the Working Woman* is a long title, but one that's successful. *Everyone Poops,* a picture book, received mixed reviews, but the title sold books.

Exercise: Title Shock

The Sweet Potato Queens' Big-Ass Cookbook (and Financial Planner) promises fun, but is outrageous in its verbiage, compared to other cookbook titles. *I, Fatty* is the title of a biographical novel. Its short and rather surprising title will force book buyers to pick it up.

What outrageous or shocking title would you give your cookbook? How about your autobiography? Or your article on shock jock Howard Stern? Or your short story about the pet store owner who was actually a pirate?

And So . . .

Clever, bold, funny, startling, gripping, titillating . . . these adjectives may describe titles that grab the attention of readers, but the one that captures them all is *memorable*. For a title to be memorable, it must be easy to recall, provocative or intriguing in some way, and it must provide a clue of the contents.

Of course, not all excellent books, stories, or articles bear memorable titles. In like manner, many tempting titles aren't worth the shelf space allotted them. But for writers—whether the venue is book, magazine or newspaper, the importance of a memorable title is not only crucial for potential readers, but for the editor who precedes them. Ho-hum titles that provoke no imagery, no hook, no inquiry of any kind might very well lead no where. The goal is to push the reader to the next step—that of opening the magazine or book and reading the first line.

Where's Papa Going with That Ax? Memorable Openings

O pening lines provide the essence of a novel or the theme of a biography or the gist of a poem, a speech, a newspaper article. Openers set the tone, the substance, the pace of the journey to come. In every way, opening lines need to invite the reader along for the ride. Whether a short piece or a tome, if the reader is not caught up in the first few lines, the rest of what might be a very fine story will be lost to a wider audience.

In our family, there was no clear line between religion and fly fishing.

So begins *A River Runs Through It, and Other Stories,* by Norman McLean. The juxtaposition of religion and fishing is an intriguing correlation that piques the curiosity. The use of the adjective *our*, a possessive, self-referential word, tells the reader that the story will be told as a first-person narrative, that it is an intimate telling of one family's life. That single opening line tells a story about a family of individuals who find their spiritual solace and look for the answers for their lives in fly fishing.

Tone Evokes Reader Reaction in Adult Fiction

Successful opening lines trigger a reader's interest in an unexpected way, forcing a reaction. They do this with two important ingredients: an interesting voice or tone and the hint of the story to come. *Voice* is not easy to define, but for our purposes here, it is the idea of the author (or the author's created narrator or character), and the manner in which that idea is expressed. The voice emanates someone who sets the stage and relates story.

No matter the genre, no matter the length of the first paragraph, a compelling narrator behind the promise of a story stimulates a reader's delight, curiosity, horror, or empathy. Each word of a successful opener matters; each is chosen with intention and thought and often revised numerous times.

J. D. Salinger opens *The Catcher in the Rye* with the disdainful, irreverent, no-holds-barred-I'm-not-backing-down voice of Holden Caufield.

> If you really want to hear about it, the first thing you'll probably want to know is where I was born, and what my lousy childhood was like, and how my parents were occupied and all before they had me, and all that David Copperfield kind of crap, but I don't feel like going into it, if you want to know the truth.

If you really want to hear about it begins the book with a challenge. The *it* hangs heavy in that opener, a word that can't help but force the reader to wonder. The David Copperfield allusion reveals both Holden's education and his disdain about life. Six decades after it was written, this book is still being read and discussed in classrooms, largely because readers are hooked by Holden's voice and, in the opener, by his hint at a story. A reader does not stop after that first line because this voice, this attitude, attracts attention and oddly commands respect, like that of the high school bad boy everyone has known.

The tone or voice disclosed by an opening line—distant or personal, formal or casual—sets the stage for the rest of the story. Arthur Golden brings readers into *Memoirs of a Geisha* with a voice far different from Holden Caulfield's, and yet just as effective:

> Suppose that you and I were sitting in a quiet room overlooking a garden, chatting and sipping at our cups of green tea while we talked about something that had happened a long while ago, and I said to you, "That afternoon when I met so-and-so . . . was the very best afternoon of my life, and also the very worst afternoon."

As in *A River Runs Through It* and *Catcher in the Rye*, a first-person narrator speaks in *Memoirs of a Geisha*, but this voice is softer, more obsequious. Notice the same kind of opening phraseology in *Catcher*—*suppose that you and I were sitting*—the words inviting an intimacy between the narrator and the reader, promising a story that may be purer, more reflective, more objective than Holden's. Though her words are soft and polite, she doesn't suggest a lovely story. *The very best* and *the very worst* are ominous themes in this gentle, clear speaker's voice because of their antithesis. We're more than curious about the narrator and the particular afternoon to which she's referring.

The opening of Alice Walker's *The Color Purple* is a one-two punch:

> You'd better not never tell nobody but God. It'd kill your mammy.

This threatening voice by an abuser informs the thoughts and actions of the memorable narrator, Celie, for years to come. As narrator, Celie's next statement is her own:

> Dear God, I am fourteen years old.

With such an opener, most readers' hackles are raised; they are hooked by what's being left unsaid.

Sometimes it's a close-up—and in this case also a bird's eye view—that creates a riveting opening:

> The naked parrot looked like a human fetus spliced onto a kosher chicken.

This simile either delights or repels the reader, but the reading won't stop. The tone seems almost straightforward because the sentence is so basic in construction, but the effect is startling because of the image. Even though the voice seems to be missing, it's there. *Fierce Invalids Home from Hot Climates* author Tom Robbins is promising close-up shots with compelling detail to push the reader into the next line and the next. The first page continues to detail the parrot, as well as the reactions of the human characters around it.

In two short clauses, Lois Lowry's *The Giver* pushes a middle-grade reader into worrying about a character he has yet to know:

It was almost December, and Jonas was beginning to be frightened.

The story is told in third-person narration, a distancing that allows a more omniscient perspective than the first person, but the sentence has the feel of the ominous. The sentence combines the cold and dark suggested by December with the approach of something. *Almost* and *the beginning of fear* imply dread of more to come. The sentence introduces a boy, who is named and therefore has a reality. An effective mix of 11 words hooks the reader in the first line.

Mary Doria Russell's futuristic tale *The Sparrow* begins like this:

On December 7, 2059, Emilio Sandoz was released from the isolation ward of Salvator Mundi Hospital in the middle of the night and transported in a bread van to the Jesuit Residence at Number 5 Borgo Santo Spirito, a few minutes' walk across St. Peter's Square from the Vatican.

The concrete details of the bread van, the names of places, date, and time, and the sense of mystery (Why an isolation ward? Why the middle of the night? Why a bread van?) indicate a reporter-like narrator who seems to have a story that has already been lived and now will be revealed. In the first line, the reader is transported into the future by the specifics, by the scene, itself, and by the intrigue.

A *disjunction*, or jarring of the sense of logic, is another way of hooking a reader, especially in fantasy or science fiction. George Orwell's *1984* offers this compelling opener:

It was a bright cold day in April, and the clocks were striking thirteen.

Exercise: Jump into the Future

Create your own new world in just one sentence, a memorable sentence that could be the start of an entire story. Copycat George Orwell's memorable opener to *1984* in some way: "It was a bright cold day in April, and the clocks were striking thirteen."

Normality of the day, in any year, is set down in the first half of the sentence, while the second half jettisons the reader into the future. There, not just one clock (which could indicate merely one oddball household)—all the clocks in the kingdom are striking 13. The reader immediately has a sense of the everyday as jarringly foreign. A whole new world is about to unfold.

Children's Classic Openers Use Rhetorical Devices, Action, Detail

There are as many ways to open a story as there are expressions on a face. Here are three beautiful opening countenances.

J.R.R. Tolkien begins his epic tale *The Hobbit,*

In a hole in the ground there lived a hobbit.

Like the fairy tale quality of the classic opener *once upon a time,* the line establishes a reliable storyteller's voice. It promises at least one fairy or folk creature, an otherworldly setting, and surely, a series of interesting events. Instantly curious, the reader moves to the next sentence and dives into this world:

Not a nasty, dirty, wet hole, filled with the ends of worms and an oozy smell, nor yet a dry, bare, sandy hole with nothing in it to sit down on or to eat: it was a hobbit hole, and that means comfort.

The storyteller pushes the reader into the hole and into an adventure. Tolkien does it by beginning with several negatives: This is what it is *not*, then he states simply and embracingly what it is—*comfort.*

Immediate action is a great way to begin fiction. Christopher Paul Curtis does this through the main character's viewpoint in his Newbery winner, *Bud, Not Buddy.* The first line leads to the second, the second to the third. Like a fly to the web, the reader is enticed into the story.

Here we go again. We were all standing in line waiting for breakfast when one of the caseworkers came in and tap-tap-tapped down the line. Uh-oh, this meant bad news, either they'd found a foster home for somebody or somebody was about to get paddled.

At night the animals
came out of the woods.

So begins the story
"Foxy," by Helen Griffith
(*Cricket*, July 2000). What
experience can you reveal in
a single, succinct line—an
intimate revelation—that
would entice a young audience?

Ouch! That hurts. The
very thought of having
shoes nailed to your feet is
enough to make you
cringe.

That's a nonfiction opener
by Earl Weber in the same
issue ("Horseshoes Are Lucky
. . . for the Horse!"). What
subject would you like to
share with a young reader?
Create the article's enticing
lead—a lead that holds
drama.

Without reading further, the reader
suspects that the main character is
going to be the *somebody*. Bud's
memorable voice engages the
reader by inviting him directly into
the middle of a story.

In another Newbery winner,
Missing May, Cynthia Rylant uses
concrete detail to capture the reader's attention:

When May died, Ob came
back to the trailer, got out of his
good suit and into his regular
clothes, then went and sat in the
Chevy for the rest of the night.
That old car had been parked
out by the doghouse for as long
as I could remember, . . .

Immediately the reader is alerted to
a death—a word that draws attention. Then there is the odd reaction
by someone who was evidently
close to May, someone with the
curious name of Ob. Through details
(*the trailer, his good suit, old car*), an
impoverished lifestyle is implied.
The next line reveals that this observation is being offered by the young
narrator and main character. In two
lines, three characters are revealed
and a story of grief is begun.

Charlotte's Web opens with conflict in the middle of action, conveyed in dialogue:

"Where's Papa going with that ax?"

The first draft of E. B. White's opener could have read something like this, written by someone less masterful: "Fern saved Wilbur's life, a pig doomed to end in the frying pan." Though there's nothing wrong with this line, it doesn't have a speck of action in it. The sentence is passive and doesn't move with what is happening. White knew that a passive opening wouldn't capture a young reader's attention nearly as well as one that places a main character squarely in the middle of conflict. This kind of opening owes some to the narrative tradition anciently called *in media res*, telling a story from a middle point.

Whether fiction or nonfiction, classic or contemporary, children's authors must economize their words. No lazy, lengthy detail is tolerated or the young audience will disappear. Every word of every sentence counts, and none more than the first line of the picture book. These opening lines are generally straightforward, appropriately for children, but they may capture readers by asking an irresistible question, setting up a mystery, even making a broad statement that the reader may want to argue with. The openers engage straightway.

Phyllis Root sets an entertaining tone that promises a world to come in *Big Mama Makes the World:*

When Big Mama made the world, she didn't mess about.

Exercise: Beginning in the Middle

Janisse Ray's memoir, *Ecology of a Cracker Childhood,* probably should have opened with the first line of her second chapter:

A junkyard wasn't a bad place to grow up.

Instead, the first chapter begins:

When my parents had been married five years and my sister was four, they went out searching among the pine-woods through which the junkyard had begun to spread.

Sometimes it happens that a story needs to begin farther into the story. The actual beginning is merely background material. It's the looking back at what's important that matters more than the actual beginning.

Write a story, then choose its beginning—you'll find it somewhere in the middle.

The reader is delighted and pulled in by the narrator's no-nonsense intent to tell the story straight out.

The adventure of a cat and a little girl is immediately set into motion in Janet Lawson's picture book, *Audrey and Barbara.*

"Barbara," asked Audrey, "how would you like to ride an elephant?"

Yes! responds a young reader to a question that pushes the action and the imagination. The first page of *Strange Creatures That Really Lived,* by Millicent Selsam, bears only one line:

Strange animals have always lived on earth.

Such a line suggests page after page of weird, but real, critters. The tone carries some authority. A child will turn the page, either hopeful or doubtful of the sweeping statement. The same goes for the first line of David Bouchard's picture book *If You're Not From the Prairie:*

If you're not from the prairie, you don't know the sun, you can't know the sun.

The amplification is a wonderful blend of authority, emotion, and revelation and suggests truths to be revealed in pages that follow.

Because word count is limited, children's magazine stories and articles hold true to the same formula of immediacy as picture books. The lure arrives in the form of intimacy, a question, the hint of mystery, or trigger words that create emotion. Here are a few samples from *Cricket:*

> ‣ It's true—I did tell a lie once. "McBroom Tells a Lie," Sid Fleischman, September 1973 and September 2003
> ‣ I was about your age (if you are not quite ten) when a buffalo nickel changed my life. "Meet Your Author: Sid Fleischman," September 2003
> ‣ Timothy, our tiger cub, was found by my grandfather on a hunting expedition in the Terai jungles near Dehra, in northern India. "The Day Grandfather Tickled a Tiger," Ruskin Bond, September 2003
> ‣ Things were just as bad as they could be for Mom and me. "Thanksgiving Gumbo," Janet Graber, November 2000

Mysteries Entice through Storms, Action, Conflict

Longer works often begin at a more leisurely pace yet they must still lure the reader. By their very nature, mysteries especially must intrigue their audience from the first words. Through concrete detail, Mary Casanova introduces action and conflict in her historical middle-grade novel, *Curse of a Winter Moon,* which begins with a date line, December 24, 1553:

> All night, the Mistral wind blew down from the Alps, damp and chill, and howled through cracks, despite windows shuttered tight against December.

It is not just any wind, but a *mistral*; not just the mountains, but the Alps. Personification—in the form of December—makes the month come alive with its threatening power. Will the reader shiver from the cold, the howling, and something more? Perhaps, but he will not stop reading. A mystery is in the making.

Veteran writer of adult thrillers Robert Ludlum also uses the weather to provide action and the promise of conflict in *The Icarus Agenda:*

> The angry waters of the Oman Gulf were a prelude to the storm racing down through the Strait of Hormuz into the Arabian Sea.

Trigger words like *angry, prelude,* and *racing* foreshadow harrowing forces at work, and not just in the storm. They leave no doubt in the readers' minds that the story to come is big, bold, and believable.

The theme of action and something ominous brewing opens this short story mystery from 1962 by the king of mystery writers, Ellery Queen, really two cousins named Frederic Dannay and Manfred B. Lee who wrote under that pseudonym:

> An early account of the death of Don Juan Tenorio, fourteenth-century Spanish libertine—who, according to his valet, enjoyed the embraces of no fewer than 2954 mistresses during his lifetime—relates that the great lover was murdered in a monastery by Franciscan monks enraged by his virility.
>
> "The Death of Don Juan,"
> *Ellery Queen Mystery Magazine,* 1962

215

Each line begs further reading for two reasons. Words like *libertine* and *valet* and phrases like *enjoyed the embraces* suggest culture, finesse, wealth. The great number of mistresses suggests the apparent wealth of this patron and a personality worthy of further exploration. The reader will also be intrigued by this valet, the man who kept the numbers. More to the story is declared by the mention of a violent murder . . . by a gang of monks, no less. The hook is in place.

A more intimate voice is that of an actress who finds herself unintentionally drawn into a crime. The reader is drawn by the emotion and the lure of the opening line of "Parties Unknown by the Jury; or, The Valour of My Tongue," by P. M. Carlson, a story from the collection, *Women on the Case:*

> Please, I beg you! Don't ask me to recount the story of that cruel night in 1892 . . . I have nightmares to this day!

The emotional voice suggests an eagerness to tell the tale, even as she protests telling it (a *litotes*).

Methods of hooking a reader:
- concrete detail
- mystery or suspense
- juxtaposition
- disjunction
- enticement
- character introduction
- familiarity or intimacy
- action
- plot theme
- a factual detail
- an ominous setting
- humor
- a line from the classics
- a dictum or axiom

Classic Openers Set the Stage for Modern Writers

Classic openers, often more formal, have set the example for contemporary authors. They offer voice and the promise of a story.

It was the best of times, it was the worst of times.

That recognizable opener from Charles Dickens's *A Tale of Two Cities* uses a powerful rhetorical device, *antithesis*. In a few words, Dickens also manages to incorporate the tone of the work with a somewhat formal, distant narrator; he gives a clue to the story to come—romance and violence, peace and war; and the opener indicates the story looks more to the social complexities of the times than to character development. Readers have always responded to the intriguing contradictions Dickens established in those few words.

Another very suggestive first Dickensian line, even shorter, comes from *A Christmas Carol:*

Marley was dead: to begin with.

The reader is surprised, maybe shocked by these six words that suggest much more to come. The bit about Marley is only a trifle—*to begin with*—compared to the rest of the story, which the narrator will unfold in the ensuing pages. With a distant storyteller's voice that is saying *I've got a tale for you!* and hints of a narrative of death, suspense, and much more, the reader is morbidly curious to read on.

Call me Ishmael.

So declares the narrator of Herman Melville's *Moby Dick*. An authoritative voice that commands

Exercise: Collect & Mimic

Gather a pile of books or magazines and look at opening lines. Which lines attract your attention? Choose one of them to imitate and then write the first paragraph of a new story, one of your own.

Example: "It was the best of times, it was the worst of times" becomes "My senior year—it was the best of times, it was the worst of times."

Exercise: Start with an Axiom

Either choose an old axiom or create your own to begin a story, a one-liner that provides a general summary before the story begins.

Try this one from Washington Irving's "Rip Van Winkle" and write your story around it:

A sharp tongue is the only edged tool that grows keener with con-stant use.

the reader to listen up, Ishmael's voice also suggests an intimacy in the telling of the tale to come; he directly addresses the reader. A century and a half later, Sena Jetter Naslund wrote *Ahab's Wife* about some of Melville's characters in that same time period. Naslund's opening is almost as economic:

Captain Ahab was neither my first husband nor my last.

Both novels begin by introducing a no-nonsense narrator who has a whale of a story to unfold, although Naslund's narrator hints at far more of hers than Ishmael does. For this reason, a contemporary reader may be drawn more quickly into *Ahab's Wife* than into *Moby Dick*.

In a much more proper but subtly humorous tone, Jane Austen firmly establishes a narrator in the first line of *Pride and Prejudice:*

It is a truth universally acknowledged that a single man in posses-sion of a good fortune must be in want of a wife.

Here the narrator is omniscient, introducing a dictum of the times to tell a story. While many of the previous examples show that the narrators are very much a part of their stories, Austen's narrator remains the unseen author, unknown and not a character. Yet this first line provides a sense of the fine eye, perceptions, and humor of the storyteller, who provides such an insightful hint about the plot and provokes such a smile with the remark's audacity.

Leo Tolstoy employed the same kind of declarative opening —an axiom of the day—in *Anna Karenina:*

All happy families are like one another; each unhappy family is unhappy in its own way.

Nonfiction Openers Also Need Voice & the Promise of a Story

The openers of each of the novels discussed introduce some kind of narrator—distant or actively involved—who firmly sets the stage with the promise of a story. Through morbid curiosity, horror, or intrigue, the reader's interest is piqued. Do successful nonfiction openers employ the same ingredients? They do.

Memorable first lines are as essential in nonfiction, as shown in the following choice openers from a random assortment of genres and forums. Successful nonfiction authors think long and hard about their opening lines, wanting a reader to come along for the whole journey. Biographer Doris Kearns Goodwin began an article about Franklin Delano Roosevelt:

> From Warm Springs, Georgia, where he died, the funeral train moved slowly through the rural South to a service in Washington, then past the now thriving cities . . . and finally to Hyde Park, where he was born. Wherever he passed, Americans by the hundreds of thousands stood vigil, those who loved him and those who came to witness a momentous passage in the life of a nation. Men stood with their arms around the shoulders of their wives and mothers. . . . A father lifted his son to see the last car, which carried the flag-draped coffin. "I saw everything," the boy said. "That's good," the father said. "Now make sure you remember."
>
> "Franklin Delano Roosevelt," Doris Kearns Goodwin,
> *Time*, December 31, 1999

The reader trusts the author to tell the exact truth about the entire story. Why? Because of her detail, her reverence for the subject, her implication that every reader should remember this man.

Dale Carnegie's *How to Win Friends and Influence People,* written in 1936, is still on the shelves today (updated and revised), but with an opening line that remains the same:

> On May 7, 1931, the most sensational manhunt New York City had ever known came to its climax.

Who could not read further? The first line seemingly has nothing to do with the title, suggesting that the book is not your average,

219

Exercise: Concrete Facts

The concrete detail of dates, numbers, names, and mileage provides the passage with an authoritative voice that promises an accurate accounting.

A December 31, 1999 issue of *Time* begins a story about Genghis Khan like this: "Temiyin was born clutching a blood clot the size of a knucklebone." Imitate that line and begin your own nonfiction article about something you're familiar with.

Example: Baby snappers are born clutching layers of dirt, darkness, and siblings, each the size of a quarter.

plodding how-to, but rather a book stocked with interesting anecdotes. The voice is established. (This teacher is going to be intelligent, even provocative.) The direction is obvious. (This class is going to be fun, even riveting.) The reader is ready to sign up!

The memorable opener in Frank McCourt's *Angela's Ashes* illustrates the voice or tone of the book's narration along with a strong clue of the story to come. It almost has an echo of *Anna Karenina*'s opening:

When I look back on my childhood I wonder how I survived at all. It was, of course, a miserable childhood: the happy childhood is hardly worth your while. Worse than the ordinary miserable childhood is the miserable Irish childhood, and worse yet is the miserable Irish Catholic childhood.

The reader is delighted by the unique blend of humor—established by the repetition and buildup of key words *(anaphora* and *amplification)* and an Irish childhood of poverty. The first-person speaker sets an intimate tone for the telling of a memoir. The humor and voice promise to deliver the goods without leaving the reader in misery.

Even an information-packed, large-indexed travel guide, *Traveler's Turkey Companion,* by Donald Carroll, can hook a reader in the first two lines:

Each morning on our blue cruise we dive from the side of the boat into the clear blue sea. Immersion in the transparent liquid washes away the fog from our brains—induced perhaps by the previous evening's onboard entertainment—and juices up our vital life forces.

This reference book promises to be a narrative—not just a listing of tourist spots—by authors with an opinion and a turn of phrase. The word choice is not simple and direct. In fact, it's almost ornate: *immersion in the transparent liquid.* Note how the images of sea/liquid/liquor/juices mirror each other, even though *water* is never used. The reading promises to be entertaining if not informative.

A collection of reflections by western women ranchers entitled *Leaning Into the Wind: Women Write from the Heart of the West* (edited by Nancy Curtis, et al.) begins like this:

> Flood, drought, wind, hail, tornado, fire, financial trauma—we suffered them all, each in turn slicing still another sliver from my heart until I thought my heart was dead, it must be dead, had to be dead, for survival depends upon courage and resilience and fortitude and I had none of those.

Many rhetorical devices give this opening its rhythm and beauty: *asyndeton*, in which the author has established a seemingly endless list of the horrors that ranchers face; *antistrophe*, which heightens the debilitating effect through the use of a single repeated ending word; dead, *polysyndeton*, the suggestion of an endless listing of survival traits. The author adds lyricism to her writing by incorporating *alliteration*: "slicing still another sliver." In a sentence, the reader knows the narrator is a person of courage and considerable experience, who has withstood great hardship, and remained humble. Who would not follow this kind of voice, this kind of direction into the rest of the book?

Articles Must Open with a Hook, like Humor

Not unlike a table on which dozens of books vie for attention, dozens of articles try to hook a reader in the pages of a magazine. Voice and the promise of a story are the magic ingredients.

> The stage was set for another international showdown Monday, when chief U.N. weapons inspector Hans Blix confirmed that the remote, isolationist state of North Dakota is in possession of a large stockpile of nuclear missiles.
>
> "North Dakota Found to Be Harboring Nuclear Missiles,"
> *The Onion,* February 5, 2003

Though this opener employs many nonfiction components similar to those in other newspaper articles, the article is not what it may seem. The average reader is hooked into reading on, for the reference isn't to a rogue nation, but to a rogue state within the Union. The tone is authoritative, the details promise the revelation of more concrete details, and the reader's reaction is assured: shock by those who are unaware of *The Onion*'s tongue-in-cheek reputation, and giggles from those who are.

Time directed half of its July 7, 2003 special issue to the subject of Benjamin Franklin. The provocative title of one of the articles— "Why He Was a Babe Magnet," by Claude-Anne Lopez—attracts readers because of the juxtaposition of a historic figure with contemporary slang. The article's opener continues with that same rather sardonic voice:

> More than two centuries after his death, people are still trying to figure out how a paunchy, balding, bifocaled septuagenarian managed to get French ladies in a flutter.

The author's list of specific less-than-attractive aging modifiers provides an entertaining contrast to the final words of alliteration, action, and rhythm—*the French in a flutter.* The opening phrase— more than two centuries after his death—provides a leap in time to today's people who are still trying to figure it out. From this point onward, the article is firmly placed in Franklin's time period.

Another way to attract a reader's attention is through contrasting images. Here are opening lines with three different voices and directions from three articles in (*Yoga Journal,* January/February 1999), each promising an interesting few minutes for the reader:

> ▸ In a dusty riding ring amid the bare hills of California's Sonoma County, Ariana Strozzi Heckler is telling a small group of business people why working with horses will help them learn to be better leaders.
>
> "Our Pets, Ourselves," Susan Davis

> ▸ I like to sit on the floor when I shuffle paperwork around; it gives me the illusion that I'm doing something earthy and primitive, like shucking peas.
>
> "Marketing the Soul," Anne Cushman

> Tutankhamen was buried with it to guard him from evil spirits in the underworld. Greek and Roman legionnaires chewed it to quench their thirst as they marched through the desert. Even the Kama Sutra recommended drinking it with milk and sugar as an aphrodisiac.
>
> "A Candy and a Cure," Blake More

And So . . .

Coal lumps of dull, unmemorable openers abound. They're printed in celebrated work and in the obscure. Gold nuggets of first lines can be found on the same shelves, but not as often. How does the author craft the memorable opener? By digging for it, panning for it, traveling long distances to uncover it. By knowing the story's narrator, by knowing the story, by determining the tone that best suits the story to come. That nugget opener is not easy and it's not magical (though it may seem so by the reader). The opener—like the title and like the ending—are honed and hewed after many drafts, choosing the exact set of words that reveals the essence of the entire work.

Leave a Lasting Impression

M ore difficult than titles, more difficult than beginnings and middles are endings. When and how to end? This chapter doesn't address when to end a piece, but rather the reasons why successful endings resonate long after a story is finished. The chapter focuses on several types of endings and even touches on chapter and paragraph endings. In studying strong closings, a writer can determine why they leave a lasting impression, why it's successful in leaving the reader satisfied.

An ending that leaves a lasting impression satisfies the reader (even if all the threads aren't neatly tied) and provides a nugget of inspiration, an inquiry, a point to ponder. Whether fiction or nonfiction, successful story endings can arrive in a variety of forms: an amen, an analytical conclusion, a full-circle wraparound, a surprise, a succinct summary, or a dangler.

Amen Endings

Like the close of a prayer, an ending might arrive in the form of a satisfying amen—or as in fairy tales, an actual and definitive *the end*. Those specific words may not necessarily be used, but the implication is there. All threads are neatly tied. If fiction, the main character is satisfied, and so is the reader. If nonfiction, the author has spelled out the point he wanted to make and the reader gets it.

The last scene on the last page of Beverly Cleary's children's

Exercise: Amen Ending

An unusual amen ending is this final line from a newspaper column:

> After all, real life is not in the dour headlines. You know this. . . .
> Real life is where you launch forth, right now, just after this period
> coming, this one right here.
>
> "Please Write More About Rape," Mark Morford,
> *San Francisco Gate,* May 14, 2004

The period is the amen. A punctuation mark is the amen to all
sentences, paragraphs, chapters, and books, but in this excerpt the
preceding words underscore it. Sometimes an author or speaker will
emphasize the period, by stating the word: Period. *The End* or *That's all,
folks* are other forms of amen endings. Can you think of more? Create
a few lines of dialogue for a fiction character or create a few lines to
end an essay. The narrator is emphatic about his or her feelings on a
certain topic (politics, corporal punishment, gas hogs, highway litter,
muscle-shirts or mini skirts, pettiness, cell phones).

---

book, *Ramona and Her Father,* shows Ramona at the Christmas
pageant, where she plays a sheep:

> Ramona was filled with joy. Christmas was the most beautiful,
> magic time of the whole year. Her parents loved her, and she loved
> them, and Beezus, too. At home there was a Christmas tree and
> under it, presents, fewer than at past Christmases, but presents all
> the same. Ramona could not contain her feelings. "B-a-a," she bleated
> joyfully.

The *b-a-a* is an entertaining amen, happily spoken. The author
has amplified the meaning of Ramona's joy by detailing its causes,
succinctly summarizing the character's conflict throughout the
story: Despite her father's job loss and the resulting problems, her
parents love and support her, even if she is only a lowly sheep in
the Christmas play.

Now here's a real amen for you.

But I don't think us feel old at all. And us so happy. Matter of fact, I think this is the youngest us ever felt. Amen.

The narrator in *The Color Purple* now has hard-earned freedom in every sense of the word. With that freedom arrives the lightness of spirit, the youth she never enjoyed the first time around. Author Alice Walker's final paragraph leaves a lasting impression: The reader is satisfied because the main character is finally *so happy*. The ending also provides an important point to ponder, that no matter one's age or circumstance, lost youth can be regained. Walker's last sentences grow by degrees: The first set of words is somewhat tentative—*don't think, at all*; the second adds a modifier, *so*, that heightens her happiness; and the final sentence uses the superlatives *youngest* and *ever*. The expletive *matter of fact* adds strength to Celie's final declaration, while the *amen* makes a not to be ignored exclamation point, not only to the end of a letter to God but to the end of a story and a human struggle.

In unusual historical fiction, Anita Diamant tells the story of a barely referenced biblical woman, Dinah, the sister of the twelve sons of Jacob. *The Red Tent* begins with Dinah's eloquent, memorable voice speaking to the reader about herself and her invisible life:

We have been lost to each other for so long. My name means nothing to you. My memory is dust.

Dinah's beautifully detailed "autobiography" of a nomadic desert life ends with these final lines, words from a woman many years dead, once again addressed directly to the reader:

My heart brims with thanks for the kindness you have shown me by sitting on the bank of this river, by visiting the echoes of my name. Blessings on your eyes and on your children. Blessings on the ground beneath you. Wherever you walk, I go with you. Selah.

The voice of *The Red Tent* is both narrative and philosophical. It carries the weight and the tone of the Old Testament that informs it. The ending continues that tone in a summing up, not of the long story of Dinah's life—although its essence is surely there in *the echoes of my name*—but of her well-earned philosophy about life and death. The reader is thoroughly satisfied about a woman's life well-lived in a male-dominated world, about the blessing she bestows on the reader who has journeyed and shared this life with her. Use of the second-person pronoun, *you*, gives the impression of intimacy and sacredness between the narrator and the reader. A specific Hebrew word, *Selah*, which means *pause and think on it,* aptly ends the story.

The Dalai Lama ends his *Ethics for the New Millennium* with a prayer infused with the Buddhist philosophy revealed throughout the book, but that asks blessings on the general reader:

> May I become at all times, both now and forever
> A protector for those without protection
> A guide for those who have lost their way
> A ship for those with oceans to cross
> A bridge for those with rivers to cross
> A sanctuary for those in danger
> A lamp for those without light
> A place of refuge for those who lack shelter
> And a servant to all in need.

Once again, an author satisfies with a coming together, leaving a final amen. The listing in this ending takes on the effect of universal blessing, of the wisdom of adages. It uses powerful metaphors and personification. The language is elevated through a parallel structure of contrasts, *antithesis*—often employed in sacred texts, from the Beatitudes to contemporary prayers like this one.

Concluding with Analysis

Sometimes, rather than tying all threads neatly and leaving the reader sighing happily, an author concludes by offering an analysis of some kind, an adage, a point to ponder, a message. The irreverent storyteller's voice that opened *Catcher in the Rye* carries through to an ending that shows the feeling of the protagonist and narrator, Holden Caufield, in his own indomitable style:

> D. B. asked me what I thought about all this stuff I just finished telling you about. I didn't know what the hell to say. If you want to know the truth, I don't know what I think about it. I'm sorry I told so

Exercise: Broccoli Inspiration

In a light tone, Anne Lamott ends each anecdotal chapter in her writing book *Bird by Bird* with a witty conclusion about a particular topic. The chapter "Broccoli" concludes:

> If you don't know which way to go, keep it simple. Listen to your broccoli. Maybe it will know what to do. Then, if you've worked in good faith for a couple of hours but cannot hear it today, have some lunch.

Lamott uses broccoli as a metaphor for intuition, the still small voice inside each of us. Sometimes faith and lunch, Lamott says, are needed to access that broccoli, to give it time to surface. These word choices are no accident. They're needed to give the metaphor some meat (pun intended).

Listen to your broccoli. Think about the ways to end a story or article you're working on. Which kind of ending would best serve your work: a dangler? A summary? A full-circle wrap around? An amen? A surprise or twist? An analytical conclusion? If your broccoli isn't talking, go eat lunch, then come back and try several different endings.

many people about it. About all I know is, I sort of miss everybody I told about. Even old Stradlater and Ackley, for instance. I think I even miss that goddam Maurice. It's funny. Don't ever tell anybody anything. If you do, you start missing everybody.

This conclusion presents the narrator's feelings, but it's not a tidy ending. The listing of some of the characters acts as a summing up. Notice that the tone and words are confessional *(if you want to know the truth, I'm sorry)* and once again, spoken through the first- and second-person pronouns, making the tone intimate—between you and me. But J. D. Salinger's ending leaves the reader wondering what will happen to Holden, what he means by the last comments, spoken in his unpolished youthful way *(it's funny)*. He's offering a truism or his own axiom—recalling the memories of specific people makes one yearn for their presence. He also offers a depth of perception, an insight that readers may interpret in different ways, but perhaps most obviously that when we open up to people, they in some sense take part of us with them.

Law professor Randall Kennedy ends *Nigger: The Strange Career of a Troublesome Word* with this paragraph summing up the book, and he also leaves a universal point to ponder:

> There is much to be gained by allowing people of all backgrounds to yank *nigger* away from white supremacists, to subvert its ugliest denotation, and to convert the N-word from a negative into a positive appellation. This process is already well under way, led in the main by African American innovators who are taming, civilizing, and transmuting "the filthiest, dirtiest, nastiest word in the English language." For bad or for good, *nigger* is thus destined to remain with us for many years to come—a reminder of the ironies and dilemmas, the tragedies and glories, of the American experience.

Multiple antitheses elevate this paragraph—negative and positive, bad and good, ironies and dilemmas, tragedies and glories—which is especially effective in an ending when a lasting impression is important. Notice, too, Kennedy's repeated usage of trios of words: *taming, civilizing, and transmuting; filthiest, dirtiest, nastiest.* The first sentence uses a trio, in the form of triple infinitive clauses: *to yank, to subvert, to convert.* The final sentence has its trio of antitheses. These kinds of repetitions and listings not only give the writing rhythm, but builds the argument and provides a parallelism that helps the reader remember.

Each chapter in *Nickel and Dimed: On (Not) Getting by in America,* Barbara Ehrenreich's study of on-the-job, low-wage America, covers one state in which the author traveled, and researched, as a minimum-pay worker. The final chapter is an analytical overview and evaluation of her experience. She ends paragraphs in this final chapter with summary observations such as these:

> ▸ It's a lot harder, I found, to sort out a human microsystem when you're looking at it from the bottom, and, of course, a lot more necessary to do so.
>
> ▸ You don't need a degree in economics to see that the wages are too low and rents too high.

> And that is how we should see the poverty of so many millions of low-wage Americans—as a state of emergency.

Notice how expletives *(I found, of course)* in the first example; a parallel construction with repetition in the second example; and a parenthesis in the third add emphasis to each of her points.

Short fiction, too, can offer an analytical conclusion. Saki's "The Open Window," from *Beasts and Super-Beasts,* is the story of a man's disturbing visit to the home of an excessively imaginative young girl who tells him a horrifying and totally false story about his friends. The story concludes with another of the girl's fanciful stories, told in response to her aunt's question about why the man has left so suddenly. Note the concluding line:

> A most extraordinary man . . . dashed off without a word of good-bye or apology . . . One would think he had seen a ghost.
> "I expect it was the spaniel," said the niece calmly; "he told me he had a horror of dogs. He was once hunted into a cemetery somewhere on the banks of the Ganges by a pack of pariah dogs, and had to spend the night in a newly dug grave with the creatures snarling and grinning and foaming just above him. Enough to make any one lose their nerve."
> Romance at short notice was her specialty.

Full-Circle Wraparounds

Stories, articles, verse, fiction, and nonfiction books can also end by going back to the beginning, creating a full-circle effect. Drawing the beginning into the end wraps the story around in a most interesting way.

The listing of names at the end of *Fair Weather,* Richard Peck's middle-grade novel, provides a summary, especially about the rascally, embarrassing grandfather. His grandchild is the narrator:

> And Granddad? He never died. He lived on and on, in our hearts. I see him yet, stumping along the Midway in his old ice-cream traveling togs, parting the common people with his stick. Or there he goes in his terrible wreck of a buggy, the buzzard's feather in his hatband to ward off rheumatism and the epizootic. Tip's there on the seat beside him, and they're going to town for the mail, in case one

of us children has written a letter home. And, of course, it's always fair weather.

The succinct listing of images created through distinctive descriptive words moves the reader back, back, back to the beginning, in this case, to the title, *Fair Weather*. The reader is left satisfied, for despite the death of a primary character, the author implies that memories keep people alive after death.

A short nonfiction meditation by Sharon Dardis, part of the collection *As I Journey On: Meditations for Those Facing Death,* begins:

> My father used to dip his hands in melted wax.

Astonishing because of its opening imagery, the piece moves into memories of a parent who suffered arthritis most of his short life. The narrator, his daughter, ends the meditation:

> In my memories, I sometimes slip once again into my father's waxen gloves, remember his lessons, and thank him. And that's comfort enough, I suppose.

This conclusion is a blend of endings. It is an amen ending in that a child has recognized a parent's importance and pays tribute with memories, remembering lessons, a thanks. It is a full-circle ending with its repeated imagery of the waxen gloves. And yet, the ending has analysis, too: The expletive, *I suppose,* implies to the reader that missing a loved one lasts a long time.

Children's author Lois Lowry ends her futuristic story about memory, *The Giver,* with lines that linger in the reader's mind. The ending is not neatly tied up; it leaves the reader wondering. In the closing scene, the exhausted main character sits atop a sled, clutching a baby he has rescued from certain death, speeding downhill, feeling himself losing consciousness:

> He was racing toward the final destination, the place that he had always felt was waiting, the Elsewhere that held their future and their past. . . . He could see light—red, blue and yellow lights that twinkled from trees in places where families created and kept memories, where they celebrated love. . . . Suddenly he was aware with certainty and

Exercise: Full-Circle Wraparound

A column in *Reader's Digest* (October 2000) highlighted the career of novelist Michael Crichton, author of *Jurassic Park, Disclosure, Timeline*. Columnist Jane Gross ended the four-paragraph "personal glimpse" with an analogy Crichton makes about knowing which one of his many research jaunts will morph into a book:

> "I think of it like farming," he says. "I have planted these seeds and eventually, after many years, there's a crop I can harvest. But the subjective experience is: I start to think more and more about a particular subject, and I can't let go. Usually I'm not sure why."

Gross drew a metaphor from this analogy for the column's title: "Fertile Imagination." And she plucked six key words for an emboldened crosshead: "There's a crop I can harvest."

Often, the title of a work doesn't appear until the work is finished; it's pulled from the ending, rather than the other way around. Searching the closing paragraphs for a title or even a first line is a way to give a piece a full-circle effect. Here's the ending to another "personal glimpse" in the same magazine, this time about Steve Case. who built America Online into the world's leading interactive services company:

> Case continues to value perseverance, and looks for it in the people he hires. "I want to find people who have had to work hard and who have learned from their failures," he says. "Perseverance is no guarantee you'll succeed. But without it, it's almost guaranteed you won't."

Create a title to make the piece circular. Look at some of your own nonfiction and come up with titles that do the same.

joy that below, ahead, they were waiting for him; and that they were waiting, too, for the baby. For the first time, he heard something that he knew to be music. He heard people singing. Behind him, across vast distances of space and time, from the place he had left, he thought he heard music, too. But perhaps it was only an echo.

This ending sums up the main character's increasing longing for the things he has glimpsed though never experienced in his life: love, color, joy, music, life. With that last tentative line, the reader closes the book wondering if the boy was rushing to his life or to his death, for in his former world, beautiful scenes and soft music were part of euthanasia ceremonies, the very thing from which he was saving the baby. The reader is left to wonder if he was achieving their freedom or their death, an ultimate irony.

Poems are famed for their final lines—lines that encapsulate a point, sum, or offer a twist on the poem's thread, all of which when well-done may provide satisfaction for the reader. Gerard Manley Hopkins's "Spring and Fall, To a Young Child" addresses a girl who is apparently upset that the foliage is leaving in the autumn. The speaker tells her she will become less sensitive to that leaving as she grows, but note how the brief, 15-line poem turns the meaning:

> Margaret, are you grieving
> Over Goldengrove unleaving?
> . . .
> Now no matter, child the name:
> Sorrow's springs are the same
> Nor mouth had, no nor mind, expressed
> What heart heard of, ghost guessed:
> It is the blight man was born for,
> It is Margaret you mourn for.

The speaker answers his own initial question by saying to this child, or to himself and the reader, when we are saddened by the passing of the seasons, it isn't the leaves or the sun that grieves us, but ourselves. It is an analytical ending, a full-circle ending, and perhaps in its way, even an amen ending, sad as that seems.

In children's verse, *Just Us Two,* by Joyce Sidman, is a picture book collection of poems about animal dads. In a most satisfying way, the final verse of the final poem "Hangin'" about South American Titi monkeys swings back to the book's beginning:

> Dad lets out a scream
> that scares that sorry snake
> half-silly.
> And we're gone. Outta there.
> Hangin'. Just us two. Hangin' all day long.

This verse is a double accomplishment: Sidman has ended both the poem and the book by going full circle, back to the book's title. This double ending is emphasized with a repeated idea: *gone, outta there.* Rhythm and movement is provided through anaphora, a repeated word (*hangin'*), and alliteration in the form of a scream that scares that sorry snake half-silly.

Surprise Endings

Endings do not always go full-circle, analyze, or breathe *amen.* Sometimes they conclude with a surprising twist. Surprise endings delight both readers and editors, but they're difficult to pull off. Mysteries almost by definition conclude with a twist. O. Henry stories like "The Gift of the Magi" typically end with a surprise. Even the rebus, a children's picture-word story, often hangs on the surprise ending. Short or long, fiction or nonfiction, surprise endings take a good deal of plotting to pull off.

Earlier in the book examples from Guy de Maupassant's memorable French short story "The Necklace" provided examples of situational irony. Matilda, an unhappy young woman who suffered from poverty most of her life, attends an elite party with her husband. She borrows a diamond necklace to complete her outfit. Alas, the necklace is lost or stolen. The couple change lodgings, "haggle to the last sous their miserable" earnings to pay back the 36,000 francs it costs them to replace the necklace. Ten difficult years later, the final scene has the barely recognizable main character meeting the still attractive owner of the necklace. Matilda openly blames Madame Forestier for her hard life, informing her that the necklace she'd returned to her wasn't the original. Madame replies:

Exercise: Surprise Ending

The final line of a poem often bites a reader with its surprise. Here's a child's verse by Dick King-Smith from *Big, Bad, and a Little Bit Scary: Poems That Bite Back:*

> If you fall into a river that's full of Piranha,
> They'll strip off your flesh like you'd skin a banana.
> There's no time for screaming, there's no time for groans,
> In forty-five seconds you're nothing but bones.

Exquisite simile, the anaphora (repetition of leading words), and the rhyme make this a verse to love. But it's the final summation line, its specific detail (*forty-five seconds*) and final shivery word (*bones*) that will stick with a young reader for a long time.

Using King-Smith's verse as a model, create your own shivery poem about a scary topic like snakes, sharks, black-widow spiders, closet monsters, back-alley gangsters, schoolyard bullies. Jolt the reader with the last line.

"You say that you bought a diamond necklace to replace mine?"
"Yes, you did not perceive it then? They were just alike."
"Oh my poor Matilda. Mine were false; they were not worth over five hundred francs."

The story is finished right there, on that twist of an ending, an irony, in the middle of action. No final tie-ups by the author or narrator are needed. But de Maupassant implies much: Is one night's happiness worth a decade of debt and deceit? Does one's life turn on one small event? The story is told in third-person narrative. Madame Forestier—a character who's seen only briefly in a much earlier scene—has the last word.

Readers don't usually think of the paragraphs of a nonfiction article or a short story as mini-chapters, but sometimes that's exactly what they are. For "Death of a Chef," William Echikson wrote a stunning opening paragraph whose final lines leave the reader reeling:

Poularde Alexandre Dumaine, a two-hundred-and sixty-seven-dollar chicken offered at La Cote D'Or, Bernard Loiseau's gastronomic temple in Burgundy, is filled with julienned leeks and carrots, lightly basted and seasoned with salt and pepper, and baked in an earthenware pot. Truffles inserted under the skin give the bird an earthy flavor, and the meat is tender and pungent. Early on the afternoon of February 24th, Loiseau watched his team of a dozen chefs prepare the poularde for two American chefs who were completing internships in France. After the dish was served, he went home for a siesta. Sometime later that day, he shot himself in the mouth with a hunting rifle. He was fifty-two.

"Death of a Chef," William Echikson,
New Yorker, May 2003

The vivid word choices in the opening lines lure the reader into thinking and salivating about food. The equally vivid details in the stunning final sentences lead into a more traditional *rest of the story*, a profile of this tragically ended life.

Saving a key fact until the very end provides an interesting way to pull off surprise in nonfiction particularly, though it can be risky. Earl Shorris's "The Last Word" is the story of the survival and demise of various world languages. The lengthy and provocative article moves in and out of dozens of obscure languages but ends by discussing Maya, and an attempt to save it from extinction. The author describes the alighting of a butterfly next to him in Mexico, and its vivid, almost indescribable blue. He concludes the article in this memorable way:

There are nine different words in Maya for the color blue in the comprehensive *Porrua Spanish-Maya Dictionary* but just three Spanish translations, leaving six butterflies that can be seen only by the Maya, proving beyond doubt that when a language dies, six butterflies disappear from the consciousness of the earth.

"The Last Word," Earl Shorris,
Harper's, August 2000

The specificity and literal colorfulness of the insight underline the authority and profundity of this conclusion. Fresh and surprising, this ending lingers long after the magazine is shelved.

A four-paragraph sidebar in *Yoga Journal* ends with a surprising anecdote, intriguing enough to propel the reader into discovering the rest of the story in the main article. More could easily have opened with this sentence but instead ends with it:

> In a move that probably delayed our acquaintance with Indian culture by at least a millennium, the yogi chose to set himself aflame on a funeral pyre rather than go along.
>
> "America Revisits India," Blake More,
> *Yoga Journal,* January/February 1999

The sidebar's goal? To entice readers into informing themselves about Indian culture. The hyperbole—the equation of the thousand-year delayed connection to Indian culture because of immolation—charges the entire piece.

Endings That Summarize

In a sense, the opposite of a surprise ending is the summary. Biographies, science articles, histories often use this kind of wrap-up, concluding with key points. Here's the finale to Jane Resh Thomas's middle-grade book, *Behind the Mask: The Life of Queen Elizabeth I*:

> Yet the sixteenth century has never been known for Mary Stuart, or even King Henry VIII. It is primarily the accomplishments of the great Elizabeth Tudor, Gloriana, Good Queen Bess, the maiden queen who married England—that we remember. And we honor her name by giving it to the Elizabethan Age that was in large part her creation.

Besides the comparative listing of other key figures, Thomas evokes respect for her subject through words such as *century, accomplishments, honor, remember, Elizabethan Age, creation.* The queen lived a most uncommon, often harrowing life in a time that did not respect women, let alone female leaders. By listing who the sixteenth century is *not* noted for—a form of *litotes*—the queen's legacy gains more mythical proportion. The words *we honor* are inclusive, indirectly asking the reader to spend time with this woman, because she's worthy of attention.

A biologist can effectively end his scientific inquiry and analysis with profound summary. In 1974, Lewis Thomas wrote this ending to *The Lives of a Cell: Notes of a Biology Watcher:*

> Each day, millions of meteorites fall against the outer limits of the [atmospheric] membrane and are burned to nothing by the friction. Without this shelter, our surface would long since have become the pounded powder of the moon. Even though our receptors are not sensitive enough to hear it, there is comfort in knowing that the sound is there overhead, like the random noise of rain on the roof at night.

Lewis sums up, he satisfies, and he leaves a lasting impression. The imagery could so easily have been mundane: Scientific writing often is clinical. That explains why this book's essays first appeared in the *New England Journal of Medicine* and why, on the strength of their writing, were reprinted in a collection that is still on today's shelves. The writing is made memorable and lyrical because of the integrity of Thomas's imagery and other rhetorical devices, like alliteration (*millions of meteorites, pounded powder, random noise of rain on the roof*). They give the piece rhythm and movement, life.

Danglers

No piece of writing, whether a novel or a short periodical piece, should suffer from thoughtless final lines. After all, this is the author's final chance to leave a lasting impression—whether the goal is to impel readers to turn the page and begin the next chapter or to motivate the readers on to other work by the same author or merely to tickle their inquiring minds.

Endings that dangle, leaving the heart racing or the mind wondering, can leave the reader either frustrated or motivated. April Prince ends her review of the children's book *They Came from the Bronx* with this line:

> But beware: the ghost-like images of buffalo that haunt Waldman's end-papers will stay with you long after you've put the book away.
> *The Five Owls*, No. 4, 2002

The reader, through direct address, is given an image of a ghostly buffalo and with it, an invitation to check out this book. Despite the brevity of the article, the dangler serves as a motivator.

A chapter in *Death in Holy Orders,* by the consummate mystery writer, P. D. James, ends in this way:

> And now I expect you would like to see where he died.

This final line has everything a good fiction ending needs in its provocation to start the next chapter. The reader now knows about the apparent suicide but, like the protagonist, Adam Dalgliesh, wonders if there's not more to the story, perhaps even murder. The reader wants to get to the death scene just as fast as the inspector and by choosing words that imply a question, the reader, like Dalgliesh, nods his head. It's as though the author is saying to the reader, "And now I expect you would like to see where he died." "Yes!" says the reader, for no murder mystery is complete without a visit to the scene of the crime. With that chapter dangler, the reader is hooked into turning the page to the next chapter.

Chapters in middle-grade fiction can also end with a lure, a dangler, pushing the young reader into the next chapter. Two of Katherine Paterson's chapters in her Newbery Medal-winning book *Jacob Have I Loved* end like this:

> ‣ "I wonder—" Momma began, but we were turning in at our own gate, and she didn't finish the sentence.
> ‣ If he was not a spy, if he was indeed Hiram Wallace, why had he come back after all these years to an island where he was hardly remembered except with contempt?

Paterson uses an *aposiopesis* (a-pos-io-*pee*-sis) in the first example, a rhetorical device that abruptly stops the words mid-sentence, leaving the statement unfinished. The second example makes good use of an *aporia,* an expression of doubt about an idea or person or behavior.

Chapter endings cannot all end with a dangler or a lure into the next chapter. Maintaining that kind of intensity for an entire novel would be exhausting for both the reader and the main character. The chapters in *Jacob Have I Loved* end, just as often, on a down note, a conclusion, a respite:

▶ I excused myself from the table. The last thing I needed to hear that day was the story of my sister's life, in which I, her twin, was allowed a very minor role.

▶ I did not press her to explain. I was too grateful for that one word that allowed me at last to leave the island and begin to build myself as a soul, separate from the long, long shadow of my twin.

Did you notice the action followed by an interior thought in the first example? The second directly follows action conveyed through dialogue. The repetition of a single word, *long*, is *epizeuxis*, a repetition for emphasis.

Franz Kafka's novel *The Castle* ends in a very bizarre way, with a corker of a dangler. The bizarre, nightmarishly complex, illogic of Kafka's writing doesn't necessarily explain the run-on of commas:

> She held out her trembling hand to K and had him sit down beside her, she spoke with great difficulty, it was hard to understand her, but what she said—

And that's where the novel ends—forever out of reach (especially since the author died in 1924). The debate is ongoing about whether this ending was purposeful or not. Can you think of other books or films that end with a dangler, an unfinished scene? In each case, would you consider the ending successful or not?

And So . . .

The final verse, the final chapter, the final paragraph, each should end the writing piece with a conclusion that leaves an impression. Not always, but often these final lines circle back to the beginning, maybe even back to the title. Just as often, an ending will surprise—even shock, succinctly summarize, analyze, or lure. Ultimately, a successful ending needs to satisfy the reader, even if all the threads aren't neatly tied or even if the closing is unhappy or sad. And finally, if well crafted, the ending will leave the reader with something to chew on. These successful, memorable endings are neither easy nor simple, though they may appear to be so. The authors have written and rewritten those lines. And the payoff is a story that may be read again and again.

Bibliography

Adams, Henry. *The Education of Henry Adams*. A classic available in many editions.

Angelou, Maya. *I Know Why the Caged Bird Sings*. New York: Random House, 1969.

Austen, Jane. *Pride and Prejudice*. A classic available in many editions.

Babbitt, Natalie. *Tuck Everlasting*. New York: Farrar, Straus, Giroux, 1975.

Barr, Nevada. "Beneath the Lilacs." From *Women on the Case,* edited by Sara Paretsky. New York: Delacorte Press, 1996.

Barry, Dave. "A Forest of Lights Can Only Mean That It's Christmas in Miami." *Miami Herald.* December 7, 2003.

Bauer, Ann. "The Drunkard's Gait." *The Sun.* April 2004.

Bauer, Marion Dane. *On My Honor*. New York: Clarion Books, 1986.

Bell, Madison Smartt. "Small Blue Thing." *Harper's.* June 2000.

Beowulf. A classic available in various editions.

Bond, Ruskin. "The Day Grandfather Tickled a Tiger." *Cricket.* September 2003.

Book of Common Prayer. Available in many editions.

Bouchard, David. *If You're Not from the Prairie*. New York: Atheneum, 1995.

Carlson, P. M. "Parties Unknown by the Jury; or, The Valour of My Tongue." From *Women on the Case,* edited by Sara Paretsky. New York: Delacorte Press, 1996.

Carnegie, Dale. *How to Win Friends and Influence People*. New York: Simon & Schuster, 1936.

Carroll, Mary. "The Lady Saddle." *Cricket.* July 1, 2003.

Carroll, Donald. *Traveler's Turkey Companion*. Helena, Montana: Globe Pequot, 1999.

Casanova, Mary.
—*Curse of a Winter Moon*. New York: Hyperion, 2000.
—*One Dog Canoe*. New York: DK Pub., 1999.

Chabon, Michael. *The Amazing Adventures of Kavalier and Clay.* New York: Random House, 2000.

Chmielarz, Sharon. *Down at Angel's*. New York: Ticknor & Fields Books for Young Readers, 1994.

Cleary, Beverly. *Ramona and Her Father*. New York: Morrow, 1977.

Clifford, Hal. "Nightfall over the Deadly Bells." *National Geographic Adventure,* Winter 1999.

Coleridge, Samuel Taylor. "Kubla Khan." A classic poem available in many editions and anthologies.

Covert, Calvin. "Director Foley a Talent Magnet." *Star Tribune*. April 25, 2003.

Curtis, Christopher Paul. *Bud, Not Buddy*. New York: Delacorte Press, 1999.

Cushman, Anne. "Marketing the Soul." *Yoga Journal*. January/February 1999.

Dahl, Roald. *James and the Giant Peach*. New York: Knopf, 1961.

Dalai Lama. *Ethics for the New Millennium*. New York: Riverhead Books, 1999.

Dardis, Sharon and Rogers, Cindy. *As I Journey On: Meditations for Those Facing Death*. Minneapolis, MN: Augsburg, 2000.

Davidson, Diane. *Dying for Chocolate*. New York: Bantam Books, 1992.

Davis, Susan. "Our Pets, Ourselves." *Yoga Journal*. January/February 1999.

Diamant, Anita. *The Red Tent*. New York: St. Martin's Press, 1997.

DiCamillo, Kate.
—*Because of Winn-Dixie*. Cambridge, Mass.: Candlewick Press, 2000.
—*The Tale of Despereaux: Being the Story of a Mouse, a Princess, Some Soup, and a Spool of Thread*. Cambridge, Mass.: Candlewick Press, 2003.

Dickens, Charles. These classic titles are available in many editions.
—*Bleak House*.
—*A Christmas Carol*.
—*David Copperfield*.
—*Hard Times*.
—*The Old Curiosity Shop*.
—*A Tale of Two Cities*.

Dickinson, Emily. "Because I Could Not Stop for Death." A classic poem available in many editions and anthologies.

Dillard, Annie. *Teaching a Stone to Talk: Expeditions and Encounters*. New York: Harper & Row, 1982.

Donne, John. "Holy Sonnet XIV." A classic poem available in many editions and anthologies.

Echikson, William. "Death of a Chef." *New Yorker*. May 2003.

Ehrenreich, Barbara. *Nickel and Dimed: On (Not) Getting by in America*. New York: Metropolitan Books, 2001.

Enger, Leif. *Peace Like a River.* New York: Atlantic Monthly Press, 2001.

Erdrich, Louise.
    —*The Last Report on the Miracles at Little Horse.* New York: HarperCollins, 2001.
    —*The Master Butchers Singing Club.* New York: HarperCollins, 2003.

Eugenides, Jeffrey. *Middlesex.* New York: Farrar, Straus, Giroux, 2002.

"Farewell, Concorde." *International Herald Tribune.* April 14, 2003.

Fleischman, Sid.
    "McBroom Tells a Lie." *Cricket.* September 1973; September 2003.
    "Meet Your Author: Sid Fleischman." *Cricket.* September 2003.

Fonseca, Isabel. *Bury Me Standing: The Gypsies and Their Journey.* New York: Knopf, 1995.

Franklin, Benjamin. *Memoirs.* 1790. A classic available in various editions.

Franzen, Jonathan. "Caught." *New Yorker.* June 16/23, 2003.

Friend, Catherine. *The Perfect Nest.* Cambridge, Massachusetts: Candlewick Press (publishing date pending).

Frost, Robert. "The Road Not Taken." From *Anthology of Modern American Poetry.* Edited by Cary Nelson. New York: Oxford University Press, 2000.

Golden, Arthur. *Memoirs of a Geisha.* New York: Alfred A. Knopf, 1997.

Goodwin, Doris Kearns. "Franklin Delano Roosevelt." *Time.* December 31, 1999.

Graber, Janet. "Thanksgiving Gumbo." *Cricket.* November 2000.

Gray, John. *Men Are from Mars, Women Are from Venus.* New York: HarperCollins, 1992.

Gray, Paul. "Johann Gutenberg." *Time.* December 31, 1999.

Griffith, Helen. "Foxy." *Cricket.* July 2000.

Gross, Jane. Personal Glimpse of Michael Crichton. "Fertile Imagination." *Reader's Digest.* October 2000.

Harris, Joanne. *Chocolat.* New York: Viking, 1999.

Hawthorne, Nathaniel. *The Scarlet Letter.* A classic available in many editions.

Haynes, David. *Right by My Side.* Minneapolis, Minn: New Rivers Press, 1993.

Hemingway, Ernest.
 —"Hills Like White Elephants." From *Men Without Women.* New York: Scribner's, 1927.
 —*Death in the Afternoon.*
Henry, O. "The Gift of the Magi." Available in many collections and anthologies.
Herman, Linda. "Dragon's Down Under." *Cricket.* July 1, 2003.
Hoffbeck, Steve. "A Visit from the Babe." *Minnesota Monthly.* June 2003.
Hopkins, Gerard Manley. Classic poems available in many editions and anthologies.
 —"God's Grandeur."
 —"Spring and Fall, To a Young Child."
Horyn, Cathy. "Wearing America on Their Sleeves." *New York Times,* July 1, 2003.
James, Henry. *The Golden Bowl.* A classic available in many editions.
James, P. D. *Death in Holy Orders.* New York: Knopf, 2001.
Kafka, Franz. *The Castle.* Available in many editions.
Kennedy, John F. Inaugural Address. January, 1960.
Kennedy, Randall. *Nigger: The Strange Career of a Troublesome Word.* New York: Pantheon Books, 2002.
King James Bible. Available in many editions.
 —*1 Corinthians.*
 —*Ecclesiastes.*
 —*Isaiah.*
 —*Luke.*
 —*Matthew.*
 —*Proverbs.*
King, Martin Luther Jr.
 —"Facing the Challenge of a New Age." December 3, 1956 speech.
 www.stanford.edu/group/king/publications/papers/vol3/contents.html
 —"Letter from Birmingham Jail." www.stanford.edu/group/king/popular_requests/frequentdocs/birmingham.pdf
King, Stephen. *Hearts in Atlantis.* New York: Scribner's, 1999.
King-Smith, Dick. *Big, Bad, and a Little Bit Scary: Poems That Bite Back.* New York: Viking, 2001.

Kingsolver, Barbara. *The Poisonwood Bible.* New York: HarperCollins, 1999.

The Koran.

Lahiri, Jhumpa. "A Real Durwan." *Interpreter of Maladies.* Boston: Houghton Mifflin, 1999.

Lamott, Anne. *Bird by Bird: Some Instructions on Writing and Life.* New York: Pantheon Books, 1994.

Lao-tsu. *The Way.*

LaRochelle, David. *Absolutely, Positively Not . . . .* New York: Arthur A. Levine Books (publishing date pending).

Lawson, Janet. *Audrey and Barbara.* New York: Atheneum, 2002.

Leaning into the Wind: Women Write from the Heart of the West. Edited by Nancy Curtis, et al. Boston: Houghton Mifflin, 1997.

Lederer, Richard. "English Is a Crazy Language." *Crazy English: The Ultimate Joy Ride through Our Language.* New York: Pocket Books, 1989.

Lincoln, Abraham. Second Annual Address to Congress, 1862. Available in many editions and anthologies.

Lockerbie, Catherine. "Green, Unpleasant Land." *New York Times Book Review*, December 22, 2002.

Longfellow, Henry Wadsworth. "The Song of Hiawatha." A classic poem available in many editions and anthologies.

Lopez, Claude-Anne. "Why He Was a Babe Magnet." *Time*, Special Edition on Benjamin Franklin, 2003.

Lowry, Lois. *The Giver.* Boston: Houghton Mifflin, 1993.

Ludlum, Robert. *The Icarus Agenda.* New York: Random House, 1988.

Maupassant, Guy de. "The Necklace." A classic available in many editions and anthologies.

McCourt, Frank. *Angela's Ashes.* New York: Scribner, 1996.

McLean, Norman. *A River Runs Through It, and Other Stories.* Boston: G. K. Hall, 1976.

McPherson, James A. "Reflections of Titus Basfield." *Harper's.* June 2000.

Means, David. "It Counts as Seeing." *Harper's.* September 2000.

Melville, Herman. *Moby Dick.* A classic available in many editions.

Miller, Florence Fenwick. *Harriet Martineau.* London, W. H. Allen & Co., 1884.

More, Blake.

  —"America Revisits India." *Yoga Journal.* January/February 1999.

  —"A Candy and a Cure." *Yoga Journal.* January/February 1999.

Morford, Mark. "Please Write More About Rape." *San Francisco Gate.* May 14, 2004.

Naslund, Seta Jetter. *Ahab's Wife, Or, The Star Gazer.* New York: William Morrow, 1999.

Nesbitt, Marc. "The Ones Who May Kill You in the Morning." *Harper's.* August 2000.

Nye, Naomi Shihab. "Kindness." *The Words Under the Words.* Portland, Oregon: Eighth Mountain Press, 1995.

O'Brien, Tim. *The Things They Carried.* Boston: Houghton Mifflin, 1990.

O'Connor, Sheila. *Where No Gods Came.* Ann Arbor: University of Michigan Press, 2003.

The Onion. "North Dakota Found to Be Harboring Nuclear Missiles." February 5, 2003.

Orwell, George.

  —*Animal Farm.* New York: New American Library of World Literature, 1961.

  —*1984.* New York: New American Library of World Literature, 1961.

Paterson, Katherine. *Jacob Have I Loved.* Grand Rapids: Eerdmans, 1962.

Peck, Richard. *Fair Weather.* New York: Dial Books, 2001.

Petit, Charles. "Pulsing Stars." *U.S. News and World Report, Special Edition,* 2003.

Piers Plowman. A classic available in various editions.

Plath, Sylvia. *The Journals of Sylvia Plath.* New York: Dial Press, 1982.

Poniewozik, James. "Trading Places." *Time.* July 2003.

Prince, April. Review of *They Came from the Bronx. The Five Owls.* No. 4, 2002.

Queen, Ellery (Frederic Dannay and Manfred B. Lee). "The Death of Don Juan." *Ellery Queen Mystery Magazine.* 1962.

Quindlen, Anna. "Playing God on No Sleep." *Newsweek.* July 2, 2001.

Ray, Janisse. *Ecology of a Cracker Childhood.* Minneapolis: Milkweed Editions, 1999.

R., Fred. "Honoring Our Hunger for the Ecstatic." *The Utne Reader.* October 2001.

Robbins, Tom. *Fierce Invalids Home from Hot Climates.* New York: Bantam Books, 2000.

Roosevelt, Franklin. Message to the American Booksellers Association, April 23, 1942.

Root, Phyllis.
    —*Aunt Nancy and Old Man Trouble.* Cambridge, Mass.: Candlewick Press, 1998.
    —*Big Mama Makes the World.* New York: Walker Books, 2002.
    —*One Stuck Duck.* Cambridge, Mass.: Candlewick Press, 1998.
    —*What Baby Wants.* Cambridge, Mass.: Candlewick Press, 1998.

Rowling, J. K. *Harry Potter and the Chamber of Secrets.* New York: Arthur A. Levine Books, 1999.

Russell, Mary Doria. *The Sparrow.* New York: Villard Books, 1996.

Russo, Richard. *Empire Falls.* New York: Alfred A. Knopf, 2001.

Rylant, Cynthia. *Missing May.* New York: Orchard Books, 1992.

Safransky, Sy. "Sy Safransky's Notebook." *The Sun.* April 2004.

Saki (H. H. Munro). "The Open Window." *Beasts and Super-Beasts.* London, New York: John Lane Company, 1914.

Salamon, Julie. "A Widow, but Spare the Pity: Resisting Pressure to Sentimentalize over Daniel Pearl." *New York Times.* October 6, 2003.

Salinger, J. D. *The Catcher in the Rye.* Boston: Little, Brown, 1951.

Salzman, Mark. *Lying Awake.* New York: Alfred A. Knopf, 2000.

Schama, Simon. "The Unloved American." *New Yorker.* March 10, 2003.

Sciolino, Elaine. "The New Next-Door Neighbors." *International Herald Tribune,* April 14, 2003.

Sebold, Alice. *The Lovely Bones.* Boston: Little, Brown, 2002.

Shakespeare, William. Shakespeare's plays are available in a variety of editions.
    —*Hamlet.*
    —*Julius Caesar.*
    —*A Midsummer Night's Dream.*
    —*Richard II.*
    —*Romeo and Juliet.*

Shorris, Earl. "The Last Word." *Harper's.* August 2000.

Sidman, Joyce.
    —*Just Us Two.* Brookfield, CT: Millbrook Press, 2003.
    —*The World According to Dog.* Boston: Houghton Mifflin, 2003.

Slater, Lauren. "Dr. Daedalus." *Harper's*. July 2002.

Spinelli, Jerry. *Maniac Magee*. Boston: Little, Brown, 1990.

Spy Stories. *U. S. News & World Report*. Special Edition, 2003

Stegner, Wallace. *Crossing to Safety*. New York: Random House, 1987.

Stocker, Carol. "Rediscovering Rhubarb." *Boston Globe*. May 16, 1996.

Strunk, William and White, E. B. *The Elements of Style*. Revised, 4th ed., Boston: Allyn and Bacon, 1999.

"Survey: The Beast of Complexity." *The Economist*. April 2001.

Swift, Jonathan. "A Modest Proposal." A classic essay available in many anthologies.

"Theodore Roosevelt: Dakota Adventure," *National Geographic Park Profiles*

Thomas, Jane Resh.
  —*Behind the Mask: The Life of Queen Elizabeth I*. New York: Clarion Books, 1998.
  —*Daddy Doesn't Have to Be a Giant Anymore*. Clarion Books, 1996.

Thomas, Dylan.
  —*The Poems of Dylan Thomas: New Revised Edition*. New York: New Directions, 2003
  —"Do Not Go Gentle into That Goodnight." 1951.
  —*A Child's Christmas in Wales*.
  —"Notes on the Art of Poetry."

Thomas, Lewis. *The Lives of a Cell: Notes of a Biology Watcher*. New York, Viking Press, 1974.

Thoreau, Henry David. *Walden*. A classic available in many editions.

Tolkien, J. R. R. New York: Ballantine, 1982. Published by arrangement with Houghton Mifflin.
  —*The Hobbit*.
  —*The Lord of the Rings*.

Tolstoy, Leo. *Anna Karenina*. A classic available in many editions.

Toole, John Kennedy. *A Confederacy of Dunces*. Baton Rouge: Louisiana State University Press, 1980.

"Toughing It Out." *Reader's Digest,* October 2000.

Twain, Mark. "The Celebrated Jumping Frog of Calaveras County." New York: C. H. Webb: American News Co., 1867.

"The Universal Means Test." *The Economist*. March 6, 1999.

Walker, Alice. *The Color Purple.* New York: Harcourt Brace Jovanovich, 1982.

Warner, Sylvia Townsend. *Scenes of Childhood.* New York: Viking Press, 1981.

Weber, Earl. "Horseshoes Are Lucky . . . for the Horse!" *Cricket.* July 2000.

Wharton, Edith. *The House of Mirth.* A classic available in a variety of editions.

White, E. B. *Charlotte's Web.* New York: Harper & Row, 1952.

Williams, Theresa. "Jane." *The Sun.* April 2004.

Woolf, Virginia. *Mrs. Dalloway.* A classic available in a variety of editions.

Glossary

Alliteration: the repetition of the same initial sound in successive words.

Allusion: a reference, often literary, to a famous person, place, event, book, or fact in order to provide an instant image.

Amplification: the expansion of a single detail by repeating a word or expression, to add more detail.

Anadiplosis: the rhetorical repetition of one or several words that end one clause, line, or sentence and begin the next.

Analogy: the comparison of two things, an unknown to a known, but with several points of similarity, to explain further or deeper.

Anaphora: the repetition of the same word or words at the beginning of successive phrases, clauses, or sentences.

Anthropomorphism: the attribution of human form or personality to nonhuman things; not a language device like personification but rather a story line or character decision.

Antimetabole: the repetition of the same phrase of one clause in reverse grammatical order in the next clause.

Antiphrasis: a one-word irony.

Antistrophe: heightens the debilitating effect through the use of a single repeated ending word.

Antithesis: the juxtaposition of contrasting ideas or themes, sometimes in the same sentence and often in a parallel construction.

Apophasis: a statement that pointedly pretends to ignore or not to mention something.

Aporia: an expression or question of uncertainty or doubt—often feigned—to establish argument or relationship; a debating with oneself.

Aposiopesis: a sudden halt in the midst of speaking, often to portray emotion.

Appositive: Often set off by commas, a noun, noun phrase, or noun clause that follows a noun or pronoun and renames it so as to clarify.

Apostrophe: an abrupt interruption that turns from the general audience to address someone or something completely different (another audience present, absent, or inanimate).

Assonance: the repetition of the same internal vowel sounds in successive words.

Asyndeton: a series, uninterrupted by a conjunction, implying multiplicity.

Brachylogy: a condensed speech pattern of short, quick words.

Climax: the arrangement of words, clauses, or sentences in ascending order of importance or emphasis.

Conceit: an extravagant use of language; a far-fetched or bizarre metaphor, simile, or analogy.

Consonance: the repetition of the same internal consonant sounds.

Dangler: a chapter or scene ending that either lures the reader on or leaves him hanging.

Disjunction: a jarring of the sense of logic.

Ellipsis: an omission of words that allows a smoother flow and added emphasis.

Epistrophe: a partner to anaphora; the repetition of the same word or words at the end of successive phrases, clauses, or sentences.

Epizeuxis: the emphatic repetition of one word, without other words between.

Eponym: the name of a person that has become so common in usage as to be a part of the everyday language.

Euphemism: a milder or more delicate substitution of words for a stark reality.

Expletive: a single word or short phrase that interrupts normal syntax to give emphasis to preceding or succeeding words.

Exposition: the explanation or background information for character, setting, plot.

Hyperbole: a deliberate exaggeration; an extravagant overstatement.

Implication: a subtle text that offers more than the concrete narration states.

Inference: the action taken by the audience. An author implies or enfolds a point; a reader infers or guesses.

Irony: language that leaves a gap between what is stated and what is meant (or between what happens and what is expected to happen); a subtle or bold discrepancy with a twist.

Litotes: a deliberate ironical understatement that denies the opposite of the thing being affirmed.

Metaphor: the comparison of two dissimilar objects or actions that have some quality in common, a quality that can relate one to the other.

Metonymy: a renaming, the substitution of one word or phrase for another that bears the same meaning.

Onomatopoeia: the naming of a thing or action by the imitation of the sound associated with it.

Oxymoron: a two-word paradox; a short phrase that seemingly contradicts itself.

Paradox: a statement opposed to common sense and yet containing truth; someone or something with seemingly contradictory qualities.

Parallelism: the balanced construction of a sentence through a similarity of structure in a series of related words, phrases, and clauses.

Paraprosdokian: the unexpected or surprising ending to an expression, a sentence, a poem, a story.

Parenthesis: set within a pair of punctuation marks, an interruption or an aside that offers new information or a quick explanation.

Parody: the mimicking of another's work.

Paronomasia: a wordplay or pun that plays on the sound or meaning of words.

Pathetic Fallacy: a personification that attributes a person's strong emotions or motivations to the natural world.

Personification: a comparison that gives human characteristics to an object, a force of nature, or an abstract idea.

Pleonasm: a superfluity or redundancy of words.

Polysyndeton: a series that places a conjunction between each and every word, phrase, or clause.

Sententia: an interrupter that inserts a wise saying or a maxim, bringing a general truth or pithy summary to the passage or situation.

Simile: the direct comparison of two dissimilar objects or actions in which a word of comparison is used or implied.

Style: the unique flavoring or design of a text: the voice, pacing, fluidity, rhythm, figurative language.

Synecdoche: a shallow metaphor or metonymy that exchanges a part for the whole, a whole for the part, the genus for the species, the species for the genus, the material for the thing made.

Toponym: the name of a place that has become so common in usage as to be a part of the everyday language.

Understatement: the deliberate expression of an idea as less important than it actually is.

Zeugma, or **Syllepsis:** a single word, usually a verb, that governs two others, providing two meanings, one figurative and one literal.

Index

267